DISTRICT LEADERS

POLITICAL CULTURES

Aaron Wildavsky, Series Editor

Political cultures broadly describe people who share values, beliefs, and preferences legitimating different ways of life. This series will be distinguished by its openness to a variety of approaches to the study of political cultures; any defensible comparison, definition, and research method will be considered. The goal of this series is to advance the study of political cultures conceived generally as rival modes of organizing political and social life.

A single set of common concerns will be addressed by all authors in the series: what values are shared, what sorts of social relations are preferred, what kinds of beliefs are involved, and what the political implications of these values, beliefs, and relations are. Beyond that, the focal points of the studies are open and may compare cultures within a country or among different countries, including or excluding the United States.

Books in the Series

Cultural Theory
Michael Thompson, Richard Ellis, and Aaron Wildavsky

The American Mosaic: The Impact of Space, Time, and Culture on American Politics
Daniel J. Elazar

District Leaders: A Political Ethnography
Rachel Sady

The Science of Political Culture and the Culture of Political Science
Michael E. Brint

DISTRICT LEADERS
A Political Ethnography

Rachel Sady

Westview Press
BOULDER, SAN FRANCISCO, & OXFORD

Political Cultures

This Westview softcover edition is printed on acid-free paper and bound in library-quality, coated covers that carry the highest rating of the National Association of State Textbook Administrators, in consultation with the Association of American Publishers and the Book Manufacturers' Institute.

Copyright © 1990 by Westview Press, Inc.

Published in 1990 in the United States of America by Westview Press, Inc., 5500 Central Avenue, Boulder, Colorado 80301, and in the United Kingdom by Westview Press, Inc., 36 Lonsdale Road, Summertown, Oxford OX2 7EW

Library of Congress Cataloging-in-Publication Data
Sady, Rachel Reese.
    District leaders : a political ethnography / Rachel Sady.
      p.   cm. — (Political cultures)
    Includes bibliographical references. (p.   ).
    ISBN 0-8133-7944-X
    1. Political leadership—New York (State)—Greenburgh.
2. Politicians—New York (State)—Greenburgh.   3. Democratic Party
(N.Y.)   4. Greenburgh (N.Y.)—Politics and government.   I. Title.
II. Title: Political ethnography.   III. Series.
JS894.G5953S23   1990
324.2747′06—dc20   90-12051
                                                                        CIP

Printed and bound in the United States of America

The paper used in this publication meets the requirements
of the American National Standard for Permanence of Paper
for Printed Library Materials Z39.48-1984.

10   9   8   7   6   5   4   3   2   1

To Daniel, Stephen and Nathan

Contents

Discussion, 130

The Forty-Seven: Part Four, 132

Acknowledgments

This study grew out of a conversation with anthropologist Margaret Lantis after we had returned from a political breakfast. Her questions and comments on what she had observed there led to the idea of an article about Greenburgh's district leaders. Years later, the "article" is this book. Throughout that time Margaret read it piece by piece, asked more questions and made more comments. To her I express my deepest appreciation.

Others have read versions or parts of the manuscript during its evolution, and I have benefited from their reactions, whether they were encouraging or urging me past my capacity to deliver. I thank, then, without their imprimaturs, anthropologists Sol Tax and Ronald Cohen; political scientists John Kincaid, Samuel J. Eldersveld and Donna Kirchheimer; and district leaders Fay Beauchamp (Philadelphia) and Carol Ettlinger (Greenburgh).

I am also grateful to the Hastings Public Library for its help in my research, particularly to reference librarian Janet Murphy, who tracked for me books and articles not only in Westchester libraries but also from far reaches of the state.

Dorothy Shannon processed the final manuscript and the ultimate corrected and coded version with her customary élan and efficiency. Mildred L. Beece provided the figures and tables. I thank them both wholeheartedly.

I feel privileged by my association with Westview Press and Aaron Wildavsky's series on political cultures. I thank senior editor Jennifer Knerr for making this publishing experience so smooth and gratifying, as well as Lindsay Schumacher, who guided the book through the final production process.

Rachel Sady
Hastings on Hudson, New York

CHAPTER 1

Introduction

Politicians are fork-tongued people who enter the partisan fray to feed their egos and fill their pockets. So goes one popular stereotype of the political breed. An antithetical but far weaker image is of selfless citizens concerned about the commonweal. Such one-dimensional portraits have been repeatedly proven false by serious reporters and students of the national and state scenes, yet they persist as commonplaces.

Politics is in part a debate about values and goals. This is an important argument in which moral and pragmatic issues are discussed and acted upon. It seems worthwhile, therefore, to transcend caricatures of participants in the debate, whatever the level of politics at which they play their parts.

This study seeks to cast light on the roles played by a selection of people who make up the lowest layer of elected party office holders and the one closest to the voters. These people are a sample of Democratic District Leaders of the Town of Greenburgh in Westchester County, New York. Who are they? What do they think they are doing? Why do they do it? What are the linkages between the district leaders and the party structure on the one hand, and the areas they represent on the other? What are the effects of their activities? The answers to these and other questions make up an ethnographic case study of the political beliefs and behavior of a specific group of local politicians and their relationship to the wider American scene. Many anthropologists are using their training to build up, piece by piece, detailed information about various aspects of life in their own society, and this is part of that general effort.

Foremost among more specific purposes in writing this book is to describe and interpret a role that most people do not know exists, to introduce what may seem a strange, indeed dying, breed. As will be seen, the political status of most of the actors in this play is not only organizationally low-level, but peripheral rather than central in their own lives. Paradoxically, this makes it more important to learn about them because, except for their part-time political activities, they are much like the rest of the nation's public; that is, they are not movers and shakers but part of the multitude whose day-to-day concerns relate to deep contradictions, historically rooted, in the social and political life of the nation.

A second reason for the study, then, is to explore its implications for practical politics. Ironically, democratic societies, particularly the United States, face serious problems in engaging their publics in the very democratic processes upon which the nations depend. Three interrelated themes emerge from the ethnographic data: participation in the political process, the role of the parties in the process; and parapolitical factionalism, which refers to intra party conflicts that help shape the role. Observing micro political processes at a local level aids in exploring these themes.

Another contribution of the research should be to add some theoretical insight to the development of political studies. I claim no breakthrough. Political anthropology and political science burgeon with conflicting hypotheses and competing theoretical frameworks. I have not tried to cut my material to fit preconceived causative formulas (this is not a denigration of theory-building, only a recognition of limitations in that area) but have used those approaches and ideas that seem to make the most sense of it.

THE ETHNOGRAPHY OF A POLITICAL FIELD

Ethnographic fieldwork has been the bedrock of twentieth century anthropology, and participant observation its distinctive method. Procedures in the field started out ad lib, and to a large extent have remained so. Early subjects of study were small, autonomous (or assumed to be) societies: hunters and gatherers, tribal people, and villagers. These groups often lived in faraway, exotic places and their cultures were almost always markedly different from the ethnographer's own. Written findings tried to give a picture of the whole culture and tended to be neutral—understanding and not judgmental—about that culture.

Over time ethnography became variegated to an extreme. The unit of study ranged from large scale to small and was located at home as well as abroad. Most research became problem or situation oriented, no longer aimed at the impossible telling of the whole story. Written accounts were naturalistic or interpretive to different degrees, presentations notably individual in style.

Studies of isolated whole societies have, out of historical necessity, given way to interest in part societies (peasant and pastoralist) and rural or urban segments of complex nation states. This in turn has led to concern about the linkages between the parts and the whole—that is, how social microcosms interrelate with their macro matrix.

People defined by certain statuses or roles have also frequently been the subject of ethnographic study. A few examples are old people, prostitutes, elites, construction workers, school children, poker players and immigrants. The research here is also about a particular role—the political party district leader—and the unit is the "field" in which they carry on their activities.

The People and the Field

The data used here result from two empirical research activities, as well as cited sources. First, during twenty years of intense participant observation, first as an election inspector and then for a longer period as a Greenburgh district leader, I have systematically collected material on a variety of local politicians in a range of political settings and activities. Second, during three of the twenty years (1977 to 1980) I also interviewed forty-seven Greenburgh Democratic district leaders. Although these years are the basic time frame of the study, the text is also informed by events observed and attitudes expressed both prior to and after those dates.

A political field has been defined as composed of the groups within which political processes can be observed (Swartz, Turner, and Tuden 1966). It is a flexible concept since its "social and territorial scope and the behavior it involves change as additional actors enter into the processes or as former participants withdraw and as they bring new types of activities and/or abandon old types" (Swartz 1968:6). Although the field as a unit of study has not caught on with many political anthropologists, it seems made to order for use here, where the situations and settings (field) in which the district leaders meet each other and their constituents face-to-face vary so greatly. This context includes their home communities and several intricately related levels of governmental and political structures, formal meetings and informal gatherings, and such activities as campaigning for and serving in public or party office. Also, since the study is semi-longitudinal, the actors do indeed come and go and local political activities change accordingly.

Some of the anthropologists who use field as the unit of study have tried to specialize "arena" in connection with it, but in such different ways (some say it is within and some without the field) as to create confusion. The usage here is that an arena is the space where particular episodes of conflict are played out; it is within the field because of the latter's fluid boundaries, which include wherever the group interactions are taking place.

The interview respondents were not randomly selected. All but two were friends or acquaintances before our talks (usually at my home, sometimes at theirs), and I had seen even those two at public meetings. The choices were made out of a desire for diversity and personal curiosity. No one was selected for being a political ally or opponent— positions that change from one situation to another, at any rate. Our dialogues and shared reflections varied with the kind of past experiences and relationships I had with each, and with the extent of curiosity they had about me and what I thought. Nevertheless, the same subjects were covered with each of the forty-seven. These were:

1. Their political self-perceptions. This includes the shaping of their political attitudes, significant interests and social relationships, and the effect of their political activity on their self-images.

2. Their political goals. This includes their value orientations and political world view, the ends for which they try to influence events, areas of conflicting interests, evaluation of political figures and their own personal ambitions.

3. Their individual experiences and adaptations in the leadership role. This includes their conceptions about political power and their beliefs about decision-making, political expediency, interpersonal relations and how the role-experience has affected them.

The interviews were taped. They ranged from forty-five minutes to a little over two hours, with the exception of one. Over a period of weekly meetings we racked up nine hours, most of which I intend to use in another way. Only one prospective interviewee suspected dark things and turned down my request. A few others I let slip after a postponement or two, feeling that they may have been ambivalent about being interviewed. As for the respondents, the taping seemed to turn them on, except for two who appeared uncomfortable and relieved when the experience was over. One hazarded a guess that he had said more than he meant to, and the other obviously had not. Readers should not expect consistency in all that the informants said and what they are sometimes described as doing. Time, events, and caprice change minds—a fact that many of the forty-seven commented on years after their interviews.

There were seventy-eight election districts in Greenburgh at the time, each entitled to two Democratic leaders (and two Republicans, of course). In ideal grassroots party politics there should have been, then, a Greenburgh Democratic committee of 156, but there is always a steady turnover and several vacancies. When interviewed all but a handful were in office or only quite recently resigned. They are not a statistical, but an ethnographic sample of about thirty percent. The composition of the committee has changed over time in ethos and ethnicity. This is reflected in the interviews, but again not quantitatively. Qualitatively there is scope, however. There are in the sample old-timers and tyros; radicals, liberals and conservatives; deeply committed politicians, dilettantes, and some who are still in mild shock and tentative about their leadership roles.

I have tried my best to present the leaders as they presented themselves to me. The ethnography is emic; that is, it is from the points of view of the informants. This leads to a problem when doing anthropology at home.

Emics and Etics

Before World War II, ethnographers had not worried too much about differentiating the natives' own views of their lives and times from their own comments and conclusions about the culture, relying on the reader's common sense to sort it out. Since then, however, some sociocultural anthropologists borrowed the emic-etic distinction from their more precise linguistic colleagues (phonetics is about the objectively-determined way the organs of speech are used to produce phones—sounds; phonemics is about the range and contrast of phones that the speakers have defined as meaningful to them). Not all anthropologists are happy with the innovation but others have found it useful enough to give it a firm place in the anthropological literature today.

An emic description is an "inside" view of a culture, of how the people partaking in the culture define its terms and their meanings. Ethnographers, of course, only approximate this view through their empathy and the professional skills they have developed. Some ethnographers have taken emic observations further, or rather deeper, into the "thick description" of Clifford Geertz (1973). This method uses symbolic interpretation to tease out meanings from the data that the culture-bearers themselves may not be conscious of, or if they are, rarely put into words.

An etic analysis is an "outside" view, but of a special kind of outsider—one trained in the sciences of the Western world. It is an explanation of the culture, or the portion of it being examined: how it works and how it got that way. It is usually attempted within a given theoretical framework. This view is not only an approximation, it is also tentative since it is to be tested against alternative generalizations and over time modified or discarded. Many anthropologists have given up on this kind of effort and still others postpone it. It has been suggested, for example, that emic studies are the first priority in the political anthropology of complex nation-states (Britan and Cohen 1980).

In short, emics is what ethnographers think the people think and etics is what the anthropologists think they know about why the people think what they think. In this study, emics is not "thick description" nor etics broad scale theory, on the grounds that both are too difficult to do. The data are emic, based only on what I saw, heard and thought about over two decades and what I learned in the last of those years. The analysis is etic only to the extent that I have been able to bring other information and insight to bear on the data.

Making the emic-etic distinction is complicated by doing anthropology in one's own country (in this case, even in my own community and among fellow political partisans). Of course, one can never completely separate one's ingrained value system from objectively-meant conclusions, but the point of anthropology is to make the effort. I found this most difficult in handling some aspects of the labeling problem.

Using party labels is not a problem. A Democrat is someone enrolled in the Democratic party, a Republican someone enrolled in the Republican party. At one time these people so defined themselves (although a few in my election district, at least, have forgotten they did, or if they did why they did). The difficulty is introduced with the words "left" or "liberal" and "right" or "conservative," as well as "neos" of both stripes and "moderates," "radicals," or small-p "progressives."

Thinking in terms of a left to right continuum is thoroughly embedded in the political culture of Western democracies. In the United States, the range of usage seems to involve the extent to which the government should be responsible for people's welfare and the extent to which the mass of its citizens should be involved in its decisions. Political scientists use it, pollsters use it, even the public and its politicians use it. The left-right mind-set in general seems consistent, structurally significant, and symbolic of class interests. Concerning the latter, a good deal has been made of the fact that European political parties are clearly based on these interests while the United States two-party system is far less polarized by class. Still, aggregate data on self-identification (therefore emic) of United States voters place them and their parties differentially on a left-to-right continuum: there are substantially more liberals among the Democrats and more conservatives among the Republicans. Furthermore, anecdotal evidence is that voters freely make the same kind of placements of people they know and of candidates they consider for office.

The significance of left-right labeling is also indicated by denial. Many politicians, frustrated by being pigeon-holed and fearful of electoral reaction to their current label, protest the practice, preferring to be judged by their good intentions or issue by issue. Political self-identification as "independent," "moderate," or "neo-whatever" is indeterminate in thrust and often simply manipulative public relations.

For example, the fledgling neo-liberals are, according to a foremost advocate, mostly Democrats who cannot be told from liberal Democrats by their voting records, but only by their emphasis on one or more of a variety of approaches to problem-solving (Rothenberg 1984). The neo-liberals vary so much among themselves that the denial of the old liberal label seems most salient in defining them.

There is, then, a solid emic Western view that the continuum under discussion exists, but it shatters into multiple versions in its application to selves and others. Left and right (or in its attenuation, liberal and conservative) have different references in contexts that vary from nation to nation, group to group, individual to individual, and according to focal issues (see Dominguez 1984 for an analysis of "the language of left and right" in Israel). Referential complexity does not leave these terms devoid of broad symbolic meanings; it only means that one must know the specifics of time, place and situation to interpret them.

Left and right are pervasive ways of thinking about social and economic issues that the United States inherited from the old world and adapted to the less polarized way of our historic democratic political tradition, and then as one way to distinguish positions on changing problems and situations. Dominguez comments of Israel, "As indexes of polarity, left and right can readily be used to refer to any contrasting political positions. The flexibility of their (shifting) referentiality makes them linguistic 'work horses'. . . ." (107).

Political labels in their multi-faceted emic sense are frequently used in the ethnographic text here. To the extent that they describe broad contrasting political positions, they are also used in the analysis. I make no excuse for interpreting there my emics as etics.

POLITICAL ANTHROPOLOGY

Another constant of traditional anthropology, besides ethnography, has been the vision of developing a unifying, encompassing theory of culture and society. Instead, in the last score or more years, anthropologists have repeatedly noted a fragmentation of theoretical interests and approaches to research. A good many of them decry this "crisis" in their profession, others push all the harder their own brand of theory, and still others—perhaps from necessity—make a virtue of diversity and celebrate eclecticism. The subdiscipline of political anthropology, of course, shares in these hopes, disappointments and current theoretical battles.

There is a multitude of ways, then, to do political anthropology, and researchers debate about the paths of choice. Two of the major ongoing debates developed out of the mainstreams of early political anthropology: the evolution of political structures and how these structures functioned.

The first concerns cultural (including political) evolution, which continues to be a mainstream subject of study. The question originally was, which aspect of culture was the most important in shaping how humans adapted to the environments and situations of their lives? Was it by the fruits of their minds—ideas—or the fruits of their needs—material things that kept them alive, if not always comfortable? The opposing positions are, therefore, called "idealism" and "materialism." Although no proponents cited ideas or needs as the only cultural evolutionary forces, their opponents frequently reacted as if they had. There is no question, however, that a strong difference in emphasis exists.

In recent years some idealists have given up on discovering universal theories of causation, opting instead for the interpretive ethnography mentioned above, which seems content with delving diversity. Materialists of many persuasions (e.g. cultural ecology, cultural materialism, dialectical materialism), although often mutually contemptuous, all continue to stress the central Marxist point of the primacy of the mode of production, a subsistence pattern, in cultural evolution. The writings of idealists, as well as other anthropologists, have clarified my views about political culture and the work of materialists has contributed to an appreciation of the pervasive importance of economics in political affairs.

The other mainstream concern was how political structures function, and it at first focused almost entirely on non-Western societies.[1] Indeed, political anthropology has been described as "the consideration of political exoticism and [its] comparative analysis" (Balandier 1970:5). The model for these seminal studies was structural-functionalism, which laid the ground for later, more process-oriented research. Structure and process are concepts basic to this work. Of the concepts mentioned above, I take up these first because they have been most prominent in political anthropological research.

Structure and Process

The unit of study in structural functionalism was analyzed, essentially, as a closed or self-sufficient community in terms of consistencies of behavior that explained how the local system kept going. While such a model yields valuable information about stability and continuity, it was not designed to throw much light on political change. The local institutions seemed divorced from the broader structures within which they were situated and by which they surely were affected. Many of these early studies, however, carried the seeds of the process-focused approach which flowered in the late 1950s and continued into the 1960s and 1970s (Lewellen 1983, Vincent 1978).

In the early 1960s, when the "state of the art" of political anthropology was reviewed for a symposium (Swartz et al. 1966), a trend away from what was called "the static nature of structural-functional analysis" was discovered. In its place was a growing concentration on the study of political processes such as decision-making, competition for power, and conflict expression and resolution. "Dynamic" and "processual" ideas seemed to be replacing the old "equilibrium" model. Recommendations were made for more process-oriented local studies in as many cross-cultural situations as possible (R. Cohen 1970).

The various studies constituting this new approach have been called "action theory" because they focused on individual actions in local situations. They used such explanatory or expository frameworks as social drama (Turner 1957, 1974), "game theory" (Bailey 1969), transactions (Barth 1959) and group action (Boissevain 1974). In the review mentioned above, the authors define the entire field of political study as the "study of processes invoked in determining and implementing public goals and in the differential achievement and use of power by the group concerned with the goals. . . ." (7). They further name the processes to be focused on as "marshaling support, undermining rivals, attaining goals and achieving settlements."

Since *District Leaders* is a very small ethnographic slice, this focus on individuals is not only amenable to the work but is the major part of its substance.

As processual studies piled up during the 1960s and 1970s, some of them tended to focus so sharply on individual acts in small settings that the larger cultural and social environment in which they occurred, if present at all, was at the blurred edges of the picture—the same fault that had been found previously with structural functionalism. By the early 1980s, structuralism had resurged in the form of an open-society model, which some of its proponents called neo-structuralism to distinguish it from the older closed-society version. Individual acts, they said, are not meaningful when torn from their wider context. Moreover, they wrote analyses demonstrating their point by linking the processes observed in their local units of study to larger political entities encompassing or touching upon them (e.g. Baber 1985; E. Cohen 1974; Strauch 1981, 1983). Important forces explanatory of local action included historical and political economic ones.

The value of these insights is obvious, their application a little like keeping several balls in the air at one time. My intention in this study is, while centering on process at the local level, to regard the wider structural elements as an integral part of that scene, both constraining the action and providing opportunities for it. In doing so, I have also tried to clarify how I think about the concepts of process and structure and the relationships between them.

The notions of structure and process are distinct only in emphasis; they overlap in meaning. Structure, in general, covers how any entity is made up of parts, which are related to one another and the whole. It is *form,* how that whole is constructed, be it concrete or abstract. In anthropology it has been applied to phenomena as diverse as social organization (the roles and statuses of individuals and groups in a society) and thought processes considered to be universally human (French Structuralism). Structure often stands for the bare-bones model of an entity rather than for the seemingly unruly behavior patterns from which it is abstracted.

Process is a more inclusive concept than early individual-based action theory would indicate. It can also be discovered in institutional proclivities and cultural drift in general, and stems from countless unobserved individual and group choices. Choices are always taking place, but they include cooperation as well as competition and continuity as well as change (Antoun 1979, Moore and Myerhoff 1975). Many cultural norms prescribe ways to behave or proscribe ways that should not be followed, but there are also options and abundant ambiguity in the cultural milieu. Elements of culture can be "indeterminate," in Moore's terminology,[2] and thus subject to various individual interpretations. Or there can be "loop holes" in the norms that individuals can take advantage of in adapting to different situations (LeVine 1982:157). Even when the norms are considered rules to live by, they are in fact manipulable—"rules for breaking rules" are ever present (Harris 1975:242).

The making of behavioral choices, whether observed closely in individual action or at a distance in the study of institutions—that is, as micro or macro phenomena—is process. Indeed structure itself, viewed over time, becomes macro process. LeVine describes such large-scale trends as demographic changes, urbanization and social mobility by that term. Other examples are shifts in the world balance of trade and in our own market economy, technological breakthroughs, and specifically in this case, legislative changes and judicial interpretations of state election laws. In a synchronic case study, structure is simply caught in a freeze-frame, a rigidity that should be tempered by historical data and thinking in terms of ongoing systems—structural dynamics, in fact.

When looking at systems, including the political, analysis of a single event is not sufficient, no matter how much background is provided. It must be replaced by an examination of the relationships between events or series of events, some of which are micro and local and others macro and external to the unit of study. Several anthropologists have called attention to the need for research on these relationships, on the links—often called nexus—between micro and macro (structural) processes (J. Bennett 1967, 1985; DeWalt and Pelto 1985). The effort here to look for linkages between local political encounters and interactions and a particular, historically developed national political system, is in line with this call.

Political Economy and Political Culture

At the same time that some political anthropologists were focusing on process, two other research developments were taking place: interest in political economy was increasing and the idea of culture as a system of symbols was being explored. More than a few students of politics have been concerned with establishing a relationship between these two aspects of political systems, one a materialist perspective and the other idealist.

Politics and economics go hand-in-hand by virtue of their relationship with power, and with the roles in the social structure that provide access to wealth and other political resources. Anthropologists working on political economy have been described (by one such) as considering "inequality, poverty, underdevelopment and the nature of capitalism" critical issues of the age (Rothstein in Leons and Rothstein 1979). That social justice is motivational in their work attracts one to it.

It is widely accepted in social theory that, in all kinds of societies, political and economic development tend to run parallel (Levinson and Malone 1980:38). Also recognized is the need for more data on local access to resources and power, which then must be integrated with what is known about national and global political and economic systems. Collecting the local data is a familiar task; it is not so clear how to go about the integration. To establish such micro-macro linkages, for examples admittedly torn from stimulating texts, anthropologists have been urged to advance interpretive anthropology by experimenting boldly in the presentation of their data (Marcus and Fischer, 1986:37–44), and to at least start thinking about the way economic anthropology might contribute to understanding the effects of world-wide capitalist domination (Clammer 1985:53–85). In spite of their lack of specificity, the authors in both instances suggest macro research and analysis agendas far beyond the scope of the present study.

I assume that my purpose in writing and my choice of field do not, luckily, require establishing global connections of the political activities of Greenburgh's Democratic district leaders. They very well might require clarifying the fit between political economy and political culture as evidenced in this field: mutual impacts of the market economy, class structure, political system; and if or how the parties represent economic interests. But this would be overreach for one not schooled in economic nor class analysis, and whose interest is incremental political democratization in a nation where class consciousness is relatively dim and revolutionary change perhaps visionary. I do, however, include in the ethnography socioeconomic data—as New York Senator Daniel Patrick Moynihan once put it to his constituents (1987)—on a "how people make a living has a very great deal to do with how people think" level.

Traditionally anthropologists have defined culture as the learned patterns of behavior and belief that make up a community's whole "way of life," and, many have added, its unique mode of adapting to the world about it. They have filled out this definition by listing various cultural categories, some in small units and some under such broad rubrics as subsistence practices and technology, social organization (including political) and religion or ideology. Whatever the categories, they are thought of as held together by a number of constituent, interlacing activities (hence, "culture patterns"). In using this conception, the emphasis is on people-in-action—mentally or physically, consciously or not, and whether they reflect or differ from the ideal norms of the group.

A growing number of anthropologists have rejected such a conception as too diffuse and prosaic, and instead think of culture as a shared system of symbols and their meanings. Or, to reverse the order, culture is a system of ideas about the cosmos, the world and the self—ideas to live by—that can be discovered by deciphering the symbols that stand for them. Symbols have a variety of forms: things, people, acts and language, written or oral, all of which can be combed over for their various meanings and the emotions they elicit. Thus, scholars have written about American kinship as a cultural system (Schneider 1980), religion and ideology as cultural systems (Geertz 1973), and have offered a bewildering diversity of symbolic analyses of bits and pieces of various cultures (Dolgin, Kemnitzer and Schneider 1977; Shweder and LeVine 1984).

Political anthropologists and political scientists (who have long accepted the concept of culture as basic to their own research) adapt to this symbolic approach in different ways. Some simply add symbols to their cultural inventories along with and close to the familiar concepts of values, ethos and world view. Others stress the importance of finding the relationship—the fit—between political ideologies (cultural meanings) and some particular aspect of people-in-action (process) such as individual and group interests deriving from their places in the social structure or the economic system—in other words, the political economy (e.g. Aronoff 1980, 1983; A. Cohen 1974; Davis 1980). This "two-dimensional" view of studying meaning and action together reflects the desire to understand cultural change, which is initiated in individual choices and social action.

The above approach is theoretically attractive. Some of its results, however, flash warning signals for practically-oriented researchers. Myth and ritual are significant symbols of religious anthropology that have been secularized for other purposes (Myerhoff and Moore 1977). They have been heartily welcomed in political research as symbolic statements, one in words and the other in action, of enduring cultural themes; one might even say that they have been over-worked in some instances. Sometimes it seems to be a game to discover how many elements in a series of political incidents can be analyzed as mythic or ritualistic. Still other analyses seem to mystify rather than clarify political processes, or to satirize rather than understand.[3]

The main problem for practical anthropology, however, is that the scholarly meaning of myth as conscious social charter and unconscious value system, with no onus attached, differs from the common usage. The American public has been trained by what they read and hear to think of myth as opposed to fact, as fiction or misconceptions perpetrated either because of ignorance or malevolence. At best, they are any politician's reading of opposing politicians' premises. Although "myth" has been embroidered in ways too divergent to be useful here, "ritual" is more commonly understood in either its guise of cohering ceremony or mere formality. Symbols appear in this ethnography as parts of political culture patterns, but they do not stand for the patterns themselves, as in the symbolic analyses mentioned above.

Patterns of political belief in the United States are complex cultural creations. They are widely shared but idiosyncratically experienced in ways that lead to various emphases and even changes in the patterns themselves. Many social scientists stress an underlying consistency in the national political culture, a consistency traced to the liberal ideals of the European enlightenment as expressed in the founding documents of the nation and allowed to flourish by an expanding economy and individualistic traits presumably fostered by the exigencies of frontier life (e.g. Burnham 1967; Devine 1972). Early examples of work on political culture were directed toward comparing national political systems on a global scale (Almond 1956; Almond and Verba 1965), borrowing some of their inspiration from anthropology's still earlier national character studies. Although these political scientists tried to avoid some of the excesses of the anthropologists, the attempts from both disciplines have been criticized for over-simplification and, perhaps, an ethnocentric bias.

Almond and Verba describe for the United States a political culture that is homogeneous on the surface in its ideology of freedom, concern for the general welfare and experimental pragmatism, but pluralistic below the surface in attitudes about the government, which spread from nil to acceptance to participation. Douglas and Wildavsky (1982)—one an anthropologist and the other a political scientist—recognize a different kind of pluralism. They see an admixture of three types of political cultures, along with their distinctive associated activities. The sectarian choice is egalitarian and voluntary organizations, public interest values, emphasis on social criticism and avoidance of responsibility for governing. The other two choices are individual market (egalitarian in regard to opportunity but not result) and hierarchy. Both of these types balance the sectarian view by emphasizing a stronger, responsible central authority. (The authors admit their own cultural bias for hierarchical organization.)

Other political scientists and anthropologists add to the picture a political culture filled with ambivalence and ambiguities resulting not only from the historical past but also changing contemporary situational pressures (Lipset 1960; Pye and Verba 1969; Eldersveld 1982; Kelley 1981; Kellerman 1984b). Taken together, they present a melange of cultural predispositions, of overlapping and opposing values and attitudes: individualism, egalitarianism, pluralism, populism, elitism, sectarianism, anti-authoritarianism, and pragmatism. The tradition of protest and hostility toward government strains against a desire for order and central authority; distrust of democratically chosen leaders coincides with admiration for the powerful person who is self-interested and self-made. Clearly, there is more than one political culture in the United States. And this fact is not easily explained by aggregate polling statistics nor large scale impressions left unlinked to other cultural experiences and locale.

To handle this situation, one school of political scientists, fathered by Elazar, has abandoned both the macro or national view of political culture and mere recognition of diversity to study regional variations throughout the country (e.g. Elazar 1970, 1972, 1982; Savage 1982; Kincaid 1982a, 1982b). They have identified three basic political subcultures in the United States:

1. The moralistic political culture, rooted in and spread from New England. The common welfare is the political goal, public issues are important, political participation is a civic duty and political parties are merely one vehicle for participation.

2. The individualistic political culture, rooted in and spread from the Middle Atlantic states. People think of politics as a business and the political arena as a marketplace for competing private interests. Since people often think of politics as "dirty business," it is left to professional politicians, from whom a certain amount of corruption is tolerated. The parties can mobilize voter participation when major issues arise, and they consider party loyalty important. Political innovation is more likely to occur in response to public pressure than from elected officials or politicians.

3. The traditionalistic political culture, rooted in and spread from the South (now in the process of rapid change). Politics is characterized by paternalistic attitudes and dominated by a network of social and family elites. The goal is to maintain traditional ways of life. Voter participation is neither expected nor encouraged. Factions replace parties in organizing political activities.

The Elazar thesis is that streams of migration have distributed these subcultures throughout the nation. In many places they have been modified by particular ethnic populations. One or the other orientations can be predominant in some states, whereas in others they have intermingled. The nation as a whole is thought to be primarily individualistic. New York is characterized as an individualistic state with a strong strain of moralistic political culture. The New York metropolitan area, however, is considered definitively individualistic. Although valid tests of the Elazar theory are large scale and quantitative, and this study is neither, the analysis does provide a point from which to view the Greenburgh data.

The typology described highlights major contemporary aspects of the United States political culture or cultures that are problematic for the future of representational democracy. These aspects have been mentioned above: the extent of public participation in the political process, the role of parties in the political system, and political conflict within as well as among the parties.

Participation, Parties and Factionalism

In turning to the immediacy of these cultural themes, two points need emphasis. First, understanding micro processes of political activity entails awareness of a macro context that is both constraining and liberating, one that sets up barriers to problem-solving in some directions and provides ways toward it in others. Although an ultimate concern must be policy-making, it is not approached here substantively but operationally, through how the political system works or fails. Second and as corollary, this study is about Democrats, but the discussion is not addressed to particular partisan issues and the conclusions are not overtly partisan. Ethnographically, it is about how a political structure becomes a system through the social and personal characteristics of the district leaders.

A key value in the country's national ideology is, and has been almost from its origins, wide participation by citizens in public affairs. Participation is touted as the legitimizing force in democratic governance, as the populist underpinnings of an elitist authority system. It is most often measured by voter turnout, however, and here the real most obviously parts from the ideal. In spite of the nation's celebration of the symbols of democracy and patriotism, and civic exhortations to get to the polls, political participation does not seem a priority for most people, even on election day. And probably never has been.

The real culture of poor political participation has been amply described for the early period after World War II (e.g. Dahl 1956; Lipset 1960). A declining voting pattern, however, has been particularly noted (and monitored by aggrieved editorial writers, political columnists, and political scientists) since the mid-1960s.

It should be said that not all political observers believe that popular participation is the sine qua non of a democratic society. To some, a low voter turnout means that people are satisfied with their government. Others take the view that politics is best left in the hands of the knowledgeable. The sociologist David Riesman once touched both bases in writing that people have more interesting things to do with their time than indulge in politics and "bringing sleepwalkers to the polls to increase turnout is no service to democracy" (1959, quoted in Lipset). Dahl, too, questioned the need for "extensive citizen participation" on the grounds that the country seemed to work all right without it and—anyway—its occurrence was highly unlikely.

The more common view, and the one adopted here, is that the widest participation possible means a more democratic consensus and its lack leads to the increasing powerlessness of people already disadvantaged since government is likely to neglect their needs to care for those who do use political pressure. Almond and Verba stress participation as the very basis of the "civic culture" they describe for the United States. Others, looking to the future, assert that true democracy will not come about until people can deal with one another from similar economic and educational vantages (e.g. Bernstein 1983:214–223). Pitkin and Shumer (1982), however, argue that achieving such parity requires the very participation to which it is supposed to lead: "We ·can begin where we are." They advocate achieving democracy by practicing it in as many face-to-face groups, where people discuss matters they feel are important, as possible. Success in these small arenas, they suggest, will energize participants for the broader political struggles of the time.

The views referred to immediately above are not narrowly focused on voter turnout. They call attention to the political environment within the polity. Political party organizations are a prominent part of this environment, and the one most connected to participation patterns.

The history of the United States' unique two-party system is far too complex even to sketch here, but certain aspects of it must be pointed out as relevant to the themes under discussion. The system was not foreseen by the writers of the Constitution nor established by federal law. Incipient parties first appeared when members of the political elite (the founding fathers) formulated opposing policies and informally mustered supporters to their sides. Although public opinion was in large part hostile to such groups as divisive, competition among office holders and seekers for backing gradually established the practice of party politics. The leader-follower relationship shifted somewhat, however; parties became institutionalized as the link between the people and the government, the instrument through which individuals as aggregates could hold their leaders accountable and affect succession to office. By the 1840s parties were fully developed and entrenched in the political system: they selected candidates for office, conducted election campaigns, organized and controlled political conflict and even—although not famous for this—helped direct the drift of policy. Some of this has changed, but the two major parties are still semi-governmental bodies, empowered and regulated by state laws (federal laws cover financing of presidential campaigns), and a relatively stable part of the political structure—which does not mean that they always will be.

Three distinct but interacting entities make up a political party: the party in the electorate (enrolled registered voters), party organizations, and party members in government (Sorauf 1984). This study is about a party organization (the Greenburgh Democratic committee) but necessarily involves its relations with the voters in its election districts, elected officials, and other parts of the organizational structure. In general, the parties are organized in seemingly nesting fashion at national, state and local levels. That is, they are if the word "organized" is used somewhat loosely and hierarchical implications are largely overlooked. State committees and the tens of thousands of local committees in the nation are virtually autonomous. This is a condition that political scientists have come to call a "stratarchy" to differentiate it from the bureaucratic style of organization where orders go down and accountability and deference go upward (Lasswell and Kaplan 1950:219–220; Eldersveld 1964, 1982:133–136).

In spite of the institutionalization of party roles, a sizable public anti-party sentiment has persisted in the political culture. Opponents of the two-party system have frequently predicted its demise and friendlier critics have warned of it. The most recent "party decline thesis" dates, as do the declining-vote patterns noted above, to the 1960s. This thesis has it that party organizations have been gutted from the outside and weakened from within to the point where they have lost their primacy in the political sensibilities of the electorate.

The most cited external threat to the parties is the direct primary (indirect primaries nominate party officials), innovated early in the century by reformers to further democratize the political system. Increasingly popular since the 1960s, it has spread in one form or another into most parts of the country. The primary (assume the "direct" in this context) is an election called to choose the party's candidate(s) in the general election. It thereby breaks the party organization's monopoly on the nominating process and may generate party nominees not only independent of but embarrassing to the organization (or vice versa).

The primary has also added a new dimension to intra party factionalism. The parties arose from factions and have been characterized by factionalism at all levels. Today the losing faction in cases of split support for potential candidates can take the dispute directly to the party electorate.

More general environmental changes have also deeply affected the parties. High media technology and expertise, as well as the rise of career "consultants" or "advisers" to candidates have short-circuited traditional party control of campaigns. Furthermore, the political environment is now crowded with issue-oriented and interest-oriented groups, which compete for the audience that belonged to the parties in their heyday.

Still, the parties are often blamed for their own reputed decline. Aside from distrust because of corruption and "dirty politics," there is some sense that the parties are stuck in a time warp, that they have not been creative in the face of changing circumstances. The question about the health of the parties may take some such form as, "Is party decline due to lack of public interest in political issues or because the parties have lost interest in the people?"[4] In other words, are the parties a dependent variable or an independent variable? It seems clear that since parties are both affected by and can affect their political environment, they can be considered one or the other in particular contexts: for example, the former when they are the subject of holistic analysis (theory) or the latter when the subject is how party organizations can and do size up and take advantage of their outreach opportunities (practice).

In the last decade one begins to hear among the voices of party doom others with another message: mourning is premature. Not only has the two-party system finally achieved competitive elections in most areas of the nation but the practice is still spreading. Party organizations show evidence of being more active than ever, even while many voters are losing interest in identifying with them. In some localities, far from declining in importance, political committees seem to be on an upsurge; they have a lot to do with the traditional tasks of choosing candidates and winning elections (Eldersveld 1982, 1986; Crotty 1986; Murray and Tedín 1986; Hopkins 1986; Cotter et al. 1984; Gibson et al. 1985).

Former House Speaker "Tip" O'Neill often repeated the dictum: "all politics is local." It is time now to turn from the generalities to an introduction of the particulars of one locality and its matrix.

CHAPTER 2

The Field and the Players

STRUCTURE OF THE FIELD

The political field in which the Greenburgh district leaders are studied is one of dwindling concentric circles, from national politics inward to overlapping local political scenes. The diminution is not one of motivations or interest, particularly when it is a presidential election year or when primaries are being fiercely contested, but involves the salience of the leadership role itself. In the small inner fields personal interactions are more concentrated and there is a greater possibility of affecting outcomes. Besides these levels of governmental and political organization, each leader's own community of residence is part of the field.

Governmental and political structures run parallel. For the Democrats, for example, Westchester County is tracked by the county committee of about 1,640 district leaders, made up of two people from each election district in the county, who are theoretically elected every odd-numbered year. (The hope that they will be Noah's-Ark paired is often met but by no means all of the time.) New York State is paralleled by the state committee of a man and a woman (legally required, in this case) from each assembly district; and the nation, by the national committee consisting of delegates from each state.

New York State

The unique U.S. form of federal governance contains fifty state variations of the two-party system. The role of the parties nationwide is to choose candidates and run elections, but exactly how these activities are conducted differs from state to state according to election laws, party rules, court decisions and local demographics.

New York is distinct in several ways (see Scarrow 1983). First, its version of a two-party system is in fact a multi-party system, one that developed—unplanned—as a result of election law reforms. The Democratic and Republican organizations have been official parties since 1898, when laws were passed regulating the elections of their officers and district leaders by their electorates (indirect primaries); other parties could go about their business as they willed. Since 1922, however, any party that accrued a certain number of votes in the previous gubernatorial election also becomes an official party with a separate line on the ballot and subject to indirect primaries. Today that number of votes is pegged at 50,000. This is a very low level of access to the ballot and various minor parties have achieved it. If they cannot maintain this level in future gubernatorial elections they fall from official grace. Currently the minor parties on the ballot are Conservative, Liberal and Right to Life.

New York is distinctive in yet another way that, given its multiparty system, cuts into the competitive advantages of a two-party system. In 1985 it was one of only three states that allowed cross-endorsements of one major party by another (today it may stand alone). Sometimes in New York minor parties have run their own candidates in order to make a political point by offering an alternative choice. This is a time-honored method of "third" parties, nationwide, to send political messages to the major parties and the people in general. But more often in New York the minor parties piggyback on the major parties' choices. This gains them leverage with the major parties far beyond what their electoral representation warrants.

Because the Democrats and Republicans in New York are relatively competitive statewide, and because minor parties have easy access to a line on the ballot, cross-endorsement deals between major and minor parties for influence and patronage pervade the political system and limit the citizen's choices at the polls. Deals between the two major parties, although rarer, have even more impact in that a choice by the voter is preempted. In short, although the major parties are relatively strong in New York, their effectiveness in making the people's votes count is weakened by the state's multiparty system with its cross-endorsement provisions.

There are legislative remedies to this situation, but to date few state legislators have been interested in making them. (The Westchester Democratic leadership has not sought such changes, either. The Greenburgh committee has, however, made sporadic efforts to discourage the practice, and the Hastings committee raised the issue in one caucus.)

New York has had direct primaries since 1911, except for presidential and state supreme court justice primaries, in which delegates are selected to choose the candidates. This system has two variants in New York, one for statewide office and one for all others. In the latter, candidates, including a party's choices, have to go through the petitioning process to get on the ballot. The ballot does not single out the party's preferences from the other candidates, and the party cannot spend money on their behalf. Party candidates for state office do not have to go the petition route and are publicly supported by the party. Since 1967 they do, however, face the likelihood of a challenge primary from outside of the party organization.

The direct and indirect primaries are conducted at the same elections and under the same rules. Over half of the states, including New York, have closed their primaries to voters outside of the party (as opposed to open or comparatively open primaries). However, New York makes it much more difficult than do the other closed primary states for non-party people to enroll in a party in time to vote in its primaries. Except for this, the parties' control of the nominating process has weakened, as elsewhere, through the increasing adoption of the primary option.

The state has consistently, since 1954, tried to make it easier for its citizens to vote. Before, all people not living in rural areas had to register annually to be able to vote in the general election. That year the state legislature enacted a law to permit each county to carry out permanent personal registration (PPR). In the counties that did so, citizens registered, and then as long as they voted at least every two years (and did not move), were maintained on the registration lists. This relieved them of the yearly extra trips to the polls. In 1965 the language requirement for registration was dropped; in 1967 the election law was amended to *require* that the counties impose PPR; in 1970 residence requirements were changed from ninety days to thirty days; in 1971, the age of franchise was changed to eighteen years, preceding the national change by one year; in 1975 the election law was amended to provide for mail registration (now used by ninety percent of new voters); and in 1981 the years of voting inactivity before removal from the registration lists were stretched from two to four years.

Through all but the initial years of this history of electoral reform, designed to make the franchise more accessible, voting declined. Fewer and fewer citizens registered and fewer and fewer registrants voted.

New York State has usually been described geographically and politically as upstate and downstate, the latter including as part of the metropolitan area the suburban counties ringing New York City. In recent years, however, suburban politics have taken on a life of their own, as a third division of the state. Westchester tends to be independent in statewide races and in gubernatorial politics it is considered a swing-vote county. Although traditionally Republican, in the last several years Democrats have achieved parity in enrollment, if not in election victories, with the other party.

Figure 1
WESTCHESTER COUNTY IN NEW YORK STATE

Adapted from New York State Map

Westchester County

The County is about 450 square miles of cities, suburbs, rural estates and farmlands sandwiched between the Hudson River to the west and Connecticut and the Long Island Sound to the east. It reaches from New York City's Bronx at its southern border to Putnam County at the northern (see Figures 1 and 2).

County historians describe how, during the first years of the twentieth century, Westchester "communities became fragmented, with rich against poor, native against the foreign born, country life against urban life and labor against management" (Comstock 1984:48). Most of the "foreign born" mentioned were unskilled workers from Ireland and, later, southern and eastern Europe. Still later immigrants have added to the ethnic mix.

Figure 2
TOWN OF GREENBURGH IN WESTCHESTER COUNTY

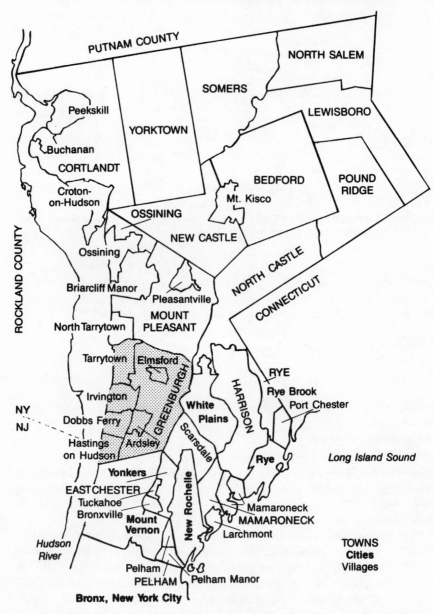

Adapted from *WESTCHESTER COUNTY MAP*

A Community Profile of Westchester County (Westchester Community Service Council 1983) describes a demographics in which there is increasing evidence of social differences between classes based primarily on income and social mobility. During the decade before the 1980 census, the county's white population declined to 84.2 percent and all "non-white" categories increased. The black population has risen to 12.2 percent. The new migrants—Latin Americans and Asians—represent 5.3 and 1.7 percent, respectively.

Population density is high in the county's southern tier, amounting to just about half of the total population. In the past decade, however, it has declined faster than has the number of all county residents. The central tier or region circling White Plains, the county seat, is much less heavily populated. About one-fourth of the population is in the central region and another fourth in the northern tier, but in the latter people are spread over a much larger and mostly rural area. The Westchester population is growing older due to economic factors and demographic rates. Nevertheless, minority youth in the southern and central tiers show a relatively high growth rate.

Social scientists weight income heavily when determining socioeconomic status or class. The median family income in Westchester is above the New York State level. Mean family income is highest among the new ethnic Asians and the whites in that order and lowest among blacks and Latin Americans, also in that order. In 1980 the overall rate of poverty had declined but concentrations of the poor had increased. The worst socioeconomic conditions prevail in the southern and most densely populated urban areas of the county, which lower Greenburgh abuts.

The county is governed by a county executive and a board of legislators representing seventeen legislative districts. From this level downward, the political picture is similar to that described above, but more complex. Westchester is divided into six cities and eighteen towns, each shadowed by its political committees. The cities are further divided into wards and the towns may also contain incorporated villages, again each accompanied by its own political committees. The smallest political unit is the election district, not to exceed 1,000 voters (and in Greenburgh they are very much smaller). The leaders in each district compose the county Democratic committee and the Republican counterpart. They are members of city and ward or town and village committees only by virtue of their identities as elected leaders in this body (see Figure 3).

The Town of Greenburgh

The town consists of thirty-one square miles of land, with a population of over 40,000, between the Hudson River to the west and the

Figure 3
PARTY ORGANIZATION

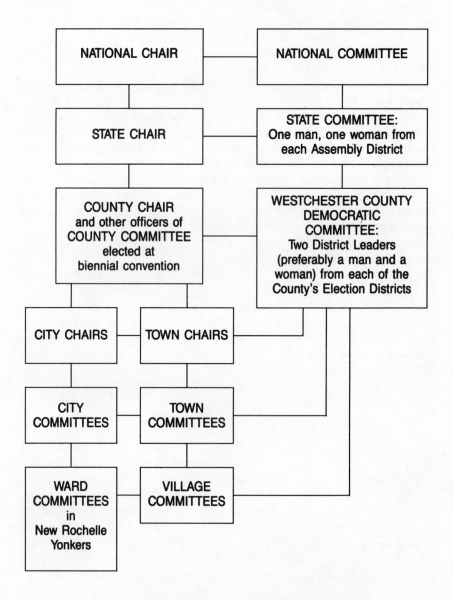

NATIONAL CHAIR

NATIONAL COMMITTEE

STATE CHAIR

STATE COMMITTEE:
One man, one woman from
each Assembly District

COUNTY CHAIR
and other officers of
COUNTY COMMITTEE
elected at
biennial convention

WESTCHESTER COUNTY
DEMOCRATIC
COMMITTEE:
Two District Leaders
(preferably a man and a
woman) from each of the
County's Election Districts

CITY CHAIRS

TOWN CHAIRS

CITY
COMMITTEES

TOWN
COMMITTEES

WARD
COMMITTEES
in
New Rochelle
Yonkers

VILLAGE
COMMITTEES

Adapted from *DISTRICT LEADERS HANDBOOK*
Westchester Democratic Committee

Bronx River on the east, extending from the north boundary of Yonkers to abut the southern edge of the Town of Mount Pleasant; it is part of the county's central tier. This stretch of land is divided almost equally between six incorporated villages and the unincorporated area. The town describes itself (Town of Greenburgh 1985) as:

> . . . a relatively unknown geographic entity. There is no "Greenburgh" railroad station, post-office, or "downtown" area; nor does it appear on New York State road maps. The Unincorporated Area with its amorphous geographic delineations remains a puzzle for its residents. . . .

The town's only railroad station and post office are in Hartsdale, and are so labeled. Other unincorporated area residents have post office addresses of five of the villages and neighboring Scarsdale and White Plains.

Before World War II unincorporated Greenburgh was a largely rural area left over after the older established communities became incorporated at the turn of the century. After the war the area was rapidly developed (real estate has been and is a thriving industry) and populated.

Four of the villages line the Hudson River, starting with Hastings on the southern border of the town and, going northward along the river, followed by Dobbs Ferry, Irvington and Tarrytown. Ardsley is nestled contiguously east of Dobbs. Elmsford floats alone in the unincorporated sea and is the seat of the town government. The villages differ in size and somewhat in character. Although a stranger driving up Broadway through the river villages might be hard put to tell one from the other, except for a few large estates to the north, parochial attitudes prevail among their residents.

Governmentally, Greenburgh is two entities, the town wide and the town outside. The town wide includes the six villages within town boundaries and the unincorporated areas—Hartsdale, Fairview, Edgemont and so on (see Figure 4). The town outside means outside the villages, only the unincorporated area.

The town is the tax-collecting agent for the county and for schools and other service districts. The town wide is assessed and taxed for these purposes in the same way throughout. The town government is run by a supervisor and a council of four legislators; a town clerk, a receiver of taxes and two judges are also elected. This government has few responsibilities for the villages, aside from collecting their taxes. The town outside is taxed substantially to support the government, but the villages minimally. (In 1986 villages were taxed $1.50 per thousand dollars of assessed valuation of property and town outside residents

28

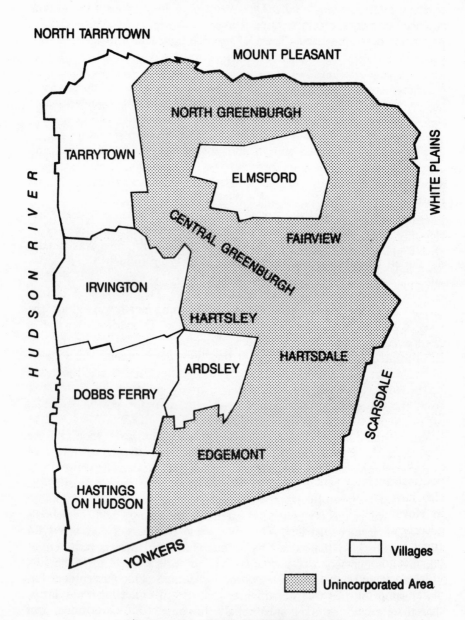

Figure 4
TOWN OF GREENBURGH

NORTH TARRYTOWN

MOUNT PLEASANT

NORTH GREENBURGH

TARRYTOWN

HUDSON RIVER

ELMSFORD

CENTRAL GREENBURGH

FAIRVIEW

WHITE PLAINS

IRVINGTON

HARTSLEY

HARTSDALE

ARDSLEY

DOBBS FERRY

SCARSDALE

EDGEMONT

HASTINGS
ON HUDSON

YONKERS

Villages

Unincorporated Area

Adapted from *THIS IS GREENBURGH*
Town of Greenburgh

were taxed at the rate of $48.90 per thousand.) Each village has its own municipal government headed by a mayor, with four or more trustees, and including a village justice, and is financed by village taxes.

Town demographics vary. Some of the villages are identified with particular early migrants—Dobbs Ferry with Italian ethnics and Hastings with Polish and Ukrainian, for example. In the town outside and in the village of Elmsford the black population increased several percentages between 1970 and 1980—18.3 and 17.8 respectively. None of the river villages has a significant number of blacks, but none has less than one percent. Only in Greenburgh outside and the village of Tarrytown is there a sizable concentration of Latin American ethnics.

The Community Profile rates clusters of census tracts comprising about forty-one each by "quality of life" or socioeconomic conditions into "Quintiles." The criteria used are income, employment, family organization, housing and education. None of Greenburgh's tracts falls in Quintile I, which has the greatest socioeconomic debilitation. Quintile II populations live relatively marginal lives and are considered vulnerable. Only two Greenburgh tracts are so characterized; one is in Tarrytown and includes a fairly high number of Latin American ethnics and the other is in the Fairview section and includes a large black population.

People in Quintile III are most like those in the county in general. Two Greenburgh tracts, all of Elmsford and the westernmost parts of Dobbs Ferry and Hastings (bordering the Hudson) fall in this category. The population in Quintile IV has a relatively higher quality of life than the county as a whole. It includes a large portion of Greenburgh outside and the east or hill section of Hastings. Quintile V contains more affluent residents. It includes all of Ardsley and Irvington, a large part of Tarrytown, the east side of Dobbs Ferry, and the east Irvington area in Greenburgh (see Figure 5).

The town wide-town outside governmental arrangement results in a political anomaly. The villages hold their local elections in March, but also have equal say in electing the town government every two years in November. Most of the village voters know little about the town government and care about the same. The villages have more than an equal voice—the village vote is large and can swing an election. The town candidates for election like their slate to include a villager or village-oriented person for this reason. During campaigns much is made of the amorphous town-village link. For example, various voluntarily shared services are stressed, and it is pointed out that traffic and community development in the town outside affects people in the villages.

Figure 5
GREENBURGH SOCIOECONOMIC QUINTILES

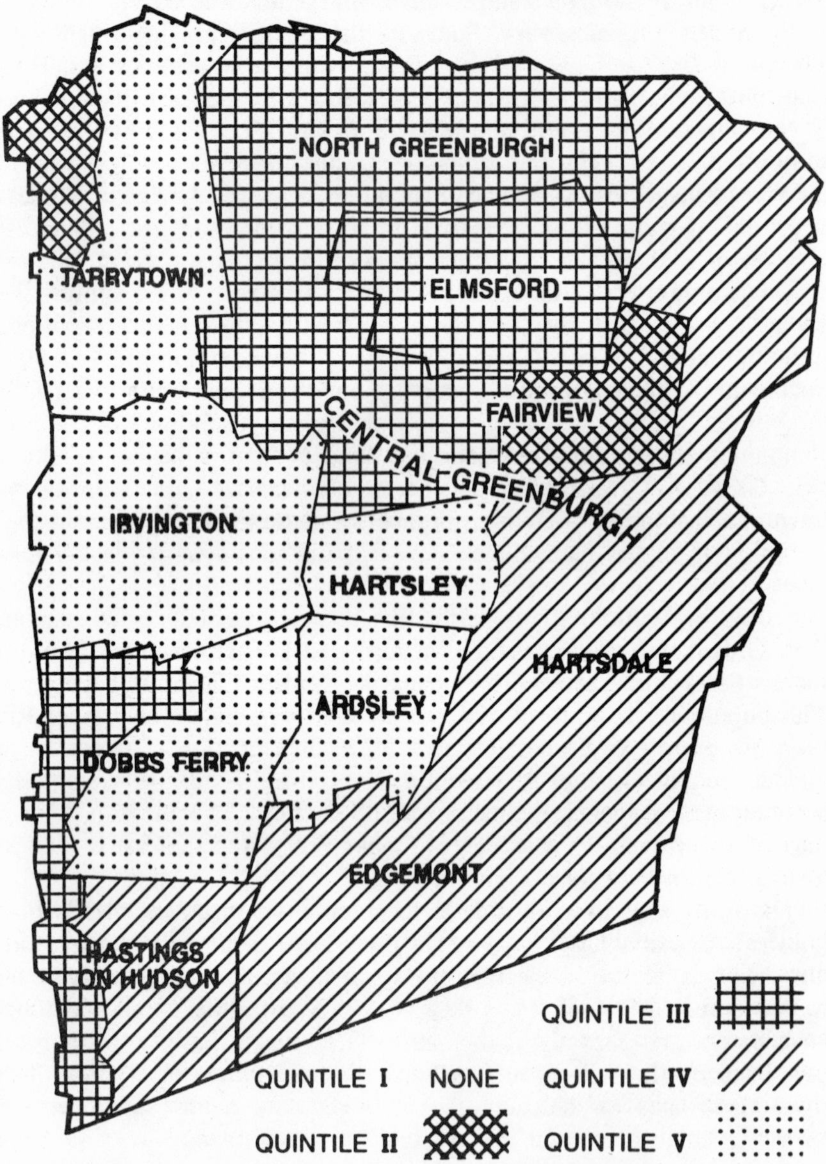

Adapted from *A COMMUNITY PROFILE OF WESTCHESTER COUNTY*,
Westchester Community Service Council

Greenburgh is the most populous of Westchester County's towns, and its Democratic committee has sizable political influence within the county organization—even at times challenging its powerful neighbor to the south, the city of Yonkers, over rights and prerogatives. The officers of the Greenburgh committee include a chair, an executive vice-chair, three other vice-chairs, a treasurer and two secretaries. These officers are elected every two years at a reorganization meeting. In addition, the two state committee people and any town members of the county executive committee are considered officers. These people and each area and village chair sit as voting members of the town executive committee.

There are forty election districts in the town outside, grouped in seven areas, and thirty-eight in the six villages; each area and village contains four to ten districts (see Table 1). Every two years they, too, elect area chairs and other officers at a reorganization meeting prior to the town reorganization (which in turn is held prior to the biennial county convention at which the county chair and other officers are elected (see Table 1).

Until 1973 the government in Greenburgh was solidly in the hands of the Republicans.[1] In that year, due to a strong candidate for supervisor at the head of the Democratic ticket, the infusion of new blood into the local party as a result of the movement against the Vietnam War, and disillusionment with the previous administration, the tables were dramatically turned. The entire Democratic ticket won office. The administration of the town has remained Democratic, with the supervisor the same man, ever since.

The village committees are organized, as are the area ones, in accordance with county and town committee by-laws. However, they may innovate beyond these provisions in their own by-laws. In Tarrytown office holders are ruled out of becoming district leaders because they have no trouble filling their leadership slots. In Dobbs Ferry office holders are not only district leaders, but—they think—the most effective ones. The Irvington committee makes their ex-leaders emeritus, with a vote on village affairs. The Hastings committee has added two categories of people aside from its sixteen district leaders as full voting members on village and internal committee affairs. Early in its history the sixteen election inspectors were included and, later, leaders were allowed captains to help out in their districts. Both decisions were made to broaden the base of the committee, but the effect has been minimal since inspectors rarely participate in committee business and few captains have been selected.

Table 1
DISTRIBUTION OF GREENBURGH ELECTION
DISTRICTS 1980

Greenburgh Outside   40

Central Greenburgh	6
Edgemont	6
Fairview	6
Hartsdale East	8
Hartsdale West	4
Hartsley	4
North Greenburgh	6

Villages   38

Ardsley	4
Dobbs Ferry	8
Elmsford	3
Hastings	8
Irvington	5
Tarrytown	10

Total	78

With increased Democratic enrollment, most of the villages have managed to win elections more frequently than they had in the past, but for Elmsford and Irvington it remains difficult.

The affairs of the committees at all levels are managed by their elected chairs and executive committees made up of other officers and the chairs of the next lowest unit, if there is one. All of the committees have regularly scheduled conventions and meetings for conducting party business.

Still other political districts cut across this ordering. In addition, the boundaries of these districts may change every ten years or so, after the census is taken, in order to approximate the "one person one vote" principle. These include congressional, assembly, state senate, and county legislative districts, each differently numbered—a source of confusion for voters. Political activities in these districts, however, are not separately organized but are mediated by the city and town committees which fall within their borders.

The governmental and political structures have been described in situ. It requires the people in positions within the structure to change it into an ongoing political system with inputs, decision-making and outputs. The following pages introduce some of those people as the system would like them to be and as they see themselves.

DISTRICT LEADERS

The Democratic District Leaders Handbook, issued by the Westchester County Democratic Committee, is a clearly written lesson in the local political structure and practice. It tells the county committee people that they also have the informal title of district leaders, and dedicates the manual to them—"the backbone of our party and its most important official."

The Handbook then explains the Democratic political organization, the technicalities of the leadership job according to the state election laws, and gives advice about "How to Be a Good District Leader." The manual has not been up-dated since 1977. Nevertheless, it stands as the party's vision of the ideal district leader.

The Ideal District Leader

The Handbook continues to address the freshman leader:

> Your job is essential to the democratic process. An informed and active electorate can prevent usurpation of power and circumvention of laws by ambitious and unscrupulous individuals and groups. . . . The mission is clear. The job is at hand. We hope this pamphlet will help you to do it properly.

A good leader will fulfill the functions of locating and informing favorable voters, registering Democratic voters, and pulling the favorable voters to the polls on election day. To perform thusly, one must do something called "setting up your district." This involves using such basic tools as enrollment lists, which are provided by the party, and ferreting out street lists, which mostly are not provided, or making oneself a card file of district residents organized by addresses. The latter is on the theory that people will leave often but houses are rarely destroyed or left unoccupied for substantial lengths of time, so one has a more permanent basis of operation.

More than this, district leaders are asked to serve in what is essentially the grassroots connection between election district and party structure. They are to report their constituents' "needs, fears and desires" and carry "the organizational message back to them." This, along with recruiting volunteer workers, is to be done by the year-round process of canvassing—that is, contacting district residents by door-knocking and phone-calling. In this way leaders are supposed to get to know their districts and be the indispensable link that will lead to the party's victory at the polls.

Some chairs at the local levels distribute the Handbook to new leaders, at least when they happen to have copies. Occasionally the county committee runs leadership workshops, and sometimes new leaders even attend them. Reactions of the leaders themselves to these admonitions are given in the next chapter.

Some Real District Leaders

It would be futile to try a reputational study of the district leaders. The overwhelming number of their constituents do not have any idea that the position exists, never mind who fills it. Within the town committee itself, reputations are easily made. A leader who does any work—pulls the vote, at a minimum—is considered good, and those who try to know their districts better are considered paragons. Leaders who work come to resent deeply those who cannot be counted on. Since these vary over time, the frequent pushes to "cut out the dead wood" are restrained by practical realization of the difficulty in recruiting better workers and the possibility of alienating good Democrats.

By chance, the forty-seven interviewees are almost evenly divided by sex. Almost one-third (fifteen) are from unincorporated Greenburgh, almost another one-third (fifteen) from five of the villages, and a little over a third (seventeen) from Hastings. Hastings, then, is represented in abundance. My experience was as a district leader in Hastings; the increased attention to the leaders there fits with the matching circumstance that Hastings is drawn on for examples of village attitudes and events more often than are the other incorporated communities.

Of the forty-seven, twenty recognize being Jewish as part of their social and/or religious identity. Ten of these are naturalized citizens or of second generation European descent; the rest are of more distant non-American origin. Eleven other leaders are ethnic Catholics, all but two being more than second generation American born. Five of the Catholics are of Irish descent (two of whom are married to ethnic

Italians), four of Italian descent, and one each of Portuguese and German heritage.

Three of the remaining leaders are black and thirteen are white with no strongly felt ethnic identity (this includes one German born and one second generation of Russian descent). Whether religiously affiliated or not, such status does not seem to carry the same identity-impact as being, for example, a Polish Jew or an Irish Catholic.

As an ethnographic sample, the forty-seven do not proportionately represent the Greenburgh Democratic committee. It is almost impossible to assess from the district leader lists the total ethnic makeup of the committee at any one time during the period of the study. Nevertheless, it is certain that blacks are under-represented in the sample.[2] Non-Jewish whites, ethnic or otherwise, are more adequately represented.

It has often been observed that the majority of the nation's citizens are middle class and that community affairs, including local politics, are middle class business. Although the socioeconomic spread of the leaders is relatively wide, it only laps at upper middle and working class edges.

A cast of forty-seven is inherently unwieldy. In spite of this, the district leaders appear in this study at least as often as individuals, identified by pseudonymous first names (see Table 2), than as anonymous aggregates. In other words, they appear with their own personas, expressing their own opinions and acting according to their own lights. Consequently, readers may feel that the names of leaders whose story they do not yet know—or cannot remember—sometimes come too thick and fast, as the forty-seven agree, disagree, take sides or are simply used as examples.

To lessen this problem and to emphasize the leaders' individualities, biographical sketches are presented in four groupings between chapters, beginning at the end of this one. An effort was made to place the vignettes of some of the actors either before or after they are featured in the narrative. But in spite of the imagery, this is not a play and the stage managing is only minimally successful. Identifying most of the leaders may not matter to most readers most of the time. For those cases where it does matter, Table 2 gives the page where each thumbnail bio starts, and there is an index of leaders on p. 203 where this is repeated and every other mention of the individual is located.

This chapter concludes with summarized material about the forty-seven: their political socialization (and resocialization) and values, their connections within their home communities, and their motivations in becoming district leaders.

Table 2
DISTRIBUTION OF THE FORTY-SEVEN INDEXED
FOR BIOGRAPHICAL SKETCHES

Unincorporated Area Leaders

Abby	133	Jack	47	Orson	50
Becca	78	John	138	Ralph	133
Brooke	77	Ken	72	Rita	72
Fay	134	Mandy	101	Sid	78
Hanna	138	Nino	135	Zoe	106

Village Leaders

Ardsley

Ann	103	Leon	132	Maria.	46

Dobbs Ferry

Ilse	105	Chester	76	Golda	136

Elmsford

Cali	47	Pepe	139	Polly	44

Irvington

Dennis	136	Faith	108	Marge	75

Tarrytown

Arthur	73	Laura	48	Nathan	107

Hastings

Cedric	137	Ella	72	Jodie	45
Charlie	49	Evan	44	Lewis	51
Claud	74	Fred	108	Nora	49
Conrad	104	Gene	105	Tess	104
Craig	77	Jane	75	Vi	101
Duke	51	Jimmy	102		

Political Socialization

Attitudes and values are transmitted from generation to generation, along with more concrete patterns of behavior. Two suggestions about specifically political socialization offer clues of what to look for in the life stories of the forty-seven. After an extensive study, Almond and Verba (1965:260–306) come to very general but significant conclusions that people who have throughout their lives had opportunities to engage democratically in non-political discussions and decision making are more likely to carry over what they learned there about process to political activities. The family and primary education are two important loci, but can be offset, in one direction or the other, by later educational, workplace or other influences—a factor in Pitkin's and Shumer's design for participation noted on pp. 16–17.

It has also been hypothesized by R. Cohen (1970) that if childhood lessons in "proper political behavior" agree in general with adult experience, the political system tends to be stable. The hypothesis adds the reverse: as societies change—gradually or radically—individuals will adapt to these changes, and particular incongruities between lessons and behavior will lessen. This leads to the question of whether the expectations of the forty-seven resulting from their political socialization were realized in their later intimate experience as leaders to the way the party system works. An answer must await descriptions of what did, in fact, happen in the field and how they evaluate the experience.

The forty-three native born Americans interviewed grew up within the broad consensus of our federally organized and democratic form of government. They experienced this consensus distally in all the explicit and subliminal versions in our complex society and proximally in multi-varied familial and other primary group contexts. Four interviewees were foreign born. All forty-seven leaders underwent resocialization of varying degrees of intensity as adults.

Over half the sample recognize strong family influences operating in their adult interest in politics and social reform. At the other extreme, eight flatly deny any political content at all in their home lives. Among the first group, many specifically mentioned the "dinner table" syndrome; that is, reading or listening to the news and discussion—or arguing—about current events and figures was encouraged by parents, usually the father.

Two of the three blacks (Abby and Fay) stressed their "racial" background as part of their significant familial political experience, and also described their religious roots as being important—two of the very few who did. Religion in a sacred rather than civil sense was not paramount as part of the leaders' political sensitivities. Ethnicity as a value was extremely strong in the cases of Jimmy and Nino, both of Italian descent. Jimmy recognizes the influence of his upbringing in the ethnic neighborhoods of the Bronx, and Nino emphasizes his desire to excel because of his minority background. Abby and Nino were the only leaders who overtly cherished the goal of integrating their ethnic confreres into a solid political force as such, but neither was sanguine about the possibility.

High school experiences, mostly because of the specific schools attended, were politically meaningful for Jodie, Becca, Leon and Nora. College added a resocialization factor for Sid, Faith, Fred, Mandy (in the form of turning her back on sorority life for, to her, more meaningful activities) and Polly (in the form of helping found the first black national sorority). Jane, Brooke and Rita became politically motivated through their husbands, who were candidates or ideologically committed or both.

The most dramatic instances of resocialization, however, resulted from World War II. For Craig and Charlie, serving in the army and the navy (respectively) meant shedding for the rest of their lives a narrow vision of people and places. Three of the four Europeans who had become United States citizens learned grimly at very young ages that, as Orson put it, "politics was being anti-Nazi." For Ilse, immigrating after the war, democracy was a dazzling discovery that reshaped her life.

Other introductions to politics of the leaders-to-be were idiosyncratic. Ella and Jimmy met mentors who encouraged them along the path of partisan politics. Lewis got bored with street corners, tried politics, and found it stimulating. Cedric covered politics as a reporter, and then began exploring personal possibilities.

Politics is an important part of the value systems of most of the leaders. To some, it was natural to follow that value system to its pragmatic conclusion (some galloping to the head of the forces for good, others dragged reluctantly in their wake out of a sense of duty) of becoming a small cog in the party of their choice, because if they did not (for a while, anyway), who would?

The political orientations of the forty-seven fall within a wide range—from radical to conservative—but with a clustering toward what they have variously described as "liberal," "progressive," or, cautiously, "moderate" attitudes. As far as civil rights and foreign policy are concerned, the dominant clustering is much heavier in the Greenburgh town committee than it was before the Vietnam War.

Even so, there are caveats. Charlie, Orson, Ralph and Nathan all claim to be waning from a liberal youth toward a more conservative present. These and others take pains to qualify their liberalism. On civil rights, all say they are liberal. Jack adds, "but conservative in methods"; Nathan and Evan, "conservative fiscally"; Duke, "conservative on welfare." Only Vi, Ann and Jimmy go for conservative, period. Pepe chooses the term "regular Democrat" and prides himself on surviving the "Concerned [Democratic] takeover." Nino, who describes himself as a moderator or conciliator, also uses words that may indicate to others an essentially conservative outlook.

A handful of the leaders thought labels were meaningless, which indeed they were in those cases. One leader sees himself, unless the interviewer was being taken for a royal ride—and he claims she was not—as basically Republican in outlook.

Community Life

In the societies that anthropologists have traditionally studied, political systems and processes are part of a community. Ideas about the public good and power relationships do not belong to a distinct category of behavior and beliefs, but are embedded with other social systems—kinship, economic, religious—in one conceptual whole. Complex societies such as ours, however, are defined by a specialization of interests, a compartmentalization of the various aspects of people's lives.

Many anthropologists, recognizing this compartmentalization, think of politics in terms of authority systems or governmental activity. Others see essentially political behavior occurring in arenas other than the one we call politics. Bailey (1969), for example, has commented that what we do in politics may have only marginal connection with our economic or religious life, where we are brought into contact with different sets of people, with different sets of rules for behavior.

Although Bailey reports on political activity in each of these broad contexts, and the field here is more narrowly defined, his comment raises the question of the extent to which the district leaders see their political roles as bearing on their other "lives," the extent to which the field flexes into community life. Again a satisfactory answer must await examination of the leaders' self-perceptions, but a start can be made in noting the range and nature of their community contacts. In other words, to what groups do they belong? Whom do they know?

As expected, the range is wide and the nature varied. Mandy, at one extreme, thinks of her community efforts, which have been many, as intertwined, as all-of-a-piece fashioned by—not in her words, but implicit in them—a sense of social justice and the common good. It was only because of the Vietnam War that her energies focused on specifically political activities. They have remained so.

Others at the gregarious end of the personal contact continuum are Rita, who joins compatible groups because bodies are needed ("If you need a job done, find a busy person . . ."), but whose informal contacts are limited, along with her husband's, because "We're happier with people we can talk politics with." And Abby: "I go to a meeting every time I turn around. It's outrageous." And Jodie, not because she is a joiner but because she has a far-ranging personal and family network. And others.

At the other extreme is Cedric who, although a communicant and lector of one of the two Catholic churches in his village, says, "I meet people through the benefit of the political system." John, too, who knows his election district well, and Golda, say they have few contacts outside of politics. Pepe, who has many contacts outside of his home village, says he has absolutely none except for political within it—"I have nothing in common with the people." Ann, Leon, Maria, Nino and Nora all indicate that their personal networks are mostly outside of the areas they represent.

About a third of the sample reported no lasting community commitments in organized form that did not have direct political tie-ins. These were appointments to boards and commissions on either town or village levels—for example, Arthur, Nathan, Dennis and Jack.

Claud, Duke and Jodie stated that they were not "joiners" (Duke: "I was a [volunteer] fireman for two months, but it wasn't me"), yet all three had greater recognition in their village than others who did "belong." Jodie's unique network is mentioned later. Both Claud and Duke, who became village candidates and briefly office holders, had spurts of activity for specific purposes that kept them in the public eye, and each had platforms from which they let people know what they thought. Claud is a consummate speechmaker and letter writer, and both gifts are sought after. Duke worked in the village business district where he constantly met and talked with customers and passers-by.

Some general statements can be made. Outside of neighborliness (strong in most cases, weak to non-existent in a few), the single most important tie within the community is the children. In Charlie's words, "the linkages are through the kids." (Of course, when the children grow up, the bonds become fragile unless mended by other affinities.) At least a third of the forty-seven have had formal school-involved associations—an excellent training ground for a similar kind of politics. This is in sharp contrast to the situation concerning church or temple affiliation. Only seven (one-sixth) speak of personally significant organized religious associations. Of course, there is a political significance in the sense of whom you know and it becomes very political when a leader becomes a candidate.

Entrance to the Field

The nature and depth of the leaders' motivations for assuming their roles correlate only loosely with the way in which they were selected. Or rather, elected, because that is the legality of the process. Every odd year a leader or potential leader is required to get signatures on a designating petition (five percent of the party enrollment in the district) in order to become a candidate in a primary election for the county committee. If there are no competing petitions, no ballot for the position appears on election day and the candidate becomes the incumbent. If no petition is carried at all, or if the number of names on one is insufficient, or if vacancies occur during the two years of incumbency, the county committee through the lower level committees appoints leaders. At any one time in Greenburgh appointees may outnumber elected members.

Whether elected or appointed, individuals become district leaders through their own initiatives or by recruitment. Of the forty-seven, over a third were recruited by foraging chairs because they had been politically or civically active or were otherwise recommended. A more sizable group was self-selected—they deliberately sought their positions, whether eagerly or casually. The remainder became leaders because of prior involvements, either through family or because they had run for or occupied public office.

It is unusual, but has happened in Greenburgh, for someone to successfully petition in challenge of incumbents. Indeed, in one notable case a challenger petitioned and won a seat, to the stunned indignation of an incumbent who claimed no one had told him there was an election.

Many who sought their positions did so in the context of a particular group's decision to fill vacancies for specific political reasons. Most were anti-Vietnam War activists. They had little difficulty getting leaderships because there were so many vacancies. As Orson, a founder of the Edgemont activists, explained, the regulars were glad to finally get committee members who would work. Polly sought a leadership as part of a push by the Black Women's Caucus to fill vacancies, and faced a barrier in the initial, camouflaged reluctance of her small village committee to accept a black.

Because vacancies are constantly cropping up, any who know the local structure and are willing to serve outside their own election district—or, indeed, outside their area or village—can usually get a position. However, when Hanna first tried to become a leader, she felt the town committee of that time was a closed clique. A few others have since also had to persist for success.

The reverse is a much more common experience. Many who have been recruited (or as Evan says, "plucked out of the woodwork") were instantly interested, but others required some mild form of persuasion. This often took the form of sins of omission, as when the recruiter is asked, "But what do I have to do? How much time will it take?" Rarely is one handed the District Leaders Handbook before being hooked.

Brand new district leaders, from the villages particularly, are likely to be taken aback at the extent of their purported town and county responsibilities. Even Vi, after years of leadership and deep political involvement, still wonders at town meetings, "What am I doing here?" Ann, too, says she feels uncomfortable at these meetings. Most leaders simply do not attend with any regularity, but a few end up enjoying the wider involvement.

Whatever the extent or lack of avidity for the leader's job, motivations for seeking or accepting it are ideological and personal, in various mixes.

Becca, who became fascinated with politics, says, "I'm an idealist. I believe in our system. I don't believe there is a better system. It's a system that will be absolutely destroyed if people are not involved." Others equally fascinated also stress the moral merit of becoming involved in the party structure—for a small sample, Brooke, Ella, Lewis and Rita.

On the other hand Nora, far from fascinated, was successfully recruited because she felt duty-bound to do some of the needed political spadework. Both she and Charlie commented that their right to gripe depended on doing something about the things that bothered them. Charlie became a leader because he wanted to affect policy, and wryly adds, "Now incidentally I was supposed to do some work."

The hope of actually affecting policy decisions and the choice of candidates—as opposed to what Nino calls the "scut work"—was a widespread motivation for entering the field that is discussed in the next chapter about role perceptions.

Personal motivations marched alongside these normative ideals. For some there were the twin enticements of finding out about something new—for example, Conrad wanted to know the "technology" of winning elections—and becoming socially involved with new people in new kinds of relationships, maybe on the brink of exciting events.

The majority of the district leaders say that personal desire for office or patronage was not a factor in taking on their jobs, or, in fact, in later staying in them. A few, however, did see possibilities inherent in developing "a power base" and a network of relationships with higher political figures. Nino and Sid, and other lawyers as well, were aware of how judicial candidates are selected by delegates (many their committee colleagues) strongly influenced by the high-level chairs, and of other possible governmental spots. Arthur had occupied patronage positions in New York City before coming to Greenburgh.

Polly states her motivations clearly:

My reasons for becoming a district leader basically are to further my own interests politically, to give myself a lever for bargaining, to be part of the decision-making, to be a part of the power. I don't have any altruistic purpose as far as other people are concerned.

From her observations, other leaders were similarly motivated. "People are involved to further their political ambitions, whatever they are. It's the way it's done. It's the ground floor."

The Forty-Seven: Part One

POLLY

Polly is a black woman who has been a state parole officer for over two decades and has lived in Elmsford for almost as long. She says about moving there, "My family was not welcome because we were living on the wrong side of the village—the south side, and most blacks were living on the north side. We were subjected to a lot."

Polly traces her activism back to her college days at a university in New York City helping build "the oldest black sorority in the country." Her next organizational participation was in village school affairs—"I went up the PTA ladder" to local president and then to district office. Later she ran for the Elmsford school board, developing a campaign organization mainly within "the black church" (through friends, since she does not belong) that pulled a record ninety-five percent of the black vote. "I didn't win but I had a hell of a good time."

Although Polly was a Republican initially, and then unenrolled, her husband was a Democrat and she tended to vote that way, too. Her first organized partisan activity was campaigning in a county district attorney race for a lawyer who had won a discrimination case on behalf of a state parole colleague. Soon afterward she enrolled in the party, became active in the Greenburgh Democratic Club and the newly-formed Black Women's Political Caucus. The caucus discovered that there were many leadership vacancies in the county and set about trying to fill them. Most committees were happy to fill their vacancies, "but in my instance it was quite different" and her offer was ignored. Polly says that her village is a "provincial, prejudiced, racist community" and neither party in the village had ever had a black district leader. Finally a new chair gave her a spot.

Polly does not think she belongs to any particular wing of the party. Although she sometimes has difficulty "going along" with the party, in general it appeals to her "sense of fair play."

EVAN

Evan is a physiologist with a medical lab in New York City. He was brought up in a family interested in public affairs, and lived at various times in different parts of the midwest, far west and east.

Evan's political bath started when he became an anti-Vietnam War activist in 1970, the catalysts being the bombing of Cambodia, the Kent State shootings, and campus turbulence at the medical school where he worked. His initiation was to be among the first demonstrators assaulted by construction workers in the city. He "figured the first thing to do was to get rid of the bad guys and elect good guys" and so worked for certain peace candidates.

When Evan and his family first came to Hastings he enrolled as a Republican. He recognized the importance of primaries and thought (wrongly, he says) that Republican primaries had "more of a future." In 1972 he changed his registration to Democratic, worked in George McGovern's presidential campaign, and was drawn into local politics. Although actively engaged in other community interests, particularly as a member of the volunteer fire department, politics became Evan's prime interest, aside from his family and job, for a few years. He worked in county, town and local campaigns, then became a district leader, and ran for trustee of his village once.

Evan says that in spite of his liberal politics he "crosses party lines gladly" (his wife is a fairly active local Republican) and his social attitudes are conservative. He thinks he has been hurt in the community by his identification as a "hill Democrat" (read "knee-jerk liberal"). Partly in response to this and other strains, Evan resigned as a leader. Eventually he took pride in serving a term as captain of a volunteer fire company, the so-called commuters' company.

JODIE

Jodie is head of the religious education program at a Catholic church in Hastings, a job for which her education and her volunteer teaching had prepared her. She was brought up in the northeast Bronx, a rural area of one and two-family houses populated by lower middle class Irish Americans with a sprinkling of German and Italian Americans. Jodie is of Irish descent, the only child of parents not politically active. The first big influence on the girl's political attitudes was two nuns at the private high school in the city that she attended. She describes these women as brilliant, liberal, attuned to politics and admirers of Franklin Roosevelt. Jodie enrolled in an Ursuline college, where she also found the nuns liberal and politically aware, although the student body was mostly upper middle class and conservative. "I associated with people whose relatives were judges who invited their friends to free $100 dinners." After college Jodie went to work for a union local "where the bids were all settled before they went in" and the union people were "thick as thieves" with the politicians.

When Jodie married and moved to Ardsley she became active in her church, then school board elections, and finally in local Democratic campaigns. The family moved to Hastings and the Democratic chair asked her to be a leader, but at this time Jodie was far too busy raising her children. Many years later she agreed to work as an inspector and then was arm-twisted into becoming a leader in her own district. She also worked on the village Democratic newsletter, served a term as vice-chair, and was campaign manager for a village election.

Jodie has a wide network of friends and acquaintances and knows more than pretty much what is going on in her village. She explains this in two ways. First, she has ten children and, as she says, "When you fan out ten people. . . ." Second, she does not drive and so does her shopping and gets her services in Hastings. She comes to know the business people and their customers as she "walks the street and checks out things." (A third factor is that she is outrageously amusing and only rarely are people more outraged than amused.)

"I chose to be a Democrat because I'm not of the rich, not affluent." Jodie says she does not delude herself that the party is totally the party of the people but on the other hand she thinks the Republican party is truly controlled by the rich. She said that her experiences on the Hastings Democratic committee "have not set me on fire to go to my grave as a district leader."

MARIA

Maria is a young elementary school teacher of children with learning disabilities in the Bronx. She was born and brought up in the northeast Bronx. She says her parents were political and that she has always known about carrying petitions. When she first registered she wanted to be an "independent" but her father pointed out the disadvantage entailed because of primaries, so she enrolled as a Democrat—"I think I would have gotten there anyway."

Once committed, Maria became active in the local Democratic club and saw there was keen competition for jobs among the Bronx district leaders. She describes a period of three years being "laid off by the board of education during which I met a lot of political people." After returning to teaching she was approached to run for the state assembly. She was tempted but felt the campaign would be too costly, both financially and professionally. "I like politics as a hobby but my first love is teaching."

Maria lives with her parents and a younger brother in Ardsley, which she calls "a lovely, lovely village where everyone cares." She became a district leader almost immediately through meeting a village trustee candidate on her door-to-door rounds. A little over a year later she—

the only new committee member—became its chair. She describes herself as "probably a moderate Democrat."

JACK

Jack is an educator, now an administrator at a New York City YMHA. Of Polish Jewish descent, he was brought up in an area of the Bronx largely populated by people from eastern Europe with a smattering of blacks and second and third generation whites. He believes his parents, who worked in the garment industry, were oriented toward social action because of their immigrant status but were too embarrassed by their lack of education to take any formal political role. His father was enrolled as a Liberal until he became an ardent Franklin Roosevelt Democrat. Jack himself remembers as a teenager campaigning and being a pollwatcher for Vito Marcantonio, the American Labor party candidate in a congressional election.

Jack and his newly-married wife, Eleanor, who is black, came to the Fairview section of Greenburgh because they thought it was a place where an interracial couple "wouldn't have to make excuses for themselves." Soon after, in the wake of Martin Luther King's murder, the resulting riots, and Eleanor's teenage daughter's distress, the couple together with other neighborhood families, both white and black, formed GROUP (Greenburgh Residents Organized for Unity and Progress). Part of Jack's activity with GROUP was as chair of a police-community relations committee. This involvement with the community led to still others. Although an enrolled Republican, Jack felt the Republican town administration was a disgrace, and most of the community service people that he worked with seemed to be Democrats. Consequently, when some Democrats asked him to run for chair of the Greenburgh Democratic club, he agreed, changed his enrollment, and was elected. He became a leader when a vacancy occurred in his own district. Eleanor has run for and won a seat on the town council twice and plans to run again. Jack ran twice for Greenburgh's "Central 7" school board, winning handsomely the second time.

Liberal in his goals, Jack feels they must be arrived at conservatively. He thinks that doing things in a liberal way has come to mean doing things sloppily, throwing money around, and not evaluating programs. "To be a liberal means to have an open mind and I know a lot of liberals who have the most closed minds in the world."

CALI

Cali works full time as a bookkeeper in New York City and has another job on Saturdays. A good student, she was unable to take advantage of a college scholarship because she could not afford clothes and other necessities. Cali is of Irish descent and married to a man of Italian descent. She lives in Elmsford with her mother-in-law, her husband and five of her six children. She describes her mother-in-law as being "the matriarch of a very large family, so we have an active social life." Her husband has a disability pension and no longer works. About the children, she says, "Well, I was a very good Catholic. . . . When I'm into something I go at it whole-heartedly. . . . I wouldn't use birth control." Cali is not sure she is a Catholic at all now. She has doctrinal disagreements, and also feels that the church let her down when she needed it most.

Cali feels that she has always been politically aware through reading and the activities of her grandfather and father, both policemen involved in police-benefit work, her grandfather in pushing for legislation and her father in fund raising and getting out "Support Your Local Police" bumper stickers.

Cali's "outs" (of the house) used to be church on Sunday and food shopping Friday nights. Then she got active in a Head Start parents' committee, joined a county cooperative agency and was put on its executive board. This kind of work called her to the attention of the Democratic village chair who offered her a leadership outside of her district, which she accepted. After an unsuccessful run for village trustee, she took over the chair herself and for the first time got interested in the town, as well as village, level of politics.

Cali now describes herself as a liberal "on the left of the platform any given year," and her husband as conservative. The family sometimes argues about issues at the dinner table, which she likes, seeing the disagreements as political and not family arguments.

LAURA

Laura is originally from Pittsburgh and suburban Philadelphia. She feels that her Democratic liberalism may stem in one way from the fact that her father and stepmother were conservative Republicans and in another from the fact that they were both psychiatrists and always helping people—"I see politics as trying to help people." Laura is married, has two small children, and is working toward a master's degree in social work. The family lives in Tarrytown in a cooperative apartment complex. At the time of the interview they were planning to move upstate because of her husband's work, but this did not materialize.

The village Democratic chair asked Laura, who was a member of the local Women's Political Caucus, to fill a committee vacancy, telling her it was not much work. Because she wanted "to get out of the house," she took the leadership in her own district. In six years she ran for trustee and won. A try for a second term failed, and she is now again on the committee.

Laura's activities before partisan politics were with the League of Women Voters and the school community. "Women's things are my interest," she says.

CHARLIE

Charlie is a chemical engineer. He was born and brought up in the midwest in what he describes as an isolated, conservative, segregated, one-party town. The prep school he attended, also in the midwest, was only a little more diversified. He feels that the best thing that ever happened to him was joining the Navy in World War II when "I first met people," particularly Jews, blacks and colonialized natives in New Guinea. This liberating wartime experience carried over into campaigning for Adlai Stevenson while taking graduate work in chemical engineering. Charlie's politicalization increased in reaction to the excesses of Senator Joseph McCarthy and, after returning to the midwest, he also experienced "the enlightenment of enjoying a sermon" in a socially-activist congregation—one far different from the evangelical circles of his early childhood.

Charlie's idealism—what he calls his "flaming liberal period"—was still at high pitch when he moved with his young family to Hastings and there became active in local village politics. He soon became a leader in the district in which he lived, participated in the Concerned Democrats' anti-Vietnam War movement, and later was chosen committee chair for two terms.

When interviewed Charlie had recently resigned as district leader after several years of lessening activity. He describes himself as burned-out and greatly disillusioned with politics and governmental bureaucracy. Now Charlie flirts with a "conservative" political label, by which he does not mean "really conservative" but "ahead of my time."

NORA

Nora is a special education grade school teacher. She was born in Yonkers of Jewish immigrants from Russia. Her mother lived in a small ghetto town and recalls hiding on Easter holidays from gangs that would come in and attack the villagers. Her father lived in a larger town where life was less repressive. In this country, he talked politics to his daughter and she has always been interested in the subject. In

junior high school Nora thought she was a Communist, in college she
joined the American Labor party for a short while, then was involved
as a Democrat in every presidential campaign from Franklin Roosevelt
through Adlai Stevenson. After marrying, her first paying job was for
Friends of Democracy "doing undercover work exposing home-grown
fascists," and she also worked for a while for the United World Fed-
eralists.

After the Stevenson campaigns and the birth of her children, Nora
found herself less and less engaged in politics, and less and less enthusiastic about candidacies, although she was marginally involved in the
Concerned Democrats movement. She sees herself as a liberal Democrat.

Nora became a district leader out of guilt for her lack of political
activity on the village level. When the chair asked her to fill a vacancy
on the Hastings committee she agreed because "how long can you sit
here just bitching?" She feels false about her leadership because she
just is not that interested about what happens in Hastings. She thought
the role might "grab" her but it has not. She does it as a chore, a
duty. She says she is not an activist, even in things she feels passionately
about, like women's rights.

ORSON

Orson is Austrian-born, his father Jewish and his mother Catholic;
he was brought up Catholic but says he is "nothing" now. From eleven
years old to fifteen, when the family came to the United States as
refugees, politics to him meant being strongly anti-Nazi. Following
stints in college and the U.S. Army (during which his first vote was
absentee for Franklin Roosevelt), he worked in 1948 for Henry Wallace,
who was running for president on the Progressive line, as an entertainer
in "Caravans for Wallace." Orson used to think of a career in acting
and music, and has a degree in chemistry, but since the early 1960s,
he has co-owned a public relations company specializing in the field
of health.

When Orson, his wife (met during the Wallace campaign) and two
daughters moved to the Edgemont area of Greenburgh the couple
enrolled as Democrats, primarily because the party was very much the
minority party. However, they did nothing political, except to vote,
until the Vietnam War. Orson was one of the founders of the anti-war
Edgemont Independent Democrats, a group that concentrated on learning the nuts-and-bolts of political action. The members of this group
were welcomed by the "regulars who were glad to get anybody to do
anything," and they promptly filled the many district leader vacancies
in the area.

Politics is a hobby for Orson, for which he is glad to contribute his public relations skills and his time as a leader and chair of his area committee. He sees himself as a "left-of-center Democrat, becoming in some ways a little more conservative with advancing age."

DUKE

Duke is a car mechanic and manager of a gas station in his village. He is of Italian descent and grew up in the Brooklyn flatlands. His family moved to Irvington when he was young and he applied for a job in Hastings where he has worked ever since. When he got married, the young couple moved to a house in Hastings.

Aside from his family, Duke has two deep commitments— conservation ("I've been a conservationist all my life without knowing it. I had the attitudes but didn't know the word") and Hastings, about which he can wax quite romantic. His family was in no way involved with politics or issues, and neither was Duke in spite of a great deal of community volunteer work. This was all project-oriented because he is not "a club-type person, a joiner." Indeed, Duke considered himself politically independent at the time the Hastings Democrats asked him to be their candidate for village trustee. He says he was naive about what the job was but agreed because he felt the seat was a place to get things done for Hastings.

Duke won. He changed his enrollment to Democratic because he found the party "people-oriented." Two years later after an unsuccessful race for mayor, he became a leader in his own district. After another unsuccessful race, he still played with the idea of running again some- time.

Duke says there are times when he acts like a liberal and times when he acts like a conservative. For example, he considers himself liberal on civil liberties, conservative on welfare. "Give me an issue and I'm opinionated."

LEWIS

Lewis was brought up in the East Bronx in a lower middle class family which, he says, had zero to do with his later passion for politics. In his middle teens, finding his life hanging out on street corners and playing pinochle boring, Lewis had his first taste of politics in the Progressive party's presidential campaign for Henry Wallace in 1948.

Lewis studied engineering at City College, but not liking "the way technicians think about issues," turned for associates to politically radical groups. He also got to know various people in folk music circles

whose bohemian life style appealed to him. After several years he tired
of both the fruitless political discussions with the radicals and the too-
narrow concerns of the musicians. Politically, he became a "Stevenso-
nian Democrat."

During the Korean War Lewis was drafted and served a stint in the
Signal Corps. Afterward he was too busy working, doing graduate work
at universities in New York City, adjusting to life with his new wife,
Pat, and "being part of the arty social scene" to work hard at politics.
When the couple moved from the Bronx to Manhattan's west side,
however, Lewis got involved in intercity politics via a concern with
low income housing—"civically, socially, politically, my life was wrapped
up in the west side for several years." His work on housing legislation
brought home to him that to get anything done in government a person
had to have politicians on one's side, and to have the right ones they
had to get elected. To do this, "I adopted internecine politics."

Lewis, Pat and their two children came to Hastings in 1973 for its
public school system. It was also close to the place where Lewis worked
as a science technician. He immediately played a central role in a local
campaign to stop a planned shopping center just south of the village.
It was successful, and Lewis thinks he made influential contacts with
governmental officials and environmental activists also involved in the
issue. He nourished these contacts and continued to be active in the
community in a range of "short-run but intensive things." Eventually
Lewis became a captain and then a district leader on the Hastings
committee, and later a secretary of the town committee. He failed in
an attempt to obtain a state committeeman post. Pat also became a
district leader.

Lewis calls himself a progressive Democrat who believes in social
reform but regrets that "what we did, we reformers, was take away the
political hacks and replace them with a bureaucracy that is impossible
to deal with." Lewis likes to think he personally can influence events,
and "I act in such a way to see that I can." In the event of an election,
Lewis works exceptionally hard for his candidate to win.

CHAPTER 3

Role Perceptions and Performance

The forty-seven vary in both their perceptions of and pleasure in their political roles. For example, Lewis, who loves politics and engages in it aggressively, says:

> I enjoy the role of district leader. I enjoy the contact with people I represent in my district to the people I contact at upper levels of government. I enjoy gadflying. I will make trouble just to start people thinking.

On the other hand, Duke, who is usually outspoken and at ease with people, is not so comfortable in the role:

> After my primary [for the leadership in his election district] several people thought that "county committeeman" was a much higher office. I got pats on the back and congratulations and wishes for good luck—"It's wonderful that somebody from our village is going to be on the county committee!" I was too embarrassed to correct them. I felt terrible just walking away without telling them I'm just Mr. Shit from Cornell Street who does nothing but call them on election day.

In the Democratic District Leaders Handbook, the leaders are exhorted not only (if chiefly) to get voters who support Democratic candidates to the polls on election day, but to relay their constituents' concerns to the organization. Leaders are told that they are the basic connecting link between party and voters, probably the only politicians most of them will ever know.

The questions addressed in this chapter are: How do the forty-seven see themselves in this particular political role that they have sought, acquiesced in, or had thrust upon them? Do they think that they are the party's grassroots connection? How do they separate the various aspects of the job, the different sets of interactions that compose it? What are their public and personal goals and how do they try to achieve them? How do they evaluate their performances and the performances of their colleagues?

Two sets of interactions are involved in the leadership role. First, there is the voter-leader interface in the election districts. Second, there are the relationships among associates on either village or area committees and on the Greenburgh committee itself. Concomitantly with this second set are connections with people at upper levels of the party and with elected public officials—icing on the cake of collegiality.

IN THE ELECTION DISTRICTS

Two remarks to journalists by ex-Westchester Democratic committee chairs illustrate doubts about the efficacy of partisan politics in the face of the independent attitudes of some candidates and office holders.[1] Max Berking asserted that, "Today there is no need to carry petitions. It's become a media blitz. A strong candidate can build his own campaign organization." And his successor, Sam Fredman, claimed, "Everyone needs the party. It provides a certain amount of exposure, it provides people to take petitions and to get people to the polls. You cannot do all that yourself as an independent."

It sounds as if the men had opposing views about the role of the party, but in fact they were making much the same point—"the times they are a-changing" as far as party politics is concerned. Specifically, they were pointing accusing fingers at the incumbent county executive, a Democrat, because of whom they had, in sequence, left their chairmanships in frustration over what they perceived as his slighting of the Democratic organization. They use almost identical words of indictment—he has "no sense" or "no feeling" of partnership with the party.

The upbeat Handbook gives no glimpse of these doubts and frustrations about party leadership roles, which only occur, of course, when a party is successful enough to have incumbents whose behavior they can worry about. The forty-seven and most other leaders do understand that they have important nominating and electoral functions that candidates and elected officials should ignore at their peril. They would agree with Fredman's words:

It's wrong for a candidate for political office to reach a political decision by himself and then say to the party, "You fan out and put it over." We want to be part of the process. We're closest to the people. Even if half of the 1,400 county committeemen and women are not out ringing doorbells, those who are know where people stand.

Becca, who has been town chair of Greenburgh and who now works in the county executive's office (it is widely believed to help mend some of his political fences), paints a stark picture about the state of political parties in general: "Nationally, statewide, all you need is decent candidates and an organization to elect Democrats, but it's a real joke." This contrasts with her view of the Greenburgh political organization. Although she thinks that the image of leaders as the grassroots link is fine "if you have people clamoring to hit the streets" and she recognizes the clamor in the town as being less than deafening, her overall assessment of performance is good. She describes the town committee as giving the county organization more support than any other Westchester town, and the candidates as knowing this. "And once elected, they listen to us."

The Grassroots Image and Reality

The duties of the leaders to their district residents are defined officially by common political terms and expectations. However, actual interactions are shaped by the leaders' own conceptions of the grassroots nature of their positions, their reactions to the messages the party wants to convey to the voters, and their own visions of how they want to affect party policies. Another consideration, of course, is the depth of their individual commitments to the role they have assumed, and to the extent that it is central or peripheral in their lives.

A few of the forty-seven not only accept but try to pattern their activities on the grassroots ideal. They are—not coincidentally—also the ones who profess enthusiasm or at least a sense of satisfaction from all parts of their leadership responsibilities. They take pride in "knowing" their districts. Lewis, in particular, likes the excitement of politics and is strongly motivated to succeed at the grassroots level. He says:

> I retain close contact with my people. You can tell that from the last primary [in which the candidate he favored swept his district]. I talk to the people in the e.d., get their opinions even when I don't agree with them. I work the area strongly and during petition time I visit every single Democrat. . . . I call several people once or twice a month and talk about politics. Most of the Democrats will follow my lead.

Arthur, too, firmly endorses the grassroots model and claims close contact with his voters—"The district is my base, where I come from. . . . It is the base of the party structure, where you deal with the nitty-gritty, get people interested in politics." He sums up his role as "caring about people," and adds that "people trust you, even sometimes asking you how to vote." Arthur, with his political past in New York City, yearns for a Democratic club house as the focus for increased leadership activity. Others who strive to live up to the ideal include Ella, Mandy, Hanna and Rita.

The following remarks are typical of the majority of the forty-seven who accept the image presented in the Handbook:

Jane: District leaders are the passers of the word, up as much as down. It's the grassroots connection, very much the heart of the whole thing.

Nino: My job is to understand my people, garner as much support for the candidates as possible.

Marge: Politics needs a connection with the public and we're where it's at.

John: Communication is of basic importance. It's a two-way street.

But acceptance of the idea is not always adherence to the role, as the people quoted above know and as the following make explicit:

Ralph: It's a laudable aim but I doubt that it works that way.

Craig: I have a feeling most people don't work that hard at it.

Jodie: It has to be that way in order to sustain the system but I don't conceive of my role that way.

Still others stress that the grassroots connection is the party's idea, not at all the view of the voters:

Gene: The voters don't look at the leaders that way, or even know who they are.

Nathan: I have no problem with the idea, but it doesn't seem to be working that way. We are certainly not important to most people.

Ilse: The leaders are the link between the people and government officials, but often it is a pretty weak link. Most people don't know who their district leader is, so how effective are you really?

In short, most of the leaders take the ideal image with varying amounts of salt. Polly's experience and reaction may be common, although she is an exception in that she had studied the Handbook before she became a leader. After a time in her hard-won new position she was surprised to discover that this publication was not the political bible. She, too, judged that many leaders were not even fulfilling their vote-pulling duty. Although she recognizes the grassroots role as an ideal, her observation that "it doesn't work that way at all" left her with little inclination to concentrate on that aspect of her position— "The job doesn't mean that much to my life. . . . I don't see this as a part of my identification. Maybe in time I will."

Only Leon, Abby and Claud refuse to give even lip service to the idea of being the party's grassroots connection. Leon says, "If that's what the county committee says, that's their privilege. But I don't start there." Where he starts and usually stays is with issues. He would like to see issues determined by parties and not by candidates who want to run or have been talked into running for office. He thinks of his real constituents as members of the partisan organization making the political decisions. Nevertheless, at election time Leon usually swings into action for the Democratic candidates "like an old fire horse." He says he sometimes reproves himself for "salivating when the bell rings without having any great feelings that it's terribly important."

Abby's reaction to the subject of the Handbook's version of the grassroots connection was a quick dismissal:

> Yeah, I read it. But we know that's a lie. The whole idea of the Democratic party is a selective one. Party officials don't want everyone to participate because it would take away your elitist few. A lot of people like that. I don't.

Claud also dismisses the importance of the leaders as being a grass-roots link to the party. He looks on his duties as leader and, later, captain as purely mechanical—identifying "pro" voters and getting them to the polls. In his opinion a district leadership is a very poor position from which to convince voters about candidates or issues because there are much more pervasive influences operating in that regard.

The great majority of the forty-seven give the ideal of the grassroots connection lip service at least, with only a handful rejecting it out of hand. Of the majority who emphasize the importance of the image, only some also make generally consistent rather than sporadic attempts to match it. Others realistically weigh family, job, and other pressures and interests against the county committee's stated expectations of them.

The Message to the Districts

The core of the county Democratic committee's expectations of the district leaders is what the leaders call the "mechanics" or "techniques" of getting people elected to office. The leaders in general accept pulling the vote on election day and carrying designating petitions for public and party offices as the minimal definition of their responsibilities. Many would add getting new residents registered and canvassing for candidates. Together these functions constitute passing on the party's message to the people. These jobs are what Evan describes as "like raking up the leaves," Jodie as "mundane chores," and Fred as "tedious and technical."

The two guiding principles for these activities are "know your district" and "work your district." Ralph, an oldtimer now serving in his second cycle as a committeeman, explains:

> The thing to do in a district has never changed. You need to know who's what in the e.d., not from registration lists but from talking with them. And you need to know how they think, who to push and who not to push so much.

Again and again the leaders acknowledge that pulling the vote is their basic job—Nathan: "Pulling the vote on election day is the key, otherwise all else is nothing"; Becca: "Elections are decided by people who don't vote"; Golda: "My role is to alert people at election time." However, as Ralph makes clear, to pull properly one must be able to identify whom to pull. That is, knowing one's district is preliminary to working it.

The paragons among the leaders have some idea of which Democrats in their districts are going to boycott their party line on particular occasions, and which unenrolled voters or, indeed, Republicans can be counted on. Paragons are rare, however, so some leaders, particularly new ones, simply do what workers outside the district do, which is rely only on the published enrollment lists—lists which, as valuable a tool as they are, are always out of date.

A campaign manager in a village election once wrote instructions for his workers which started with the bald imperative, "Pick up the phone." Obvious, yes, but for many leaders very difficult to do. At campaign meetings leaders sagely nod their heads in agreement when one of them will say—as one of them can be counted on to say— "That first phone call is hard to make." Laura, for example, says it has taken her ten years to learn to make calls to people she doesn't know "without worrying." Duke is afraid of offending people: "I hate to call people and tell them how to vote or remind them to vote, like they're dopes."

Many other leaders list making phone calls as the most onerous part of their jobs. And although rumors that this leader and that one do not make their calls may be false, confidence that they do is shaky.

There are two kinds of pre-election telephone calls. One type is canvassing calls about particular candidates or slates in order to identify pros, antis, and "who-knows," whatever the symbols used. These are usually made from election headquarters or other phone banks during the campaign weeks. Then leaders are encouraged to call district voters one to three days before an election urging support for the slate and reminding them when and where their polling place will be open. Some leaders make one kind of pre-call, some the other, and no doubt a few make both.

Early election day a district leader is supposed to "open the polls"— that is, be there when the election inspectors in fact set up the election paraphernalia, check out the ballot on the machine for any irregularities, and be sure the inspectors have paper (it used to be yellow legal pads) and carbons for making the list of voters as they come. During the day and early evening the leaders pick up copies of the list and check off from their own enrollment lists those people who have voted. In the early evening—the time varies by district—the leaders make their most important pull calls. They telephone the people they have been counting on who have not yet voted reminding them, with some urgency, when the polls close. Perhaps most leaders can be counted on to do this, and with some relish if the campaign has engendered any excitement at all. Then the leaders "close the polls"—that is, they are present when the inspectors read the votes from the machines and tally the results. They in turn report the totals to a central village or Greenburgh gathering place and compare the results in their districts with others and with their own expectations.

The state election law requires that a given number of signatures be collected on designating petitions for most candidates for public and party office. Although any party voter in the district concerned may carry such petitions, it is considered a basic duty of district leaders, particularly when their own positions are among those in question. Throughout her many years of service, Ella has maintained enthusiasm for all facets of the leader's job but particularly for canvassing her district with petitions. "I loved carrying petitions," she says. "I couldn't stop when I got started. It was delightful." This is a unique point of view. A few say that they enjoy the visiting and getting feedback once they make themselves start their rounds, particularly when they meet new people in their district. But most of the forty-seven present a united front in their distaste for the petitioning process and the limited time frame in which it must take place.

Nathan questions the basis of the election law requiring petitioning at all:

> I can't see why they are necessary when we have conventions and caucuses. Doing it the right way, canvassing and campaigning, that's too much. People don't even know what they're signing, or why you're doing it.

Other leaders range from feeling "uncomfortable" petitioning to strong dislike of it. Faith complains that "it can take me half a day to get one signature" because of the incumbent socializing. For Chester, it is an aversion to following the party line on candidates: "I dislike getting petitions signed for people I couldn't care less about." It can safely be said that of the "technical, tedious things" that leaders are supposed to do, carrying petitions is the most unpopular.

Unless, of course, it is fund raising. Leaders are more embarrassed to ask for money than they are for votes. Hanna hates fund raising, too, but "I do it because I happen to be good at it."

The forty-seven vary widely in their attitudes about serving their constituents. Golda regards her political role as ombudsman-like in mediating between the government and uninformed or wronged constituents. She thrived in that role primarily as an elected village trustee, but also thought of her concurrent and subsequent role as a district leader in those terms. Fay and John similarly feel free to pick up the phone and talk to public officials on behalf of neighbors and the neighborhood. But most leaders do not share Golda's conception of service, beyond participating in registration drives and answering occasional questions. Craig speaks for many when he says "as for helping people out with minor problems or steering them to the place for answers, I wouldn't know what to tell them if they did ask me." Nora says that some people do ask her questions and she tries to respond, but feels ill at ease in that role.

On the other hand, Rita speaks for other leaders who gain satisfaction from passing information to constituents: "I offer my neighbors a service in providing them with political information they would not otherwise have." She describes her district in the unincorporated area as tied together only by the children and the public school (her husband, Ken, adds, "and a desire for low taxes"). Sometimes, Rita says, her constituents are surprised at and grateful for the "news" that they live in the town of Greenburgh.

"Know your district" and "work your district" are the guiding principles for district leaders. But how one works the district after one knows it is a matter of some discussion. Instructions about political activities that come down through the party chain are often qualified by assurances that "But of course you know your district so. . . ." "So," the district leader is considered the ultimate arbiter of what will work and what will not, which is a comforting cushion for harried part-time politicians.

Jack believes that the Handbook provides a good framework for the leaders' activities but he also emphasizes that leaders must not only adapt to the particular characteristics of their districts, but they have to work out their own styles of dealing with the voters. He, for example, is averse to using the telephone in pulling his voters (who are not only Democrats, he says). Instead he relies on sending out letters about the candidates before the elections and about the results after them. In these letters he supports only those members of the slate he considers worthwhile.

Zoe, an area chair, describes her election district as a microcosm of the country. "One end of it is affluent, the other struggling for a living," with middle income residents in between. She uses orthodox pulling techniques but shares Jack's view that each district is different and leaders must use their common sense in dealing with people. "They must improvise, but also know when to let people alone and when to knock down doors." She recalls her most painful vote-pulling time as when calling for George McGovern for president even though she knew people were planning to vote for Richard Nixon on the Conservative line; a few voters even hung up on her. In a town election Becca had a similar experience but in her case the voters responded to her calls genially enough—it was not until the returns came in that she realized her district had received but rejected the party's message.

Charlie thinks that the leader's role can be what he calls the old-school-tie type only if the district is made up of "like-minded people." His district, however, he calls "a mixed bag" and the drumming of the message "work your district" drives him mad:

> I'm not a snob. I talk to people at the corner market, the garbage man and so on. But we're of a different world. For me to tell them to vote for somebody, they couldn't care less. I'm just a born-again Christian one time a year.

Charlie, like John who concentrates on one section of his district, thinks it may be a good idea if some of his constituents stay home on election day.

Cali's district is largely Republican and most of the Democrats that do live there are "close-mouthed" and conservative. She sees herself as the grassroots connection only with certain people that she identifies with ideologically—"They sign my petitions and we encourage each other."

Gene believes that the grassroots role is appropriate only if the leader has lived in the district long enough really to know it. This, of course, is not possible if one is representing a district one does not live in. He was much more comfortable when he eventually became a leader in his own district, transferring from one in or near the village business district made up of many apartments. Sid, too, works an apartment district in which he does not live because no vacancy has occurred in his own. He enjoys knocking on doors and talking with people who invite him in, but this is countered by the depression he feels when doors are shut in his face. And the transient nature of his population does not help—"Every time I develop a relationship there, he or she is gone the next year."

Polly brings up another point about people representing districts not their own, particularly when black communities are represented by "outsiders." Too often, she believes, the leaders actually represent the district where they live and "the district they represent be damned."

Only Nathan sees advantages in not representing one's own district. He has served three different election districts, mostly composed of apartments, and never his own. He thinks it would be more difficult to work in his district of residence "where everyone knows one another too well."

Some district leaders speak happily of their political activities and attribute this to the fact that—as so many express it—"I love people." Conrad had a different approach. He made up and maintained a card file on the district voters; that is, he had his district organized on paper. "I enjoyed this more than working with the actual people," he says.

In evaluating themselves and their colleagues in their performances in bringing the message of the party to the voters, the forty-seven are in general candid about their own failings and critical of their associates' lapses. Duke recalls that when first made a district leader no one really told him what he should be doing, but even after reading the Handbook and in spite of good intentions he found himself neglecting his duties with the exception of making his election calls, which he hates. He blames some of his neglect on a "lack of self-organization," but also on limitations of time and money—"Without a secretary and an expense account it is too hard to carry out the role of communication."

Other leaders rate themselves with any satisfaction at all only in relation to what their colleagues do. For example, Orson says, "I'm not all that good as a district leader, but I'm better than some. If you work your district even sloppily, it does pay off." In a similar vein Conrad looks back at his tenure: "I think a good leader should do more than I did, but on the other hand, I did more than others."

The path away from ideal performance is strewn with good intentions: Zoe "planned to do it right" but hasn't; Jodie would like to have a card file by streets but doesn't; Jane finds even vote solicitation more than she can handle because of lack of time; Charlie wishes he "had been more conscientious."

In spite of sometimes brutal self-assessments, leaders take pleasure in small victories. Jodie says she can sway fourteen votes whether they are Democrats or not and whether they know who the candidates are or not. "No big deal, but something." Gene remembers his exhilaration when on checking the yellow sheets he found that all the people he called had voted. Ralph says that in his first cycle as a leader he could look at the yellow sheets and tell within a few votes the election results in his district. Ken knows he gets his voters out because he "sat on his hands" in one election in disapproval of the slate and the turnout plummeted.

The fact is that many members of the Greenburgh Democratic committee do not carry designating petitions and pull the vote cursorily if at all. This is reflected in the heartfelt remarks made by a number of the forty-seven.

John, an area chair, sees himself and his wife as the only active workers on his area committee. He mildly wonders—without recrimination, he says—just why the others are there. Once his patience snapped. He asked for and received the resignation of a leader who was simply never there when needed.

Nathan sees his own village committee as divided into workers, talkers and "a third group that's disappeared off the face of the earth." Arthur, from the same village, has a kinder assessment. Out of twenty he reckons that fourteen really work and of the others, two "don't do a damn thing." Evan classifies his local committee into "a few workers and lots of drones." Hanna resents leaders who help out at election time only if they happen to feel like it. Nora narrows her complaint down to her own election district where she feels isolated because her co-leader is uncooperative.

Pepe makes a more sweeping attack on non-workers:

> Most leaders have no idea what it means to be a committeeman, any concept of democracy. . . . They make a mockery of the position, they don't know the people they represent, they don't serve the people and don't deserve the position. They are only serving their own ambition and ego. This is what I deplore. They are using democracy.

Polly is one of several who says they do not understand why some district leaders "fill their spot for years, all the while refusing to do any work." But Mandy thinks she knows why. As town chair she has come to accept as a fact of political life that most leaders do not do a responsible job. They keep the position to keep their vote on party policy and in the selection of party candidates. It is their small piece of power.

The Message from the Districts

It is clear that the party stresses and most district leaders accept that getting Democratic candidates elected is "the name of the game." The reciprocal role of carrying messages from the voters in the district to the party—communicating "their hopes and fears"—is weakly developed. This, in spite of the fact that most of the forty-seven say they like talking to people and discovering their stands on issues and candidates. The injunction to "know your district" is taken to be in the service of its corollary, "work your district," rather than purveying views upward. The ultimate message, after all, is in the election returns.

Only two of the forty-seven see it otherwise. Vi and Ella, both strong believers in the grassroots philosophy, say they should represent their constituents' opinions as well as their own by taking informal, random surveys on "hot issues" and candidates. Ella explains that "otherwise people can't depend on you to let them know things." Vi extends her view to the point that in such surveys she does not "proselytize" unless specifically asked for her opinion.

Sending messages up from the district voters and sending them up from the district leaders are, of course, two different categories of communication. The forty-seven do want to use their positions and the concomitant formal or personal contacts with the party structure and office holders to have input in the decision-making process. As Cali asks, "Why bother with the job unless you're going to have some input?"

Indeed, many of the leaders, including Charlie, entered local politics precisely to affect policy. Disillusionment is frequent. Charlie laughs at his earlier expectations: "Not in a village like this. We're a bunch of idiots. All we do is collect money for somebody who's on an ego trip. They [incumbents] aren't controlled, they don't take orders like they should." Charlie's references are to a long train of past events in the most recent of which Democratic victory sweeps seemed to break on the shoals of the victors' independent agendas.

Any leaders wishing to raise policy questions or support a particular point of view with party or government officials have a little extra leverage, of course, if they can indicate that their constituents share their opinions. Or—whether they do or not—that if "worked" they will turn out to vote.

The relationships between district leaders and incumbents (who are usually also candidates) is the subject of later review. However, it is appropriate here to bring up the thoughts of two leaders from different villages who are or have been incumbents also. Ilse, a trustee, surprisingly thinks that the messages going up from committee people are more successful than their messages going down. This is a gentle hint that she sees at least some district leaders as being more interested in having input than in getting out the vote, "the name of the game" or no.

Laura's experience as a district leader and as an incumbent trustee is instructive. She agrees that the leaders should be the grassroots connection but "in fact they are not." She sees little political activity in her committee between the election day pulls. Yet, as a district leader she thought that there should be more channels of access to elected officials. Then she ran for and won a seat as trustee. She soon found, she says, that there were too many calls on her time for her to give any priority to keeping the channels open to the leaders—"I didn't have time to listen to the committee people." At the time of the interview she was no longer a trustee but was a leader. Now she again feels that village officials should listen to the committee "but they don't."

Nathan, from Laura's village, agrees that the leaders feel that their elected officials don't consult them as much as they should. And he understands why they are not consulted. Nathan believes that the incumbents are perfectly aware of which leaders have and which have not worked for them during the election. They feel little obligation to the latter. The agendas of leaders and officials include personal as well as political complexities which are more salient within the party structure than in the election districts.

WITHIN THE PARTY

Whereas in the election districts the leaders operate in distinctive areas of the political field, with the party structure itself they have, potentially at least, a common basis of interaction. They meet one another in a variety of formal and informal situations and also maintain communication by telephone. Yet each leader's sociopolitical network is to some extent unique, shaped by personal affinities and shifting factional allegiances.

Meetings

Meetings of one kind or another form the basic field of encounter. There are the meeting-prone and the meeting-shy among the forty-seven. Arthur, for example, goes to more meetings than most. There are at least four a month that he usually attends: his village committee, the town committee, and, by virtue of being a party officer on the county executive committee, he also goes to its and the town executive committee meetings. This does not include various ad hoc subcommittees (nominating, screening, platform, campaign) in which he may be temporarily involved. He says that he loves the details of wheeling and dealing at these meetings and, in the hiatuses, phoning people and being phoned.

Claud, on the other hand, goes to as few meetings as possible and asserts that he hates them:

> It has to be true that meetings have a value by getting people together and arriving at decisions, but in my heart I resist the idea. . . . There are always a few people who want to have their say, and want it ad infinitum, and are not particularly anxious to let other people have their say. I squirm at meetings.

Others simply accept meetings as a fact of political life. As Zoe asks, "How else do you keep an organization going?"

Small working committees are enjoyed the most. Orson explains why: "It takes patience and often nothing gets done, but you have a say, get a feeling for people. I like the direct input, whether my point of view prevails or not."

Periodic village and area committee meetings receive good reports also, in spite of the fact that chairs often must strive mightily to achieve a quorum. Craig likes village committee meetings "where we thrash out what we're trying to do and where we're trying to go." Laura says of her village committee: "We get things done. We're effective." And her co-villager Nathan agrees.

"Getting things done" is important at the smaller meetings, but "getting in on things" appears to be more important to more people. Again and again district leaders express satisfaction on being on the "inside," getting "the scoop." Fay, a black, likes being "on the scene, finding out what's going on, and particularly finding out if there are some opportunities for *my* folks." Maria also wants to know what is going on in her community. "When you are a property owner, it's a vested interest. It only makes sense." Chester is less targeted—"I enjoy the gossip, chatting, the inside information."

The forty-seven also apparently enjoy watching one another. For example, Fred says "observing personalities is fascinating"; Dennis: "I enjoy seeing what the individual agendas are"; Chester: "I like watching the interplay between people." Such assessments often mention the conflict that frequently flares up. Arthur says, "I enjoy the infighting. I don't take it as serious. I like the tug of people, the drama." Charlie remarks, "I enjoyed a good, hot meeting—if I ever got there I enjoyed it." Even Jodie who thinks that meetings are tedious says, "A little intrigue now and then makes them fun." Some, however, would agree with Ann who says she becomes extremely uncomfortable at overt contention.

Town executive committee meetings have a special mystique for those who attend them. These people are village and area chairs, town committee officers, county executive committee members, town and other elected officials, and any other Democrats with a special interest in what is on the agenda. They are not often small meetings. They are held in private homes and the room where the meeting is conducted is supplied with extra chairs, but the floor must often also be used for seating. While business is being discussed over coffee and pastries, people peel off in twos or threes to the kitchen, or snag newcomers at the door, to share opinions or special tidbits of information. When the buzz of background noise becomes too distracting the chair corrals the mavericks with a few pointed remarks.

New executive committee members from the areas and the villages are often at a loss about what is going on under the surface exchanges taking place at the meeting—as outspoken as the participants usually are. With time, however, they learn who the players are, get an inkling of personal or factional motivations, and gain, as often as not, in their interest in Greenburgh politics.

The town committee's general meetings for the full roster of Greenburgh leaders are often poorly attended. Deeply involved executive committee members dutifully appear but others primarily interested at the village or area level attend only sporadically if at all. The exceptions are when there is a vote either on an issue or, more often, for electing candidates or party officials. In these cases proponents of the various sides assiduously work the telephone, wooing district leaders to their side.

Before 1978 paper proxies from leaders who could not or would not come to the meeting were permitted and their collection and notarization were a major pre-meeting activity. Some leaders expressed extreme resentment at this use of paper proxies by paper leaders, although necessarily indulging in it themselves. But in that year the town committee voted to ban proxies of any kind in town contests. Now the bodies have to be present in order to vote. Still, resentment lingers, as Ken makes clear:

> It's always bugged me when people who do absolutely nothing turn out on a vote and are accorded the courtesy and have the right to vote. . . . It's a shame to win an important contest when the majority of people are not involved, in fact have been dragged kicking and screaming to a place they don't want to be.

Ken, Rita, Hanna and Leon have yet another quarrel with the town committee general meetings. They feel that they are insufficiently policy or issue-oriented—this in spite of repeated efforts of party officials to plan such meetings. From Leon's viewpoint meetings are "pretty awful" because the talk is always about candidates and not about the politics of specific issues. In disgust, he advocates a remedy:

> Terrorize the membership by threatening them with a resolution on an issue. They'll show up to vote on it if only to change a comma to a whatever, or to deal with it in some minuscule way. We've got so damn many lawyers.

Ken and Rita think that the only way that leaders can affect policy ("have any control over issues") is to maintain regular involvement with the town committee. At the time of their interview, however, this belief was being sorely tested at the town meetings "where, instead of issues, the question is always, who can win?" Zoe's comment is collaborative:

> We were violently an issue group during the Vietnam War, and that's why we flowered. Somehow we've gotten away from this with our incumbents in that we've become very secure, they've become the end. And there's a lot of issues out there that need to be talked about.

Hanna also wishes the town committee were more issue-oriented but goes further than desiring substantive discussions about issues to say, "We ought to take stands even if we make mistakes."

Veteran leader Ralph disagrees. He is, he says, increasingly intolerant of the nonsense talked at the meetings about issues. He thinks that the committee's concerns should be with the nuts and bolts part of keeping the party an ongoing, effective organization. He sees a practice of taking stands in the name of the party as weakening the party. Since stands are rarely taken, the majority of the leaders probably side with Ralph.

Only a few of the forty-seven have frequent or substantial enough contacts at the county level to be deeply interested in the interactions taking place there. The county committee's executive meetings occur regularly but only three of the interviewees (Becca, Mandy and Arthur) attend them. County conventions are held once a year, and the excitement they generate depends on the contests between candidates being settled. Here proxies are allowed, but each leader attending is permitted to carry only one.

The county is the level at which most district leaders have the least interest, except for supporting favorite incumbents and candidates. How much this is due to the county committee's activities is questionable. Pepe, however, thinks that—their exhortations in the Handbook or not—"They [the committee] don't realize that the sap comes from the root and not the top."

Party Parties

Another scene where district leaders mingle, as well as with other stalwart Democratic supporters, is the social one of the political breakfast, dinner, picnic or cocktail party. The usual purposes of these affairs are to raise interest in the coming election (and raise money), to honor political figures (and raise money), and to celebrate victories (and raise money). An active political social life can be very costly, so only a handful of local leaders go to the broader-based but higher priced festivities.

Village leaders are more likely, but do not feel duty bound, to go to their own annual campaign parties. These are usually highly successful affairs and the few leaders responsible for organizing them certainly have a bonding experience. However, the parties are most effective (aside from the gate) as warm evidence of the local party in the electorate.

Contacts with Office Holders

County and New York state political figures are usually seen, listened to and talked with at town and other meetings, as are local congressional representatives. Some of these people are well known to the district leaders because they have risen from their ranks. Others become well known by their diligent attendance at special meetings and far-flung fund raisers in the various Greenburgh communities. Every leader has the opportunity to interact with these individuals, whether their aim is to get answers to questions or have input on policy matters.

Other personal contacts with office holders are not so frequent, but when they occur they can make deep impressions. Lewis, who makes a practice of getting to know and trying to influence power wielders, was especially excited on a particular occasion when the legendary Yonkers Democratic committee chair invited him to lunch at his favorite eatery:

> To sit there and have three waiters hovering, you know, to be waited on hand and foot. Knowing what his favorite drink is, knowing what his favorite dish is, and being treated like royalty. You know, it's an experience to sit there—this hulking man—and be served the same way that he is. A very strange experience.

More often the experience is, on the one hand, the warm one of making friends—or at least acquaintances—on the campaign trail and, on the other hand, the less personal one of lobbying particular office holders, singly or in small groups.

DISCUSSION

Clearly there is a significant gap between the job specifications, so to speak, for district leaders and the tolerated level of fulfillment. Even if the gap were narrowed, one might wonder about the grounds for relating this informal title to the concept of leadership in general. In fact, social scientists who have thought about the subject do regard leadership in ways that can contribute to understanding the district leaders' activities (Verba 1961; Eldersveld 1964; Gibb 1969; Lewis 1974; Paige 1974; Kellerman 1984a; Lantis 1987). One insight derived from much of the research is that leadership is better understood not as qualities or specifications but as part of a process: the dynamic relations between leaders and followers.

This is not the place to generalize about the patterns that these relationships may take. Elements of the situation—the field is micro and the actors are party officials (that is, constituted leaders)—go a long way toward characterizing the interactions. Nevertheless, analogies with other peoples and other places can clarify the relationship of the leaders with the people in the election districts and with their colleagues in the party local organization.

Anthropologists studying small scale preliterate societies have described a series of leadership roles as headmen, big men, chiefs of one kind or another, and even discerned leaders where the people themselves say they have none. Common to these societies is a relatively egalitarian ethos with the result that most of the above lead by persuasion and the practice of their individual skills, knowledge and generosity. Greenburgh's leaders, although natives of a modern stratified nation, have similar if not so intimate and pervasive relationships with their electorates, and for similar reasons: an egalitarian ethos, including a deep suspicion of people who would tell them what to do. The majority of their electorates would deny, as do some of their analogues, that there are any such leaders among them at all.

Another mode of leadership, the cultural broker or middleman, stems from studies of colonialized and encapsulated communities undergoing degrees of integration into larger political entities. The broker is a member of the native community who is familiar with the ways of the engulfing nation and so can serve as a communications link between the two worlds. In the colonial situation the broker interprets each culture to people of the other. In rural villages impacted by a central or regional authority, the cultural broker may more specifically be a political one, with knowledge about government, laws, political parties and factions (Silverman 1975; Strauch 1981; Tarrow 1978). The broker is likely to be a follower of leaders outside the community, sending their message down, and at the same time a leader of followers within the community, being their link upward. In a sense, Greenburgh leaders can be seen as specialized and localized political brokers.

The leader-follower relationship within the Greenburgh party organization is not one of brokerage but rather of organizing activities and carrying them out. Or, as political anthropologists have described the task of political leaders: making decisions, recruiting and maintaining as a group people who share certain values, mediating between and rewarding these followers and motivating them to compete within the political arena (Swartz et al. 1966; Bailey 1969).

"Rewarding" in politics is often thought of as patronage in return for support. The temptation here is to rely on a patron-client model for leaders and followers—a model made complex by the multiplication of what is essentially an economic dyadic relationship. As attractive as the market analogy may be, it distorts the activities and competition, and overstates the transactions that take place within the Greenburgh committee. More appropriate is the idea of action sets, where three or more leaders act together informally to galvanize and coordinate the desired activity (Boissevain 1974). But these are subjects of following chapters.

The extent to which the forty-seven have the will and ability to exploit the leadership potential of their position varies (as is indeed true of all other politically-constituted leaders of whatever rank). At their local level, many are "ordinary people" who become good leaders because they "do more than ordinary work," and good followers because they have learned to listen critically to those who would be their leaders (Lantis 1987:190, 196).

The Forty-Seven: Part Two

KEN AND RITA

Ken was born into a New York City middle class Jewish family where political issues were always discussed and "FDR was the equivalent of gospel." Rita's father "worked his way up from the East Side" to settle in Mount Vernon in Westchester with his family. They were Jewish, "nonreligious and completely apolitical." Rita says, "I was born politically when I met Ken, who talked always about world events and civil rights." Even while working his way through school, Ken had found time to campaign for Henry Wallace for President and Vito Marcantonio for Congress.

Ken is a dentist and Rita works for the Westchester Coalition for Legal Abortion, coordinating its activities with other pro-choice groups. They live, with their teenage children, in the unincorporated Edgemont area of Greenburgh. Soon after they moved there the town Democratic chair tried to interest them in becoming district leaders, but Rita did not see the connection between the world and national issues that concerned them and the local leadership role.

The Vietnam War changed this. The couple helped organize the Edgemont Independent Democrats, which slightly pre-dated and became a part of the Concerned Democrat movement. When there was a push among Concerned Democrats to become district leaders in order to be politically effective against the war, Ken and Rita decided to "become part of the establishment to make changes." Since all but one of the Edgemont leadership positions were vacant they had no problems. Both became district leaders and leaders in anti-war activism.

After the war the couple maintained their local political involvement. Ken became a state committeeman and Rita a vice-chair of the town committee. Both say that their political activity has greatly affected their lives, particularly the success of their marriage. At the time of the interview Rita was still politically and organizationally active. "I belong to all the appropriate women's rights, civil rights, abortion rights groups. I feel obliged to join all these organizations that would die without people." Ken, however, has become disillusioned with party politics and what he perceives as his waning influence. As Rita explains,

"He's a terrific leader except that often in his political career he turns around and finds his troops aren't with him." Ken has given up his state committeeman office, but retains his district leadership.

ARTHUR

Arthur's father was German, once a prisoner of war in America during World War I who after the war met and married a young Austrian woman. The couple migrated to the United States in the 1920s, settling in Ohio and raising their children there. Arthur describes his father as being "a European Jewish liberal with a keen sense of social justice." A Republican, he voted for Norman Thomas early in the depression. Then, enamored with Franklin Roosevelt, he became a Democrat. Arthur has always been politically aware, he says, because his father saw that the children were involved in political discussions at the dinner table.

While earning a degree in New York City in economics, Arthur found time to work in a series of political campaigns as a volunteer. He was active in the Lyndon Johnson campaign partly because he was told it was a good place to meet girls—which turned out to be true in that and subsequent campaigns. He took a job with the Hubert Humphrey presidential effort in 1968, and met again and married a friend from a previous campaign.

As an economist, Arthur opted for teaching for the security it would provide his family. However, he lost his job five years later, not getting tenure due to a budget squeeze, and has since done consultant work for state and county agencies. In Tarrytown, where he now lives, he again threw himself into organizing campaigns on village, town and county levels. In the midst of these volunteer efforts he became a leader in a district not his own, was appointed to the village's Zoning Board of Appeals, and then elected to a position on the county Democratic committee's executive committee.

Arthur believes in New Deal and Great Society concepts, that "government must balance out life's inequities or we live in a jungle."

ELLA

Although Ella's parents were paid election workers, they were really not interested in politics, and neither was she when young. After she moved with her family of procreation to Ardsley, however, a Democratic neighbor got her interested in local politics—"she was my mentor." Ella says that at the time there were very few Democrats around, and most of them were inactive.

Ella did some work for the party in Ardsley and Greenburgh but it was not until the family moved to Hastings in 1949 that "politics captured" her. She gave up numerous other community activities to concentrate on strengthening the Democrats and "making it a two-party system" in the area. Through her Ardsley mentor she became a district leader. Then she separated the village Democratic club from an incipient and sporadic committee, became the chair of a stable committee with at least one leader in each district, and began calling on new residents on the party's behalf. She became Hastings' "Mrs. Democrat."

After ten years of leadership, Ella first gave up the chair to a politically-oriented newcomer to the village, then resumed it after his two-year term, and finally a few years later passed the torch to Conrad. She remained a district leader until she had to give up the position in order to take a federally financed part-time job in the new Democratic Town administration. She remains deeply involved with politics at all levels—"I can't stay away from it. If no one asks me to do something, I feel shut out."

CLAUD

Claud was brought up in the Westchester suburbs. He guesses his father always voted Republican because he was for the status quo, but his mother, since the first Franklin Roosevelt administration, was "a real bleeding-heart liberal. She was always for the underdog even if the underdog was wrong." Claud was fourteen at the time and also was excited by Roosevelt as "a doer." Ever since then he has been fascinated with politics as activism.

After World War II Claud felt strongly that the individual liberty espoused by the Republican party meant liberty to get everything one could out of other individuals. He and Antonia, his wife, lived in New York City where they were part of "the activist left segment of the Democratic party." Claud believes in a strong central government and is suspicious of decisions at local and state levels because of the part played by favoritism. He is aware of the waste seemingly inherent in large bureaucracies but thinks the human gains far outweigh that cost.

When the couple moved to Hastings their first visitor was Ella, then the Democratic chair, wanting to know their party affiliation. And thus began their long interest in local politics. In the village Claud was a district leader "on and off for twenty-six years," then a candidate, then a trustee, finally a losing candidate for mayor. Claud was never attracted to town issues, but the Vietnam War brought him back for his last period as a leader because of Concerned Democratic activity at the town and county level. Claud has recently resigned his leadership but helps politically in the village as a captain on the Hastings committee.

MARGE

Marge is an administrative secretary at a large locally situated corporation. She spent her early years in Pennsylvania, in a family she describes as non-political except for her grandfather, who was an immigrant from Yugoslavia. He played with the idea of becoming a Republican district leader but did not eventually do so.

After marriage and children, in the middle 1960s Marge and her family moved to Dobbs Ferry. She met a district leader there who recruited her for making phone calls. Later she filled a vacancy on the Dobbs committee, worked hard pulling her constituency, and also served as committee secretary.

The family moved to Irvington, and after a political hiatus of three years filled with community activities, including a stint on the Volunteer Ambulance Corps, she joined the Democratic committee there. She twice ran unsuccessfully for trustee, and at the time of the interview as committee chair. Marge says she has many close Republican links in the village, some of them through her Catholic-related and other local activities.

Marge has always been a Democrat. She says, "I vote the party line only to a point. I can sit there and yes you to death but in the back of my mind I [may] disagree."

JANE

Jane grew up in a community near Albany in a family "with an authoritarian, lovely father who was against alcohol and cigarettes and way above politics which he considered dirty business. Of course, politics *was* dirty business in Albany." To Jane, Republicans were to be voted for and politics was to be read about in the papers.

College at Cornell University changed these perceptions, perhaps mostly because Jane met law student Bob who was interested in government and issues. They married. Bob got a job on the legal staff of the Tennessee Valley Authority, and the couple consider this "a great experience in our lives," particularly compared with their next stretch in a New York community which bored them. While he was working for a corporation in 1960 Jane and Bob and their children came to Hastings. Later he entered private law practice with a White Plains partnership.

Jane's community involvements in her village were non-partisan—school and the League of Women Voters. Although a Democrat since TVA days (with a Republican lapse during the boring years "because there was no point in being anything else"), Jane did not get interested in party politics until Bob ran for village trustee. He won two terms in this office. Jane characterizes her party role at that time: "I just run around with Bob. This is not my dish." Then Bob lost a race for mayor that they had expected to win. Jane plunged into the partisan fray. In spite of having taken a full-time job with a utility company, she was a leader in the publishing of a periodic *Hastings Democrat* to rally the faithful to the cause, took a captaincy and, a few years later, the leadership.

Jane feels political labels are meaningless. "I was a Truman Democrat, probably a Kennedy Democrat. Now [1980] there is only one candidate and that's Carter. . . . I think independent Democrat describes me." In another context Jane said, "I don't pretend to be a woman activist. I have opinions but not activism."

CHESTER

Chester works for a large corporation. He was brought up in rural New Jersey in a family that "was old with some little tradition. We like to dabble in things of service if we can and I consider political activity my current service in the community." Indeed, it seems that Chester's enrollment as a Democrat and service as leader and village chair do have solely to do with the local community. When he and his family of procreation moved to Dobbs Ferry in the late 1950s he became a Democrat, he says, because there were too many Republicans there. Nevertheless, "I have always been a Republican. I have no regard for Democrats whatever, they've ruined the country, as far as I am concerned, with socialistic programs and I can't see wasting my taxes on things they spend money on."

Before he became a district leader, succeeding his wife in the role, Chester was on the school board for six years, a position he sought as an outlet for community service after being offered by the village board a job on the cemetery committee, which "looks at the graves once a year to be sure the stones are up for Memorial Day."

Schooled in sociology, Chester sees himself as an observer of the political scene at the town level—"It's better than television and I don't bowl." He says "As regards politics I couldn't care less for Greenburgh, New York State or the United States." He takes more seriously having a hand in selecting his village candidates and getting them elected to the board. Since the interview, Chester has been elected a village trustee.

CRAIG

Craig is a behaviorally-oriented industrial psychologist. He was born and spent his very early years in New Jersey, his family later moving to Queens. His parents were Republicans with little or no involvement, that their son was aware of, in community or politics.

"What really changed me," Craig says, "was going off to the army. It's a broadening experience. I saw that all ·Democrats weren't bad and all Republicans weren't good. My mother said 'I understood you when you were a little boy. Then you went off to the army and I haven't understood you since.'"

Craig and his family of procreation moved to Dobbs Ferry because he was looking for a place with a sense of community. Interested in education as psychology, he became a member of the school board—his only political involvement in Dobbs. Two moves later and living in Hastings, his wife was a district leader for a short while. Craig was asked to take the same leadership (in his own district) two or three years later and accepted. He says that he was advised by his recruiter (his chair) not to take the job too seriously or let it scare him, advice that he follows. He is, however, conscientious in his role as vice-chair of the Hastings committee.

Craig describes himself as an "old fashioned liberal" with no sympathy for the "radical wing of the party."

BROOKE

Brooke's work as a district leader, although conscientious, is completely overshadowed by her experiences campaigning for her husband, Al, a successful candidate for a town judgeship. She is from Brooklyn, and she describes her family as much too busy making ends meet to have had anything to do with politics, although they were Democrats. She met Al at a Young College Graduates dance in Manhattan. He was already a lawyer when they married, and Brooke immediately got involved in politics because he was. Al became a district leader in Brooklyn and had close connections with a leading figure there. The young couple were always going to political dinners, breakfasts, and club meetings.

When Brooke and Al moved to Greenburgh, Al became a district leader through Becca, then town chair. Brooke went with him on his door-to-door petitioning rounds. She took over his leadership post when he decided to contend for nomination for a state office. He did not win it, but then became a candidate for town judge. Brooke and Al campaigned together tirelessly, "getting to know Greenburgh on foot." Al won and has since been re-elected several times.

Brooke considers herself "a liberal, middle-of-the-road, conservative Democrat," depending on the issue.

SID

Sid is a young lawyer with a general practice located in White Plains. He lives with his wife and baby girl in Hartsdale. His father was a Jewish immigrant whose whole family had been wiped out by the Holocaust. Brought up in Brooklyn, Sid used to enjoy his father's stories about the district leader there, "the one you went to see on Wednesday night if you wanted to get your mother in a nursing home or something."

Sid has always liked politics, from the high school variety through the anti-war movement in college, on to his current Greenburgh involvement that he initiated by attending a town fund raising breakfast. He has been a district leader only a few years in a district, not his own, of large apartment complexes. He serves as area chair, is active in town campaigns, and has been appointed to two town advisory councils.

On the issues Sid rates himself as moderate to liberal. He says he aspires to political office but finds some of the things one has to go through to achieve it "heavy." He is working on lessening the degree of his personal sensitivity.

BECCA

Becca is the youngest of four daughters brought up in New York City by parents who were "liberal, independent, Roosevelt Democrats." And "I didn't rebel," she states. In the "philosophical discussions" constantly going on in the house, her father enjoyed the role of devil's advocate. This family background and her high school education at a private institution stressing "free thought" are credited by Becca with "opening up" her mind more than her subsequent college career.

Becca's husband is also interested in politics. Her first campaign efforts were for John Kennedy. With two small children she didn't get deeply involved again until in 1968, after having moved to Greenburgh. She volunteered in New York City working for Robert Kennedy, but was too much of a traditionalist to be entirely comfortable in that role.

When Becca was first asked to be a district leader she demurred, saying she was interested in issues, not party structure. However, she went to a committee meeting where "this young fellow was running for the assembly and he asked for help. . . . No one else volunteered so I became his scheduler. . . . During the campaign I did everything, down to organizing a motorcade which turned out to be the driver and me—the candidate didn't show up. He didn't show up election night at headquarters either. He got slaughtered."

After this experience Becca, convinced that the committee needed something done and you had to be a district leader to do it, became one at a time when the Concerned Democrat-regular Democrat breach was widening. In two years she became chair of the town Democratic committee even though (or perhaps because) "the Concerneds thought I was a regular and the regulars thought I was a screaming liberal." It was as chair that Becca learned the political ropes. She is now an aide to an important county official, retains her leadership, and is a vice-chair of the county Democratic committee.

CHAPTER 4

Strategies of Influence

The interest of some anthropologists in comparative political micro research and their phrasing of power as influence over decisions and policy formation is amenable to the consideration of local Greenburgh politics (Swartz et al. 1966, R. Cohen 1970). Cohen raises such questions as: Are rivalry and competition among individuals universal? Is desire for power a basic motive of political action? In fact, is need for power on the part of some people, at least, necessary for political action at all? By what means, skills or attributes do they influence others and mobilize support for themselves and their causes?

The forty-seven think of power in essentially the same terms as these anthropologists—bringing influence of one kind or another to bear on any given situation—although they address questions of motivation in individual rather than general terms. They have their own ideas about power and where it is located in their political field. In this they are pretty much, if not totally, in agreement. However, the degree of their power and the strategies of influence that they use are varied.

VIEWS ABOUT POWER

It has been said that "those who talk about power lack it themselves. Lack of power is actually more interesting than power—it is more universal."[1] The district leaders do not claim a great deal of power but few of them talk of its lack. In general they think that power means the ability to influence people and events, to get things done. Important "things" that they want done are improvements in the quality of life in their communities. As Conrad puts it about his own community, "Power means being able to change the face of the village to the better. Playing a small role in this would be a nice monument to leave behind." Although this accent on the positive was pervasive in interview responses, two leaders singled out the other side of the coin for special comment, and another has an entirely different approach to the subject.

Claud adds to his definition of power: ". . . and preventing things from happening that one does not want to happen." Golda applies the same idea directly to office holders, saying that sometimes it is just as important to keep them from taking certain actions as it is to prod them into action.

Leon thinks on a grander scale and does not use the soft word "influence." "Power is manipulative. If I can develop a mass movement, then I have power, right? But as an individual I don't have enough money to have power."

In line with their role-emphasis on bringing the party's message to the districts, the events the leaders most often want to affect is, of course, elections. "The power to elect" is the power that the forty-seven consider their basic—and a few think single—piece of political action. Winning elections is only a generalized version of this power. When the leaders say such things as "power only rests with people in their votes" (Zoe) and "a vote is power" (Arthur), they are not referring only to everyone's right, but to a responsibility peculiarly theirs as a group. The committee people select their party's local candidates. Choosing whom to run is a power that limits everyone's choices on election day.

The power to elect has a corollary: the capacity to influence the people one has helped elect. The forty-seven were asked where they believe power is located at each of the three local levels of their political interactions. They were specifically asked the extent to which they think power is held by virtue of political status—that is, by the position held by the individual within governmental or party structures. They are in accord. Such responses as "always the elected person has the clout" (Evan), "the elected official has the right to make the final decision" (Becca), and "with office holders, not the party" (Gene), are representative. Claud adds the point that power within a party is with the chair of that party only when the party is out of office. At the time of the study, Greenburgh Democratic officials were the majority in the town and three of the six villages, and Democrats had been elected to the county administration and board of legislators. This is reflected in much of the following material.

Jodie and Duke were the only respondents to link the idea of personality to power. That is, they feel that the personalities of the elected officials have as much to do with their power as does their status. In particular instances, however, only one man's and two women's personalities are highlighted in the comments below—two public officials and one district leader.

Westchester County

Most of the leaders plead ignorance of what goes on at the county level. Nevertheless, they do read the newspapers and word seeps down from their colleagues on the party's county executive committee. Unanimously the leaders locate power with the county executive, a Democrat with the reputation of ignoring the party committee. Many of them describe him as "not responsive to" or "unappreciative of" the Democratic county committee. Even those who admire his independence and administrative abilities wish he were less careless about his political fences.

Greenburgh leaders, while recognizing that they have "zero influence" (Nathan's phrase) with the county administration, do think that the town is respected for bringing in the vote. For most this is enough because the county is at the far range of their political interest and experience. Craig is typical of many of the forty-seven when he says that he feels divorced from the county, "which seems more remote than Albany."

At the time of this study two county legislative districts (the eighth and ninth) were encompassed by Greenburgh—District Eight partly and District Nine entirely. Candidates for these offices run every two years in the same election as the town candidates and in cooperation with the town slate. Both incumbents win and re-win their seats with handsome margins, and the district leaders in general admire their abilities and achievements. However, these legislators' influence on events—therefore power—is lessened by the fact that Republicans are the majority on the county board of legislators. Few of the forty-seven mentioned them in the context of questions put about power.

Doris, the legislator for District Eight, is highly praised in other frames of reference ("the only politician I really admire" and similar statements), and there were a good many expressions of personal loyalty to her during the interviews. Only two of these touched on power, however, and they came to opposite conclusions. Duke, referring to her unpretentious political style, judges that "Doris is powerful because of respect, although a meek woman." Ken's conclusion is also based on her style. He says:

> Doris is one of the really decent people. I mean she's really great. She is overwhelmingly politically successful. But she has no power. She is not someone to be reckoned with. When people sit down in a room deciding how to govern on an issue, they know she will go along or oppose, but she's not going to whiplash or knock heads—she's not going to do that.

Among the Greenburgh members of the county committee itself, only one leader claims a "piece of power" in county politics. Arthur, who sits on the county Democratic executive committee, says that his "piece" lies in his access to the county chair (who succeeded the disgruntled Sam Fredman) and being able to moderate or influence some of his attitudes. Becca and Mandy, also on the executive committee, make no such claims but this probably reflects modes of self-presentation rather than self-perceptions.

The Town

Unlike the county, the town level of political activity is the focus of interest for district leaders from the town outside and even for some from the villages. And there is no disagreement at all that Vince, the town supervisor, is the most powerful political figure in Greenburgh. This judgment does not stand alone on his office but on his use of the office, his vote-getting coattails, and a personality writ large. These factors come through in the following comments:

> John: Vince is practically a dictator. He admits it. He's the strength of the party. He's stubborn and opinionated, but you always know where Vince stands. He certainly doesn't speak with a forked tongue.

> Zoe: Power in the town rests in the hands of one person and that's Vince. He's been our meal ticket and that's fine. It's kept us in and enabled a lot of people to climb the ladder. But on the other hand he very often gets his way when he shouldn't, and locks off debate.

> Jack: Power is with Vince because he is a vote-getter. Fortunately he's a good human being. He's used to doing everything himself, doesn't listen to people until after he's made a mistake and then he has to. He's done a heck of a lot for the town. I don't like his style, but he's done a lot.

> Brooke: Vince is brilliant, although he puts on an act of not being intelligent, of being one of the boys. But I heard him once on the telephone when he forgot the act.

> Sid: Power is pretty clearly in the hands of the supervisor who wields it effectively. Vince is the one who gets the contracts for any particular company—who dumps the garbage, which architect does the new bathrooms, who gets to fix the sewers.

> Golda: Vince has built a very fine political base. There's a lot of construction in Greenburgh. Vince has the builders, unions, real estate business and also talks to educated people. He's an old fashioned politician.

There is some ambivalence in these remarks, which mix personal and positional attributes of the supervisor (and which in no way sum up his accomplishments in that role). Golda evaluates Vince as being good at pleasing and placating his constituents, "but inside the committee these relationships are something else!" The "something else" varies from leader to leader and issue to issue. Fay remarks about Vince, "He's gonna do what he damn well pleases, *he'll* tell you this." Sometimes leaders find this quality in Vince colorful. Other times they call it arrogance.

Becca says that as chair she always found Vince responsive in their talks about issues or procedures. She adds, "Sometimes we argued like hell. And sometimes he even changed his position!" On the other hand, at least one district leader feels that Vince is so authoritarian that he refuses to consider a town council candidacy as long as he remains supervisor.

Leaders who disagree with Vince's substantive positions from time to time nevertheless like his outspokenness. Rita was pressing a position on pro-choice in abortion with Vince on one occasion when he stopped her with, "God gave me free will. If He'd wanted me perfect, He'd have made me perfect." In another instance Hanna communicated her distress to Vince that the town had not taken a strong stand on establishing group homes for the mentally disabled within various Greenburgh neighborhoods. Although not happy with his reaction, on recalling it she shrugs and says "But if he had taken this stand, of course he'd never get elected."

Cali is sure that "Vince calls the shots because without Vince we won't win. Nobody fights Vince." But district leaders and town council members do tackle him and sometimes they win. During the period of this study Vince backed down on at least three different issues. One instance concerned which cable television company would come into town. A town special committee studying the matter was in agreement when suddenly Vince swung his influence in another direction. But he did not prevail. Another case was his withdrawal under pressure of an appointment to an office of a black community activist who had repeatedly and intemperately attacked the town government, in particular its only black councilperson. The third case was when the town convention voted against his expressed wish as to who should be the Greenburgh committee's candidate for a council seat in one town election (see pp. 16–17). Furthermore, when at Vince's insistence, against the advice of many of the town executive committee's members that there be a referendum on the extension of the supervisor's term by two years, the referendum not only lost but he himself drew substantially fewer votes than was his custom (tax increases were the central issue, but the referendum rubbed salt in voters' wounds).

The legend of Vince's invincibility has minor flaws but most of the forty-seven would agree with Ralph that the town supervisor is "a consummate politician and extremely effective."

There are four elected town council members, all of whom are Democrats. They have their own constituencies both among the voters and within the town committee. Vince's coattails have been mentioned, but at least one seems not to have needed them although they surely did not hurt. This is Eleanor, a black, and a proven vote-puller. In any case, Vince's shadow is so encompassing that little was said during the interviews in regard to the council people's power. Vince is seen as not sharing power unless he has to.

How influential do Greenburgh committee people think they are on their own turf? Not very, apparently, in affecting town governmental decisions. Hanna thinks the committee mostly just goes through the motions of input without having any real impact. John assesses the committee's influence as minimal, just as it should be: "I think the government is decent and why should anyone want to usurp their power?"

Two leaders added thoughts about factionalism to the topic of influence. Nathan says that before Vince was elected the committee chair had power "for what it was worth" and even now he thinks that theoretically the town executive committee should have more influence than it does. But "they have thrown it away by being fractured into factions. The elected officials don't want to get into the fights." Nino thinks power in the Greenburgh committee has been won by default. "Power is in the political nuts," he says. "They win because they are fanatical. They work for what they get. Other people are not willing to give that much time."

Town officials and many of the town outside district leaders know each other very well. It is difficult to believe that the latter are quite as uninfluential as they seem to assume. They do have considerable input into town government. The decisions made there, however, cannot possibly reflect the full range of that input. In any case, input is not equivalent to control.

The Villages

Village district leaders locate power at their level, as they do elsewhere, with the elected officials. One might expect that, because of the smaller geographical area and the greater political intimacies, this would be the arena in which the leaders could best use their powers of persuasion to move the incumbents whom they have helped elect. Considering only the three villages where, in our time frame, Democratic majorities had been elected to village boards, the evidence is that the relationship between officials and district leaders is often troubled.

A few village leaders say that it is only in their home communities that they have any influence at all. There, Nathan points out, you can get on the phone and talk to the incumbents whenever you want to. "But then so can the average citizen," he admits.

The committees and the office holders make special efforts to remain in contact between elections, to discuss programs and issues. This exchange is felt by both parties to it to be important. The committee people want to be informed and the incumbents want their moral support (specifically in the form of bodies at village board meetings). Nevertheless, district leaders sometimes complain about not being consulted and incumbents of not being sufficiently supported. Three village officials offer their versions of the relationship:

> Some people can give advice and be influential, serve as a sounding board. But not the ordinary district leader. They're out of it, completely out of it. The committee as a whole has nothing to say about anything, that's just not where the scene is at.

> As an elected official you listen to the local groups rather than the committee. On development and zoning, which was the issue of the committee, the committee would not take a stand.

> Once you get to the office where the decisions are made, you feel removed from the village, town or county committees. In my village the officials go ahead without the district leaders, who are poorly informed, don't come to village meetings, plan their own meetings on the nights when we meet. I love all these people, but they don't watch what we're doing at all.

Many district leaders in the villages admit that during exchanges with their incumbents they ask questions about what is going on oftener than they proffer advice or grassroots perceptions, that they do not in fact go to village board meetings often, if at all, and that the committees themselves are made up of people not likely to be of one mind on any given issue. On the other hand, there have been infrequent occasions on which some leaders have felt that newly elected officials have somehow forgotten the platform on which the committee thought they were running. In one dramatic instance Lewis, the hard working campaign manager of a Hastings election which had ushered in a Democratic majority for the first time in years, proudly walked with his family into the hall where the winners had just taken their oaths of office, sat down, and heard the votes that his triumphant team was announcing. Immediately he and his family got up and marched out of the room in indignation. Others involved in the campaign sat on in a state of queasiness. (The campaign had been run on the predication of a switch of personnel in an important appointed village office. This did not occur.)

Even when relationships between leaders and incumbents are at their happiest there is a built-in political hitch to complete symbiosis. The parties, naturally enough, are partisan. On the village level incumbents may be much less so. In parts of Westchester there has been some interest in having nonpartisan systems of one kind or another in the area—"There is no Democratic or Republican way to run a village." Some of the village committees have from time to time had to consider the matter of two-party cross endorsements, mostly but not always because of pressure from candidates or incumbents. In Hastings this has resulted in wariness and even outright conflict between the two groups at election time.

In only three instances during the interviews was a chair of a village Democratic committee described as holding any power at all. And in one of these cases it was the chair himself who said he had it but did not use it. Cali, as a new chair with the power at least to run the affairs of the party in her village, was exasperated because "people keep telling me who is and isn't going to run for office. I'm trying to get them to give me a little respect." Other chairs of small committees, including Marge, have felt the need to assert their positions in the face of campaign managers and candidates making decisions without their clearance. The influence of chairs even on their own committees is largely a matter of personality, not position.

Becca is the only Greenburgh district leader cited by several other leaders as an individual who has real power, power beyond that inherent in the various status positions within the party structure. Orson, for example, picks her out as being influential in the county. "She's smart politically, smart period." Ken goes further:

There are people who can parley their positions at relatively low levels into positions of power. Becca, with a relatively low position, is one of the most powerful people in the state today. She worked assiduously within the hierarchy [as town chair]. Mandy [who succeeded her as chair] works down for the roots. Becca is very ambitious. She uses her power— constantly communicating, threatening, cajoling, doing lackey jobs. But she also made too many enemies.

Becca herself says she has never understood power except for the
power of a political organization to elect candidates. "Power is something I've come to understand that I don't understand." She gives two
examples in her political career of events that opened her eyes to her
own potential for influence in her position as town chair. When the
Democratic town slate swept the elections for the first time in 1973
she was advised to take the telephone off the hook. "I didn't know
what they were talking about. But they were right." Democrats called
looking for jobs, Republicans called to be sure they were not losing
jobs, and people asked her questions she neither knew the answers to
nor understood why they wanted to know. She says she realized then
that she had more power than she ever expected to use. The second
example came in the last year or two of her tenure when several
Greenburgh district leaders began criticizing her leadership. It brought
home to her, she says, that her position was being threatened because
"there was a great deal of power there that they thought they could
have."

Both critics and admirers of Becca among the forty-seven believe
that it was not merely her status as chair that brought her under
pressure. They describe her as playing very hard ball in that position,
particularly in fighting for the candidates she thought the most qualified
in town conventions and primaries. They think she used her power to
the hilt.

The views about power verbalized by the Greenburgh district leaders
are down-to-earth, pragmatic. Well aware of their lack of power on a
grand scale, they take seriously the piece of it each potentially has—
the power to elect and the power to influence those elected. Successes,
differently defined and obscure or not, are their monuments.

SELF-INTEREST AND AMBITION

No matter how many good things district leaders want for humankind
in general and their own communities in particular, altruism, of course,
is not all that political activity is about. Mandy puts it this way:

> Part of power is influence and part is political rewards. A lot of people
> want things like paying jobs, places on boards and commissions and just
> help. Everybody you help gets you a power base. And anybody who
> thinks it doesn't, doesn't understand the game.

What personal opportunities do district leaders exploit in the course
of their political activities? The areas explored here are patronage and
ambitions to hold office, and the ways both the receivers and givers

pursue their goals. The forty-seven all assuredly understand "the game" that Mandy is talking about, but it should be recalled that some are not even certain why they are district leaders, never mind biting off anything extra politically.

Patronage

The death of the two-party system and, along with it, political patronage, has been frequently heralded in a great variety of publications (e.g., Herbers 1979; Naisbitt 1984) as well as by politicians who run for office—at least the first time—clothed as anti-politicians. "Elect me . . . or get a politician" ran the message in the brochure of a winning Westchester candidate recently. Whatever is true at the national level, in Greenburgh the Democratic district leaders in general approve of patronage, as they define it. They reject a spoils system approach for distributing paying jobs but believe in "good patronage" of "the right kind." This means that they believe that "equally-qualified Democrats" should be preferred over non-Democrats and that "equally-qualified Democrats who have worked for the party" should be preferred over those who have not. The following comments indicate a range in the depth of commitment to the practice:

Conrad: I'm in principle not opposed to it.

Claud: I don't see anything much wrong with it.

Nora: You've got to live with some of it and just see that it's not abused.

Fred: It's part of the game.

Maria: People need an opportunity. It's all right to open the door a little if a person is qualified.

Tess: Patronage is what keeps a party going.

Becca: There's no reason why people who have helped elect an incumbent should not serve. They are presumably of the same philosophy and so more apt to make it happen. Everything's political.

Firmly in favor of patronage, Gene and Lewis expand on the subject. Gene sees it as an advantage not only to the party but to the whole electoral process. "People are not necessarily involved in party politics to be sure the right person is buttering their bread." He points out that politics is an education and if one has become competent in some way through that education, then it would be an advantage to have that person. He thinks that district leaders should not be limited by

their position in what else they can do, and that an office holder has
a right to judge who can be useful, whether a supporter or not.

Lewis asserts that he would not himself take a paid political job
because he does not want to "owe" anyone but that many good professional people *are* in politics because they want to get something out
of it. "Until the name of the game changes I am absolutely one hundred
percent in favor of patronage and will help people I think are qualified
in whatever way I can." Other leaders also say that they have recommended others for jobs or, as Jodie describes it, "served as a communications link between people with jobs to give and people wanting
jobs."

The people with jobs to give are public officials and administrators.
These people often deal directly with one another in making suggestions
or picking people, but in other cases the party is involved at the
appropriate level. State patronage (where there are some "schlump"
jobs, by which Arthur means jobs that have little to do with qualifi-
cations) flows through the county chair, and for Greenburgh also the
town chair. Not many of the forty-seven are aware of proper patronage
protocol at the various levels for jobs. Leon once went to the then-
county chair in reference to an appointment he was interested in and
about which he had already spoken to his state representatives. The
man, he remembers, was outraged because Leon had not come to him
first. His prerogative as a conduit to the public officials had been
breached.

Every Greenburgh district leader by party and government agreement
holds patronage rights over the appointments of their party's election
inspectors (who work at the polls all election day) in their own districts.
The town clerk makes the actual appointments but depends on the
leaders to find the people.[2] In reality some of the leaders do not know
this and those that do are usually happy to relinquish their "rights"
to their area or village chairs. Appointing inspectors is not regarded
as patronage for the simple reason that it is often hard to find anyone
able and willing to do the job. "Inspectors are doing you a favor," says
John. And, "It's not patronage," claims Leon, "since you have to beg
people to be inspectors." Nevertheless, knowing about and finding an
individual who would like the job helps not only the electoral process
but that person. Lewis wanted his chair to at least clear the appointments in his district with him. Tess, the current chair in Hastings
makes a practice of not going over the leaders' heads in making new
appointments but asks them for suggestions.

The majority of the leaders interviewed do not seem to take the
possibility of receiving paid governmental positions very seriously.
Polly, Cali, Nino and Arthur are among the exceptions, although they

do not specify exactly what they want. Polly says that although she has scoured "the red book and the green book" (she describes them as lists of government jobs) she has not found yet a position she wants. "I do know that to get something I have to work for it since I don't have the money to pay for it. Instead of money, I'm using sweat." Cali, too, says she would like something for herself but has no idea what. She thinks "patronage is something I better bone up on." But this has nothing to do with her political involvement, she adds.

Abby has a dream about patronage—she would like to be appointed to the state parole board so that black prisoners would be more at ease when interviewed. She empathizes with them, she says, because she herself would not ask white strangers for anything, "except maybe a seat in the lifeboat if I were on the Titanic."

Those of the forty-seven who have already received patronage are:

Chester, whose daughter got an internship in the office of one of his senators.

Orson, whose daughter—also his co-leader—got a similar job working for their assemblyman in Albany.

Duke, whose son got a job in the town's Department of Public Works ("I didn't use any pressure but my political position may have been a factor").

Ralph, who recalls his only patronage as occurring when a Westchester surrogate, recently appointed by a Democratic administration, referred a special guardian case to him.

It is interesting that, in spite of the overall acceptance of the idea of patronage stated by the district leaders, those whom an outsider would be likely to describe as its recipients in full-time paid jobs indignantly reject the interpretation. In other words, the acceptance of patronage as an appropriate political tool is more convincing coming from the givers than from the receivers. For example, Ella reluctantly resigned her district leadership in order to take a job with the town's nutrition program. She does not consider her job to be patronage. She got the job, she explains, by asking the town administrative commissioner (a Democrat) at a party (a Democratic fund raising affair) about available jobs with the town government, and he said, "Okay, there's this possibility," which she received on her merits.

In two other instances, Vi and Ann insist that their jobs in their Democratic assemblyman's state district office are not in the "patronage" category. Vi asserts that her position is "earned, not given," thereby separating it from her voluntary work in all of the incumbent's election campaigns. When Ann's father-in-law, Jimmy, once referred to her position as patronage she "almost chopped off his head."

This sensitivity on the part of three of the very few of the forty-seven who have received paid jobs throws some shadow over the generally positive assessment of patronage by the leaders. Even Arthur, most insistent on the validity of patronage, does not so characterize his job within the county government. "Patronage" seems to be more of a dirty word than the generally clean billing given it above would indicate.

Views expressed by five other leaders buttress this conclusion. As is clear below, the opinions they offer do not reflect on the merits of work done by Ella, Vi, Ann or Arthur—targets are made explicit—but they are probably part of a general climate that justifies their touchiness. Mandy refers to certain county-level jobs:

> I think since those departments are full of incompetent people they may as well be incompetent Democrats. All of the county commissioners are white males, and that's not good enough.

Abby, fresh from a fray with an ex-leader holding a temporary patronage job, makes a similar point:

> As long as you've got it upstairs, I'll go along with patronage. But I don't want to be insulted by having to go up and speak to a damn idiot. If you don't give that job to a black person then you be sure the white person is intelligent enough to talk to me.

Fay's objection is the elitism she sees permeating patronage, a holding-back on sharing the goodies:

> Little crumbs come down. Everyone else gets some crumbs. Let us have some, too! But how many of us ever received anything? It goes to the big shots.

Ken and Rita characterize the people that patronage too often is given to as "political sycophants" or wives of important party leaders— "Many are totally ineffectual." Rita does not profess particular interest in a patronage position but comments, "I would like, at least, to have been offered one."

Jimmy accepts the idea of patronage as fully, if not more fully, as any other leader. He is blunt about how offended he felt when a person he sponsored was passed over for an appointment; was, he says, not even properly considered. Sure that his candidate was amply qualified, he took the decision as belittling him and his two score years of toiling in the political vineyards. He fuels his rancor by thinking of other deserving applicants who have "not been taken care of."

Several district leaders speak of non-paying appointments to boards and commissions as falling under the rubric of patronage. Ralph, Nino, Arthur, and Nathan are included among those who desired and received such appointments. Leon says the closest that he has come to receiving patronage was when he was appointed by the town government as "a dollar-a-year consultant" for it on energy issues, one of his chief interests. He wanted the appointment in order to have a little more clout than he would as an individual when he attends state Public Service Commission hearings. Polly is happy to have the honor of an appointment as a delegate to the judicial committee to screen candidates for the state supreme court. Similar examples are multiple.

Tess, however, from a village point of view at least, separates giving appointments from giving patronage: "Appointments fall in the category of getting citizens involved in local government." Most village officials seem to agree, and keep their appointments from veering off into partisanship. Nevertheless, on occasion leaders feel rebuffed when their offers to serve are refused. This was the case with Vi, whose ambition to serve on Hastings' board of police commissioners was fluffed off. Also in Hastings, Charlie was appointed by a Democratic village board to its planning board while serving as the Democratic committee chair. When the next village board—no longer Democratic—did not reappoint him he felt that its members were playing politics.

While there is no barrier to the appointment of district leaders to positions at the village or county levels, there is in the town outside. After sweeping the town election in 1973, the new Democratic supervisor and the council went to work on a Caesar's-wife set of rules to govern by. The result was the passage of "A Local Law Establishing a Code of Ethics and a Board of Ethics for the Town of Greenburgh," which has been effective since January 1, 1975. Included in the article on "Prohibited Political Activities" is the provision that appointed officers, employees, members of the board of ethics, the zoning board of appeals, the planning board of paid agency members should not hold any county, town, village or state political office or position or hold office in any political club or organization.

Many district leaders, including Arthur and Sid, believe that this provision is far too stringent. They say that one would expect to find individuals best equipped by knowledge, experience and interest to serve on the boards precisely among party committee persons. The town Democratic committee appointed a sub-committee to explore the matter and it came up with several recommendations moderating the prohibitions. These were forwarded to the town council for consideration, to no avail. Throughout the following years district leaders given an opportunity to serve in the town government have had to weigh their wish to do so against their desire to retain that most-favored part of the leader's job, their vote.

Political Office

Five of the forty-seven have run in village elections and won. The same people have also run in village elections and lost. Nine others have run in village elections and never won. The temptation is to say that running for office at this level is not really indicative of political ambition since some have stepped in only when nominating committees have been unable to convince other potential candidates to run. But it takes something close to ambition even to do that, and they all wanted to win and serve. The losers state that they enjoyed the whole campaigning experience but not so much, apparently, that they would go through it again without thinking that they had a reasonably substantial chance of winning. As Evan says, "Once for fun is enough."

Election to a village office has not often served as a springboard for higher office. Only two leaders interviewed had run for office outside of the villages. Abby won a seat as a delegate at a national Democratic mini-convention. Cedric ran for a town council nomination in a Democratic primary and lost. He then ran in Hastings for a trustee seat and lost. Nothing daunted, at the time of the interview he was thinking of tossing his hat in the ring once again:

> In the primary I broadened my base, my contacts, my exposure to people in the town. If in the future an opportunity should come I've already laid a lot of groundwork . . . which will be a benefit to me. Maybe next time I'll be a successful candidate—if there is a next time.

The ways in which potential candidates indicate their availability varies in some particulars but in general each sounds out other leaders, particularly the influential people in the party. They diligently do their party jobs and help other leaders wherever they can. If their plans advance to the point of a convention or a primary, they comb the list of Greenburgh leaders for support. (For data on the making and breaking of candidacies see the following chapter.)

A few of the forty-seven indicated that, while they had no intention of seeking public office, they would not count themselves completely out. Ann says, "I don't know. It's possible, it's possible. I know I'd have support." Fay states, "I'd run for anything I think I could deal with." Becca prefers what she is doing although "there are times when

I would like to be the one making the final decision instead of electing the people who make the final decisions." Craig, Leon and Pepe and doubtless others, too, think it would be great to be in Congress. But they know that plums do not fall into laps that happen to be sitting around, so in effect they are not politically ambitious.

Thirteen interviewees have no ambitions to run for public office at all. Ralph declares, "I would do anything for the Democratic party but run for office." John says, "A politician is really not his own person. He's all things to all people. . . . I couldn't possibly do it." Jane and Brooke are interested in their husbands' advancement but not their own. Others who flatly rule out candidacies are Tess, Jodie, Nora, Orson, Chester, Faith and Maria. Arthur says he sees nothing he wants. Polly says she thinks she may be too idealistic to be "on stage." Gene is too busy with his work and family.

Contesting for party office is a different matter. Mandy, Becca, Rita, Arthur, Lewis, Pepe and Hanna all hold party positions. Becca once came close to being selected county chair. Lewis, while ruling out public office, definitely wants to go further in the party structure. Hanna, executive vice-chair of the Greenburgh committee, does not want to take the logical next step to be chair. Rita and Ken say they prefer working behind the scenes to being up front.

The extent to which politicians resort to expedient behavior can partly gauge both their self-interest and the skills they use in promoting it.

When the subject of expediency came up in the interviews, a few mildly wondered what they had to be politically expedient about. Five declared that they had not and would not ever resort to behavior that was not completely in line with their convictions. The overwhelming majority, however, were sure that they had made expedient decisions (Golda: "What other kinds are there?") in the past and would do so again. Most of this group, though, had difficulty in providing examples of their expedient behavior—possibly because, as Craig suggests, "It's a thing you tend to forget as soon as you've done it," or, in Ralph's view, "Every political decision is expedient, made to gain a result."

The examples proffered in response to the question, "Have you ever been politically expedient?" were on the order of, "Yes, when I voted for [whomever]"; "Yes, when I ran with that slate"; "In picking winners instead of the best candidate"; and "In jumping on the bandwagon of some of my least favorite people." Becca's immediate answer of "Yeah— you gonna burn this tape?" also had to do with candidate selection, the leaders' consuming interest.

Ella's philosophy about expediency was thought out long ago, when the Hastings Democrats were running candidates in favor of an urban renewal plan for a section of the village. The proposed program turned out to be exceedingly unpopular and Ella, as chair, was unhappy with her candidates' statements on it:

> I started out with great high ideals about politics. But it doesn't work. You can't be down-the-line ideal. You can hold some of your ideals— you know, not compromise them. But there really are times when you have to do things for expediency. . . . When urban renewal became an issue I thought it was more important to elect the people, and then they could do what they thought they had to do. That was expedience. I'm not sorry I took that position. Why should you show the dirty linen in public? Why tell the truth, what you wanted to do? Then you wouldn't be able to do it anyway.

Claud remembers the same campaign when "I was so uncompromisingly moral I was nosed out for mayor by three to one."

Fred, a later candidate for trustee in Hastings, muses about an important issue during his campaign, which was coming under the provisions of the New York State Emergency Tenant Protection Act. He was at first against Hastings doing so but his slate-mates were in favor of it, so he "was expedient and researched the issue. Happily, I decided I was for it and hope it wasn't a rationalization." In similar instances, Cedric says he has not been expedient, "I just don't inject myself into everything."

Ilse, as a candidate in another village campaign, sees expediency as a matter of degree. During one of her campaigns an emotional issue was support for the modernizing of a private service institution in her village. Candidates at state, county and village levels were all against it because of doubts about both the need for it and the quality of its service. Yet it was a hot issue in the community and one by one the candidates lined up in support of the rebuilding. Ilse describes shepherding one of these higher-level candidates through a throng at a village event when, in answering questions about the issue, the candidate suddenly got the drift of public opinion and "without batting an eye completely reversed his stand in answer to subsequent questions." Ilse thinks this was understandable since any candidate expressing opposition to the institution "would have been cooked."

Some conclusions about the district leaders and power result from the data. First, they define their power specifically as the power to elect and the power to influence those elected. Both powers depend on two commodities. One is votes and the ability to corral votes within the party structure affecting decisions, which all share equally and most regard as a prerogative of some importance. The other is work, or a reasonable facsimile thereof.

Persuasive action by the leaders must be based on their reputations for doing that part of their job that the party most wants done (knowing and working their districts) and assuming and carrying out the duties of chairs and other party officers. Although competition in doing so is not very fierce and tokenism goes a long way, hard work does make up for perceived lacks in other areas. Of the total Greenburgh committee, many leaders do not vie in these ways and one can only conclude that they either have no desire to greatly affect political outcomes or they are not realistic about their party roles.

Although none of the forty-seven is especially skilled in political rhetoric, it is safe to assume that particular leaders are influential in specific instances not only because of the sagacity of their advice but the persuasiveness with which they present it. Some exhibit other personal qualities in their desire to be effective that are not only observable but evident in their self-assessments. For example, and without evaluating the outcomes: it is clear that Lewis pursues his political goals aggressively—and loudly, he says, because of his political apprenticeship in the west side of New York City; that Ken and Rita cling to an ideologically principled ground that has earned them the epithet "conscience of the party;" and that Nino values the art of compromise and making deals. Leaders are depended on sporadically for their special knowledge and skills: legal advice, research ability, expertise in drafting platforms and news releases, doing mechanicals, or painting signs. Money from leaders is appreciated, but if the scale on which most leaders can, or are willing to, put their money where their mouths are encourages or discourages consideration of their views, the evidence is lacking in this study.

DISCUSSION

Points of view from the social disciplines about power, patronage and gamesmanship refine the picture of self-interest among the district leaders. Because the emics of the Greenburgh situation present influence as a subset of power, the wider implications of that concept require attention.

Scholars define power in various ways. Some emphasize its coercive nature: the controlling of people and resources through force or the threat of force (among anthropologists, e.g., Leach 1965; Adams 1975; Fried 1967). Certainly ultimate power, whether from inside or outside a society, has been coercive for at least the last twelve thousand years. Other social scientists distinguish between kinds of power, such as dominance or manipulation, or between power and influence and other related processes (e.g. Lasswell and Kaplan 1950; Merton 1957; Galbraith 1983). Whatever the particular rubrics favored, a range of processes is being discussed.

The focus on the forty-seven's micro influence as political actors and their relative freedom from party pressure (as distinguished from other forms of persuasion) does not deny less tangible social environmental impact on them as subjects. The macro political economy constitutes a "gloved" or indirect coercion, as it does in any democratic stratified society. The leaders described are middle class, and there is no surface evidence that they fear unpleasant consequences from any of their political activities—although a few of them may have become district leaders instead of revolutionaries because of pragmatic recognition of how things, like gloved coercion, work. The other side of the coin is the relationship between politics and immediate economic self-interest that takes the form of patronage.

A wisdom of some small subsistence communities is to be wary of accepting beneficence from others; "gifts make slaves" is the way the Eskimo put it. Yet exchanging goods and services is universal and these societies have their own reciprocal and egalitarian ways of doing it. In societies with complex socioeconomic arrangements, ways of effecting trade-offs are likely to be more power-ridden; these include clientage (patron-client relations) and political patronage.

Clientage is a culture pattern characteristic of some rural, developing and market economies in which a patron dispenses favors for services rendered. Nobutaka Ike (1972), for example, describes Japan—where paternalism is diffused throughout the society and loyalty is culturally ingrained—as a patron-client democracy: "Most citizens relate to the political system through patrons or mediating agents—local notables, agricultural association agents, labor union leaders, party politicians" (126). The trade-off, he says, is ballots for benefits. Political patronage in the United States, on the other hand, is located specifically in the government or parties. While "ballots for benefits" may sound familiar to Americans, traditional clientage seems similar to political patronage mainly in that they both involve motivations of self-interest—which is hardly surprising since so do most other human actions.

Indeed, the prevalence of self-interest is the basis of various economic views of democracy as a market place, including Downs' model (1957; also see Buchanan and Tullock 1962 and Buchanan 1984 for a later related economic political theory), in which politicians seek office only for power and citizens vote only their welfare. In other words, votes are maximized in exchange for material benefits. This goes beyond a simple concern with political patronage but the idea has been built on in an analysis of patronage in Chicago's Democratic political machine (Wilson 1961).

Wilson describes the ends of a machine boss as being more than— in some situations, not even—vote maximization. Survival is the goal. A machine, he says, is the kind of party organization that sustains its membership by distributing material incentives instead of by appealing to ideology, sociability, and the fun of the game. Wilson further defines machine patronage jobs as "the distributed posts the pay for which is greater than the value of the public services performed" (370).

Is it helpful to think of increasingly outmoded machine patronage as clientage? Conceivably but not clearly: the mediating politician in Ike's Japan is not the widely-influential patron, and the political boss in Wilson's Chicago is patron only by virtue of the way he manages his party position. In Greenburgh Democratic politics, one could look very hard without finding an anthropologically recognizable example of clientage. One *would* find mentors, swappers of favors and some political patronage. Unlike in the big city machine, the patronage is minuscule and cannot sustain the party organization. Other than material incentives, cited by Wilson above, must be operative.

Practitioners and researchers alike favor the metaphor "game" for politics. The emic usage is sometimes trivializing but also reflects an understanding similar to, if certainly not as developed as, Bailey's (1969): he thinks of politics as a competitive game with agreed upon prizes and sets of rules to regulate the conflict.[3] Conflict is the core of Bailey's conception; the politicians he describes "are all caught in the act of out-manoeuvering one another, of knifing one another in the back, of tripping one another up and . . . engrossed in winning a victory over someone" (xi). Bailey distinguishes between normative rules ("politics' public face") and pragmatic rules ("politics' private wisdom")—that is, tactics for winning that players can get away with.

Bailey's emphasis on conflict and winning needs tempering to suit the Greenburgh data, and the tempering comes from a fellow action theorist (Turner 1974:140), who writes that politics "is not merely a game. It is also idealism, altruism, patriotism (not always the last resort of the scoundrel), universalism, sacrifice of self interest, and so on." If politics is a game, it is a serious and complex one, and the stakes— besides achieving personal power—include influencing the turn of events toward one's idea of the public good. Economic and game models illuminate materialist motivational elements in local party politics. By their very nature, however, they leave unexplored wider ideational interests—self and otherwise—that are so clearly present in the emphasis on goals and issues in the ethnographic findings. Personal satisfactions of performing a civic duty, of being respected by peers for one's political know-how are not the same as, though doubtless linked to, personal gains involved in a successful pursuit of power.

The Greenburgh material leads to a moot judgment on the universality of competition and the need for power. Much of the district leaders' activities seem to have little to do with accumulating points in a contest for political influence. The fact that some leaders do vie in this way still leaves many others who must be indulging any need for power in fields other than local politics. Their part-time role, of course, leaves ample hours for more hard-nosed competition in other areas.

On the other hand, if there were no competitive players with their individual resources and strategies, it is hard to see how there would be any political activity at all. Rivalry among the leaders, whether in pursuit of specific political outcomes or linked to personal relationships, produces the work that makes the political system viable. This is evident in the following chapters where the forty-seven are seen going about the business of winning (or losing) elections and choosing sides on a number of issues.

The Forty-Seven: Part Three

MANDY

Mandy grew up in a northern Westchester city, her orthodox Jewish parents' "golden girl." They lived in an essentially non-Jewish community and she lives now in an integrated Hartsdale school district (Central 7) because she wanted her children also to grow up knowing all kinds of people. Mandy's parents are not enrolled in a party because her father, a professional, did not want to offend anyone, but she thinks they are basically Republican.

Mandy went off to an eastern university "with my cashmere sweaters" and the knowledge that her mother expected her to join a sorority. But "the sorority-frat scene turned me off" and a boy friend who was campaigning for a Democratic senatorial candidate (Abraham Ribicoff) turned her on to politics, in which she became active.

After marriage to an army man, Mandy had two sons and lived in various places across the country until moving to Hartsdale. There, she became involved with the League of Women Voters, the local fair housing group, the school and PTA, and local politics, soon becoming a leader in her own district. She feels that all of these activities are interrelated. With the anti-war movement, politics became the dominant interest. Her marriage broke up and she married a man equally politically motivated. He now has an important position in the town government and Mandy has succeeded Becca as chair of the town committee. Since her divorce, Mandy has worked for a service organization, in charge of community volunteers.

Mandy calls herself a liberal Democrat and feels that she has all the credentials, from her position on the Vietnam War to the boycott of lettuce during Cesar Chavez' organizing of migrant workers.

VI

Vi is a native Hastingsite of Portuguese descent. Her parents became Democrats in the 1930s because, her father explains, "they are for the working man, for low-income people." Vi is married and has two children. Her husband "lets me do my own thing," which includes not only politics but a consuming interest in American Indians and their welfare. She works for her state assemblyman in his Greenburgh district office.

Vi's first political activity was as a volunteer in the re-election campaign of her congressman because she liked the way he had handled a matter brought to him by her brother. "After that, politics became an addiction." The next time the congressman ran she was his local coordinator and in that role came in contact with her village Democratic committee. She first served as a leader outside her district but felt ill at ease there and resigned to wait for a vacancy in her own, a heavily Republican and conservative Democratic district, which finally opened.

Working on campaigns at all political levels has become almost a way of life for Vi. In the village she has run for trustee and lost—"I felt like a sacrificial lamb." Recently she was in a primary to retain her leadership and won.

Vi says she is conservative—"I believe in brotherhood and equality but I'm not liberal." She equates liberalism with permissiveness, and calls herself a traditionalist who wants rules. She also thinks the government spends too much on social programs and that there are too many welfare cheats. Nevertheless, the most striking thing about Vi's value system is her empathy with the downtrodden and espousal of their rights. Vi has a title for a book she'd like to write: "PowWows and Politics." "The more deeply I get into politics, the more I see how everything is interrelated, like the Mohawks' problems with the state. It's through government and legislation you're going to solve these problems."

JIMMY

Jimmy is retired but still works part-time as Democratic custodian of the Greenburgh voting machines, maintaining and delivering them to the polling places. This is a county patronage job that he has held since 1945.

Jimmy was the second of nine children of immigrant Italian parents who moved the family every few years between various Italian or mixed communities in the Bronx and lower Westchester. He remembers that during his early childhood, while the church was the center of community life, a competing center of activity was the saloons ("one on every corner") with their big backrooms accommodating every event from fancy balls to the dispensation of jobs and other favors by the ward bosses and heelers. His father was active in the community, and Jimmy classifies his parents as "gentile" and not "cafone" (a ruder class of Italians, he explains). Nevertheless, they were poor, and believed that as soon as their children were able to work they should go out and earn money to bring home.

After a childhood of hustling pennies and nickels and running with gangs, a slightly older Jimmy ("a gay young blade") entered the more lucrative business of bootlegging for an uncle and later for himself. Because of the risks, raids, pay-offs and "being screwed," Jimmy abandoned this enterprise. The family became more affluent. Jimmy started a trucking business, took the time to get a flying license, married Lila. Then, with his business in a slump, the family moved with the trucks to his wife's father's farm in rural Greenburgh.

Jimmy rushed to join the army air force after Pearl Harbor, leaving Lila in charge of the business. He spent the duration of the war as a flying instructor. After the war, Jimmy, thinking that there must be an easier way of making a living, sold what was left of his business and became a milkman, whose seven to eleven A.M. hours left him ample time to explore a new interest—local politics. Later jobs were also accommodated to this new involvement.

Jimmy learned about politics from two Democratic leaders who took an interest in him, and he gave the party his loyalty. He has served since then for the town and later in Hastings, as a party officer.

To Jimmy, patronage is still the name of the game in politics. He feels that when the party finally won big locally in 1973 the leadership failed him, that after years of dedicated service he has not been given his due. But Jimmy holds on to his role as a party leader. He is loyal but bitter. He describes himself as "a disgruntled" and someone "who knows where the bodies are buried." He says about politics in general that "graft, corruption and skulduggery" are inevitable. He accepts that this is the way of the world.

ANN

Ann grew up in an Irish Catholic family in Yonkers, received a parochial school education, and attended business school. She was interested in politics but not really active until, at twenty-one, she married Jimmy, Jr. At first they lived with his family, Italian Catholics, in Ardsley. She had decided not to enroll in a party when she registered to vote, but her in-laws told her "there were six Petrillos registered as Democrats, and at the same address there would now be seven." Soon Jimmy, Sr. asked his daughter-in-law to "set up the nuns at the Academy" for a Catholic candidate running for a local judgeship, and she "got a kick out of it." After that she worked at times for candidates chosen because of personal contacts.

Today Ann's deep involvement in party politics seems to depend on her personal and work-selected network of friends and acquaintances. She is close to her brother, who is a Republican office holder, and some of his friends. One of her strongest ties is to the state assemblyman from her assembly district, whom she first met at a Catholic Youth Organization basketball game both were attending because of their children. She was working for him as a district liaison officer at the time of the interview—work that she loves. Since then she has obtained a similar job in the Yonkers office of the assembly speaker.

These personal and work-related ties take precedence over her district leadership about which she feels somewhat uncomfortable, maintaining the position primarily to have a vote if one of her admired friends needs it.

Ann thinks of herself as politically conservative and, although she will take a strong position when morally aroused, she prefers not to take stands on issues. "When I don't want to get involved I just back off."

CONRAD AND TESS

Conrad was raised in the midwest. His father was a conservative Republican, very opposed to Franklin Roosevelt, while Conrad himself was apolitical throughout his years at college. After achieving an engineering degree he moved to New York City where "some of the most interesting people I met belonged to the eastern liberal ideology." As a result he developed an intellectual interest in politics. Conrad had already set out to educate himself in the liberal arts, and now added politics to his other academic interests.

Conrad and Tess met, married, and lived four years in the city. Tess had been brought up in Idaho, where her parents were educators and enrolled Republicans, until Roosevelt's first administration. Her father had gone into business, which failed during the Depression. While unemployed, the local Democrats asked him to run for county assessor, a job he won and kept for eighteen years. Tess's mother, a woman of strong opinions, was active in the community—an activity that the young girl emulated but her three older brothers did not (although one of them later sought and won public office). "Everyone read in my family. We were expected to read the newspaper and discuss it afterwards."

In New York, Tess and Conrad became involved with the Friends Service Committee. He joined a group called the Scientific Approach to Peace, and she put out its newsletter. In the early 1960s they moved with their two small children to Hastings. Two years later they attended a Democratic party at a neighbor's house and there met Ella, the village chair, who interested them in local politics. Conrad soon became a leader and Tess a captain in their own district.

When Ella stepped down from her post a few years later, Conrad replaced her as chair, only in a couple of years to step down himself in order to be the party's candidate for mayor, a race that he lost. After a time the couple's activity in local politics flagged, with Tess occupied by starting and managing a successful Hastings newspaper. Eight years later the Hastings Democratic committee asked Tess, her newspaper work behind her, to become chair and she acquiesced.

Conrad describes himself as a left-of-center Democrat. Tess thinks of herself as being politically idiosyncratic but definitely not conservative.

GENE

Gene is a native New Yorker from the Bronx. He vividly remembers the intense interest of his family in politics and the arguments they had, particularly those between his mother and an older brother during the Joseph McCarthy period. His mother "converted from being an embarrassed McCarthyite to an absolute hater of McCarthy and all he stood for."

Gene has always been a liberal Democrat, he says. Several years ago he persuaded his mother to change from an independent to a Democrat in order to have a primary vote. His father, on the other hand, is enrolled as a Republican. Neither man has ever mentioned the matter because "my father avoided controversy at all costs."

When a lawyer in New York City, Gene "knocked on a few doors for candidates who lost," but felt that there he was really not needed politically. He has lived in Hastings with his wife and several children only a few years but early found himself embroiled in school affairs and then in a village campaign. Noticed in the latter, he was asked to be a captain in his own district but when a leadership vacancy occurred outside he accepted it. He has recently switched back as leader in his district.

Although genuinely attracted to politics, Gene will not sacrifice time with his family. His children's upbringing is paramount and besides being with them as much as he can, he devotes time to searching for a compatible Catholic "home" for the family.

ILSE

Ilse was born in Berlin, grew up in Germany, and was in her teens when World War II ended. After high school she worked for the British occupation forces for a few years before attending college and then law school. She did not finish the latter, having met an American going to school in Europe under the GI Bill of Rights whom she married and accompanied back to the United States.

Twenty-five years old at the time, Ilse describes herself then as totally innocent of political activity of any kind and ignorant of any way of influencing life around her. Her political education began in 1960 when the family moved to Dobbs Ferry. Her first introduction to the community was through the school, "since I'm not a church person." Having missed the 1960 presidential election because of the timing of the move, she was determined to be prepared for future elections. "My husband was totally uninterested in political background. These days he takes my word for it." In order to learn more about how democracy in local government works, Ilse joined the League of Women Voters. She was fascinated with the league workshops on ballot issues, with the trips to Albany to see legislators, and she soaked up information about all levels of government, eventually becoming president of the Dobbs Ferry league.

For ten years Ilse was an unenrolled voter but then, determined to vote in the 1972 primary, she became a Democrat with her first presidential primary vote going for George McGovern. A year or so after her league presidency ended, Ilse decided that lobbying elected officials was too slow a process and she would work instead where the decisions are actually made, see the whole picture as an official herself. Her first try for village trustee was successful. Two years later the entire Democratic slate was defeated and Ilse then became a district leader. She has retained her leadership through her subsequent trustee incumbencies, although considering the role secondary.

Ilse is high on American politics. "To have a chance to influence—in the school, the village, a higher level—I relish that. It is the new dimension I have found here."

ZOE

Politics was served up at the table along with dinner for as far back as Zoe can remember her childhood in Marble Hill in the Bronx. It was important to the family to know what was going on in both the local and the national scene. Although very young when Adlai Stevenson ran for president in 1952, she remembers being caught up in the excitement of the campaign. After high school, Zoe majored in sociology and political science at a college in Manhattan.

Zoe, her husband and small children came to Hartsdale from Brooklyn, where she had been bored, but was now ready for community involvement. Part of this involvement was with the Greenburgh People for Peace, where she got to know Rita, Ken, Mandy, Hanna and other Concerned Democrats. Through a politically oriented neighbor she also worked on a congresional campaign, and was asked by the town committee chair, then Becca, to be a district leader. Through Hanna as well as her children, she became interested in Greenburgh's "Central 7" school, and is now a member of the school board. Zoe's third avocation is recreation—coaching, competition, and the Greenburgh parks system.

A "liberal" or "progressive" Democrat, Zoe belongs to various political and civil rights national organizations but thinks that by her local work she can have more impact on her causes. She is essentially an issues politician and is proud of her reputation for being outspoken on the issues—and on the candidates.

NATHAN

Nathan and his two younger siblings were brought up in the Bronx by lower middle class Jewish parents. The parents were liberal and although not actively involved in politics, they were interested and enjoyed discussing the subject. Nathan, who says he was "a street kid," found his own interest piqued by watching the Stevenson-Eisenhower presidential conventions on television and reading in the newspapers about the Bronx political machine.

Nathan attended a university in New York City for two years and later went to night school at a city college. He has worked at a variety of jobs, and now owns a rental business. A few years after marriage he moved with his wife and daughters to Tarrytown. There he worked on two local planning issues, helped first in the campaign of a Republican for mayor, and then helped the Democrats in a couple of campaigns.

When the village Democratic chair asked him to be a leader he readily agreed because he wanted to have a hand in the selection of village candidates and thus affect village policies. He has served in three districts not his own and as campaign manager in a town election. He has also served on various village boards and commissions. Nathan says his self-image is better because of his political activities—"That's important to me, knowing that I'm involved in the decision-making process."

Nathan finds himself growing more conservative as the years go by, at least fiscally. However, he remains liberal on civil rights and village development issues.

FAITH

Faith was brought up in New York City. She describes her father as being "basically a socialist" who came to this country from Russia circa 1906, having been disowned by his father for leading a strike against the family wheat farm. Later, during the Depression, Faith herself picketed a Brooklyn business "protesting many things." She considers both of her parents were liberal, but racist.

Faith's interest in politics started in high school and continued through college and after. Except for a brief enrollment in the Socialist Labor party, she has been a Democrat. After marriage she lived in the Washington, D.C. area, moving to Irvington thirty years ago. She was advised not to reveal herself as a Democrat in this heavily Republican village lest her children suffer. Nevertheless, after ten days of residence she became a leader in the struggling Democratic committee, with no untoward consequences for her family. She has since continuously been a leader and committee treasurer—the oldest in service on the committee, which she describes as having gradually changed from a mostly Catholic membership to mostly Jewish and more liberal.

Liberal seems to be the word for Faith—in religion (Unitarian), in general attitudes, and with her time in volunteer efforts. These latter have included working for such groups as fair housing, planned parenthood ("I volunteeered at the clinic until I got too old. Young girls don't relate to old volunteers, only professionals"), regional planning, and, of course, the party.

FRED

Fred has always been interested in politics, "the local industry in Washington, D.C." where he grew up in a Republican family. At college Fred majored in political science and belonged to the Republican Club. "As a callow youth" he campaigned for Richard Nixon in 1960. Later, as a voter Fred chose the Democratic candidates on the national level, finally deciding to enroll in the party.

After attending Harvard Law School Fred came to work in Manhattan. His work was very demanding and getting into politics seemed too difficult for him to pursue at the time. On moving with his wife and child to Hastings several years later, his interest found an outlet at the local level. He met the current village chair at a party and was rapidly recruited as a district leader. On the committee he served three times on the nominating committee, the last time becoming a candidate for trustee himself. He lost the election but was looking forward to trying again when work developments deterred him. He remains a leader, although not with his former zest.

CHAPTER 5

Winning and Losing

A heady mixture of motivations among the Democratic committee members, including a need for power, fuels the party machinery. The processes of choosing candidates for office and campaigning for them are major components of the political field. It is in these activities and in internal conflict that motivations and political strategies and skills of the leaders can best be observed.

The leadership role in election campaigns is, of course, heavily stressed by the party. However, it is an activity shared by others of their party as well as by some Republicans and unenrolled voters transiently drawn to particular candidates. Indeed, the more widely it is shared the more successful the leaders feel because it is evidence that the candidates they have chosen have wide appeal.

On the other hand, the choosing itself is a responsibility uniquely the leaders', unless the selection goes to primary and even then their influence is strong. For this reason, most of the forty-seven and probably most Greenburgh committee members take the responsibility seriously. According to each leader's assessment of potential candidates, some feel high excitement during the selection process, some are "left cold" by the choices, and still others speak of "lesser evil" options. But they know that their decisions carry weight.

CHOOSING CANDIDATES

New York Times journalist John Herbers has written that the two-party system "is little more than a hollow shell existing solely to provide the framework of nominating candidates" (1979). Herbers is interested in how the loss of party clout affects public life. What he describes as a rattling around in hollowness, the local leaders in Greenburgh see as a paramount political reason for being. As Sid claims, "We pick the candidates. That is power."

Factors involved in these different perceptions are the position of the observer, which part of the picture is being viewed, and what the observer thinks ought to be. Herbers, and others before and since, is worried about how we pick our national slates and whether "the demise of the two-party system," the rise of media artistry, and the proliferation of pressure groups bode well or ill for the country. Sid, although interested in these problems, is thinking about his local role. They are talking about the same institution—a political party—but Herbers's view is of its impact on one election held quadrennially, Sid's is of a multiplicity of elections for a whole range of officials held year in and year out.

Of the forty-seven, only Becca and Lewis volunteer criticism of the condition of their party in general that could be said to reflect concern about party discipline. Even so, they and many of their committee colleagues are reform-minded. They are in the field because they want to alter their party toward more of an issue orientation. Their view of "party" is less one of discipline and favors in order to marshal followers behind remote politicians' decisions than one as a tool to be used— within proper party procedures—to gather others to the particular standards they hold. Thus their relationship to the party is one of loyalty only to the extent that the party seems to them the best vehicle, because of its positions, to help achieve their goals.

The fact that some of the forty-seven assumed their political roles primarily to affect local government and others did so primarily to participate in the selection of national candidates and the solution of national problems has but little effect on their day-to-day activity. In both cases the political field is much the same, except temporarily when a leader goes as a delegate to a presidential nominating convention.

The questions in this chapter have to do with the leaders' immediate piece of the action. What qualities do the forty-seven look for in candidates for public office? How do they assess them? What are the processes by which they express and support their preferences? And how do they react to the final party nominations?

Sizing Up Candidates

Naturally enough, the district leaders want candidates who can win and then serve creditably in office. The forty-seven are in close theoretical agreement about the qualities a public official should possess. In brief, these are honesty, competence, willingness to work hard, and political stances similar to their own. Since their subjective opinions about who is honest, competent and hard-working differ, and since they themselves take a variety of stances on a variety of issues, the agreement on qualities sought does not mean agreement on candidates supported.

"Electability" is the other quality that the leaders desire. They make the very pragmatic judgment that no matter how exemplary an individual may seem as a potential incumbent, one's performance as a candidate comes first. Only two reject it as a criterion: Jane implicitly when she says, "I tend to go with the intelligent underdog," and John explicitly, "I do not pick to be on the winning side."

Except for Jane, the leaders minimize a brilliant mind in a candidate although appreciating intelligence when it accompanies the other factors mentioned above. Charlie says "candidates should be smart—or at least not dumb." Nathan describes his choice between two candidates for nomination in this way:

> He was highly intelligent, probably the smarter of the two. But taking one look at the man physically, there was no way he was going to win. Issues and who's the best shot are the criteria. Try to go with the winner.

Most of the time the forty-seven support particular seekers of their party's nominations for a mixture of subjective and objective reasons, but individually they weigh their perceptions of personalities and the candidates' recorded stands on issues differently.

Among those heavily dependent on their subjective judgments are John and Laura who explain their recent choices on the simple criterion "I like him." The reverse, of course, also happens—"I can't stand him," Ken remarks of someone not so far from him on issues. Some other leaders elaborate on the "I like . . ." theme:

> Nino: I use the same method as I have used in selecting juries for almost thirty years. I get a gut reaction, an intuitiveness, when I like a face.

> Jack: I select candidates as I would pick someone for my own staff—someone with the right instincts, whether we are always in agreement or not. Someone that's reachable. Attitude is more important than expertise or the smarts.

> Marge: I size up candidates the way I size up my co-workers, by observing their body language.

> Sid: I want to *know* my choice intuitively.

> Pepe: I use an eighth sense that allows me to see through people that I developed as a result of my war experience. It is not infallible, but I am rarely mistaken in a person.

Ralph also pleads a good deal of subjectivity in choosing candidates as opposed to stressing issues. In particular, he is adamantly against "one-issue litmus tests." Nor does he object if an incumbent is not entirely consistent with his mind-set as a candidate.

Leaders' subjective plus-ratings, of course, are often balanced by others' subjective-minus ratings. With one exception (see below), even the most issue-oriented and track record-perusing of the forty-seven can be strongly swayed by perceived personality attributes. For example, in a contest for nomination for a congressional office, in their interviews Mandy assessed one of two candidates as "a naked opportunist," and Nora thought he was much too opportunistic for her taste. Zoe had exactly the same criticism of his opponent.

Differences of opinion about candidential glamor also arise. Greenburgh voters have had a fair share of office seekers who are handsome, charming and sometimes even rich, which many consider a winning combination. Faith professes to be a bit suspicious of blatant charm and remarks with amusement, "First you get a picture of the candidate and family gallumphing over the green, and next it's 'Meet the new Mrs. Whoever-It-Is.'" She tries to dig below the surface glamor to dispel or confirm her initial reaction. Zoe also remarks that good-looking, rich people do not necessarily appeal to her, "especially those exuding noblesse oblige." A candidate that many other leaders considered capable, warm and electable, she dismisses with "he pissed ice." Claud, speaking of an aspiring candidate, similarly highly regarded by other committee members, comments that the more he got to know him, the more he felt he was constructed of plastic. In the political field, as elsewhere, to each his own. Varying perceptions of personalities add zest as well as generous dollops of animus to the process of selecting the party's nominees in Greenburgh.

The majority of the forty-seven describe themselves as being primarily issue-based in their selection of nominees and secondarily affected by the "I like . . ." syndrome. Most of the time this means that these leaders have looked for the most liberal candidates who have any chance of winning.

Often in village and town nominating caucuses or conventions committee members consider that local offices to be filled are different in nature from regional or national offices to be filled. For example, what do village mayors and trustees have to do with policies about war and peace? What do pro-life or pro-choice stands about abortion have to do with a town supervisor's or council members' jobs? In short, what do the life and death issues have to do with fixing the streets, picking up the garbage, and planning the amenities for suburban living? These considerations point to a way out of fractiousness for some issue-oriented leaders who want a united local electorate for efficient, service-oriented local administrations (for as low a tax rate as can be managed). Ken disagrees with this point of view:

> Substantive national stands are relevant to me even when the job has nothing to do with those issues. Otherwise you get office holders galore going up the ladder and *then* they deal with issues larger than garbage disposal. It is a fact that once elected, people fall silent on the issues. Some candidates I've backed have been disappointments. They get very cautious when the crunch comes.

Of the forty-seven only Lewis says that he picks nominees solely on the issues that are important to him. His comments about three individuals document his claim:

> I supported him because he would probably have made one of the best Congressmen going. But he's a shit.

> I can't stand the woman but I supported her right down the line because she's right on all of the issues.

> Frankly, I can't stand him. He's an arrogant, supercilious son of a bitch. But of course I worked for him.

This is a rare objectivity. However, the authenticity of the attitude is attested to by the fact that he did, indeed, energetically support the people he claimed to. And who but Lewis has the right to describe his subjective view of them?

The Selection Process

The method of choosing nominees varies by where in the overall political system the offices to be occupied fall. A distinction has been made in political anthropology between local-level politics, local politics and intra party activities (Swartz et al. 1966, Swartz 1968).

Local-level politics has to do with local activity centered on candidates and issues at national and regional or state levels. Presidential and state-wide elections, therefore, involve the district leaders in a larger political field than their usual one. Interest and emotions run high as individual leaders decide whom among the potential nominees to support. Officially, they are not engaged in supportive activities by virtue of their leadership roles: there is no party candidate until the nomination is made. In fact, however, they use their positions in pushing their selections by carrying designating petitions to get them—and their delegates in the case of presidential primaries—on the ballot. Some leaders make a virtue of carrying competing petitions for an office, but this does not necessarily mean that they are silent about their preferences.

An ambition of many district leaders is to attend a national convention as a delegate or alternate. This involves considerable caucusing among their colleagues, other supporters of the candidate, and within the party structure—or outside of it, as occurred during the revolt of the Concerned Democrats. Of the forty-seven, only Claud, Mandy, Ken and Hanna have been elected as delegates to national conventions.

The second category of political activity, local politics, has to do with county, town and village candidates and issues. Because of the degree of integration of the political system, the distinction between the hyphenated and unhyphenated versions of local politics breaks down in connection with those national and state offices for which local districts are drawn—congressional representative, state senator, state assemblyman and supreme court justices. The third category, however, is distinctive: It concerns the selection of party officers biennially at committee reorganization conventions and meetings and the filling of vacancies in interims.

County nominating conventions for public or party offices generate interest in some district leaders if there are choices to be made and not merely ritual anointings. Many, however, feel removed from happenings at that level. They find the cast of county politicians unwieldy, the parliamentary procedures and weighted voting (each district has votes in proportion to its party votes in the previous gubernatorial election) arcane and—as time goes on—the hours wee. Few of the forty-seven are county convention aficionados, but Becca, Mandy, Ken and Rita and the current village chairs, in roughly descending order, are dutifully involved. Bring a book or your knitting is the advice of veterans to new district leaders.

Town selection processes, on the other hand, are central to leadership activity. The town executive committee serves as a screening committee for the selection of nominees for town office. It interviews prospective candidates at a series of evening meetings, usually two or three at a session. Much the same questions are asked each individual by much the same screeners, the presentations are discussed after the interviewee has left and, at the final meeting, a secret ballot is taken with screeners listing their selections in order of preference. Screening discussions and the actual tally (aside from who won) are supposed to be confidential.

Meanwhile the avowed candidates may also be going the rounds of village and area meetings to acquire support. Later, at the town convention, the candidates chosen by the screening committee are placed, with its recommendation, in nomination—and so are any of the others who were screened or anybody else who has sufficient support to think that there is a chance of winning.

Convention supported winners may face still another hurdle before the election campaign. Part of the local political wisdom is "anything can happen in a primary." Convention losers—or a wild card—may think it worth their time and money to collect the requisite signatures on nominating petitions that will permit them to appeal to a wider electorate in a primary. Sometimes these challengers muster enough support to win. Nevertheless, few aspirants for nomination forgo appearing before the screening committee and few if any reject a convention's accolade for a direct primary route.

The town screening process is inherently attractive to the screeners. It epitomizes what most motivates them in their political activities— "getting things done," "being in on things," and, less important, "observing personalities." Selecting candidates is their most cherished power and screening is where they may have the most influence. The smaller the decision-making group, the more each vote counts. The interviews, the frank exchange of opinions and then the final tally give ample opportunity for participants to feel "in on" and intrigued by what is going on, whether they are satisfied or disappointed with the end result of their deliberations.

The presentations made before the committee by the potential nominees greatly influence the votes cast, especially when the individuals are unknown or not well known to the screeners. But screeners often know the interviewees, and know them well. They may even have come to the meetings with their minds pretty well made up about whom to support. Hanna, for example, on looking back on a screening session agrees that her candidate was much less effective in his presentation than was his opponent, but she felt she must go with her assessment of both individuals in other situations. Another leader was very impressed with the presentation of someone she had not particularly admired before but was admonished that "any lawyer can make a brilliant presentation, that's not enough." Whatever a screener's vote, it usually seems to be less capricious than well-informed.

Those screened are seldom as happy with the process as are the screeners, and this does not solely have to do with losing. Individual screeners come down hard on their favorite issues and candidates may not want to wholly commit themselves to them. Nino, for example, deeply resented his experience before a screening committee when he was asked—unfairly, he thought—about such controversial local issues as abortion and group homes for the retarded. His answers, he says, were met with the accusation that he was "fudging." He felt that the "extreme liberals" among the screeners had pre-judged him. "They expect every time I speak it will be reactionary, which it is not."

The rule is that screening discussions and votes are confidential. Winners are simply announced with no indication of the margin of victory. The reality is that secrets are far from well kept. One potential nominee who thought she had not done well in her interview was demoralized to discover one or two days later that "everyone knew" that the screening committee thought so also.

When the vote of the screening committee does not meet with general expectations, its deliberations are particularly open to wider debate and analysis. In one case, there was an unusually large number of aspirants for two council seats because two incumbents had decided to run for higher office instead. Town incumbents are normally renominated by a town committee grateful for the administration's accomplishments; over time a backlog of upwardly mobile local politicians had developed. Six people announced for the council and proceeded on their rounds of interviews and telephone campaigning. Vince had decided to run for county executive (the prior Democratic incumbent having gone on to higher office himself), and Eleanor, one of the vacating incumbents, had decided to run for town supervisor. She had an opponent in Rick, an ex-mayor of one of the villages. They were clearly heading for a race to primary and both had started on their rounds, too.

Then the county convention was held. Vince, who had been campaigning hard for months, was defeated by an ex-congressman who had been more quietly soliciting votes, both from outside and inside of Vince's bailiwick of Greenburgh. Vince considered a primary challenge, decided against it, and claimed the nomination for town supervisor. Eleanor and Rick, both campaign-ready, announced for the two council seats. Eight council aspirants were screened by the town executive committee, before and after Vince's decision. Rick and Sid were the two top vote-getters. Eleanor came in third and therefore lost the committee's recommendation. Although the balloting was secret, the small size and closeness of the vote (which became well known) did not leave much to the imagination of those interested in figuring out who had voted how.

It was a year for upsets in conventions. Eleanor swept the town convention in a major personal victory and Sid surpassed Rick for the second seat. Apparently the district leaders in convention weighed past service to party and community heavily. In Eleanor's case, she was viewed as a successful incumbent rejected by the screeners for reasons either not clear to or not acceptable by the majority. In Sid's case he was perceived as an able and active leader always ready to help others in their campaigns and deserving a chance now. Rick also was able and popular but without as many personal ties within the town committee as the other two, and perhaps also not running as hard as they.

Candidates for congressional, state and county legislative bodies appear before the town executive committee, the full town committee and often village and area committees and other local groups to plead their cases and answer questions. There is no formal screening in the sense of a tally, however, until the town convention. Even there, if the districts overlap—say, with Yonkers, or Scarsdale or Rockland County—Greenburgh's is not the only voice. Negotiations with county and town chairs of the concerned area often result in unified choices, but by no means always. As is their wont, Greenburgh's leaders individually select the man or woman they want. There is no party line at a local convention (there is at the state level). If a primary follows the convention, there is no party line there, either, until the votes are in. During town conventions and primary fights, sides are taken by the leaders that may reflect or lead to the hardening of cleavages among the Greenburgh committeepersons.

Party offices are also filled at town conventions during reorganization meetings. The town chair has previously sent letters to the leaders stating who is running for what office and outlining the procedure for nominating others. Sometimes there are contests, but oftener there are not. Most district leaders do not avidly seek party office but have to be sought out. On occasion, however, the cleavages mentioned above do affect reorganizations.

When sides are taken in a contested nomination charges and countercharges are frequently made and some bitterness ensues. One expression of this may be an attempt to change the composition of the executive committee by targeting a member considered vulnerable. In the aftermath of the nomination of Eleanor for her council seat, Polly, a strong supporter of Eleanor, announced her candidacy for executive vice chair, the positon held by Hanna. Her reason was that the executive committee, long entrenched, needed fresh perspectives. Although seen as probably right in general, specifically the target was considered inappropriate in that Hanna, whatever her choices for nominees, was well known for consistently dedicated service to the party. She retained her position. Nathan characterizes the committee attitude: "You don't throw incumbents out who have done their jobs, no matter what you think about 'new blood.' Dead wood for new blood, yes. People you owe for new blood, no."

Choice by Friendship

In coming to judgment about potential nominees in local elections, some leaders stress the importance of getting to know them personally instead of relying on reading about their backgrounds and positions. They count on "personal involvements with candidates to take their measure," in Ann's words. There is ample opportunity for this at town committee and other smaller meetings where the office seekers present their cases and answer questions. Candidates often also call on leaders individually to ask for advice or support. Whether or not the major parties are in a state of decline nationally, among the Democrats in Greenburgh people who want to run for office woo district leaders for their support. The rare exceptions occur among incumbents confident enough of their own vote-pulling powers to be willing to go to primary or caucus without the cushion of strong committee support.

Many of the forty-seven identify friendship as some kind of a factor in choosing candidates. This is particularly true in village and town elections, and in filling party offices at the biennial party reorganization conventions and meetings. Committee people often have friends or acquaintances vying for nomination and find their loyalties divided.

In these cases some say that they are not moved by friendship. Chester, for example, professes to pick whom he pleases regardless of personal relationships. Ilse also is sure that she would not let friendship sway her, as are John and Jack (who makes an exception of his wife: "I would support Eleanor even if she wasn't good").

The majority of the respondents say that they are influenced by friendship, but not unduly so. Craig, not widely involved in town sociopolitical networks, remarks, "Who you know tends to fit with what you know." Others more deeply involved in local political activism have made alliances that have a pull on them. Becca, Zoe, Fay, and Brooke feel that these ties are a problem in choosing candidates, but a problem that they can face up to in making their selections.

A long list of the leaders say that friendship influences their decisions "but only up to a point." Mandy lets friendship become important only for party positions. Cedric and Pepe would go a long way to remain loyal to their friends (Pepe: "Without friendship and trust one can accomplish nothing"). Lewis calls loyalty and friendship "the cement of politics" but characteristically says that if a major issue were the focus of a disagreement with a friend, "I would stick by my positional guns."

Ken and Rita see commitments made on the basis of friendship as one of the biggest problems in politics. They consider that calls on their loyalty in ongoing campaigns from past comrades-in-action come close to insulting their integrity. They would let friendship sway them, they say, only where the contenders are "mutually undistinguished." Similarly, Claud and Nora would let friendship influence them only when, in Claud's words, "it didn't make a whole hell of a lot of difference who won the nomination."

For a handful of the forty-seven, friends soliciting their support pose more of a problem:

> Zoe: My friends are my good friends and actually it would be hard for me.

> Abby: I would back a friend or make myself absent.

> Ann: Rather than hurt friends I would sit it out.

> Nathan: Once two good friends ran for the same party office and I backed one I had come to love during another campaign. The other friend was so hurt that next time I'll sit it out.

> Arthur: [About a similar experience] Taking sides hurts them and it hurts me.

Sid also has found choosing between friends for a party position, where the option is most likely to arise, "heavy stuff." With political ambitions of his own, he optimizes a situation in which "I could support a friend and at the same time help myself politically."

Several of the leaders admit to having fallen into "the friendship trap" by giving their support to the first friend or acquaintance who asks for it, without waiting to see who else might throw their hats in the ring. They soon learn to bide their time not only to have a better basis for selection but, as Becca points out, "if you jump too early no one pays any attention to you."

Friendship is one side of a political coin of which the other side is animus—the desire to curb a potential rival or retaliate for past slights. Such motivations are rarely observable and even more rarely admitted. The very nature of politics demands a certain amount of soothing hypocrisy. Nevertheless, the conventional wisdom that "politics makes strange bedfellows" is a clue to negative motivations, particularly in factional squabbles, which are discussed in the following chapter.

In the Villages

Selections of candidates for village offices savor more of search and importunement than of screening. Nominating procedures are overwhelmingly colored by anxiety about being able to field a slate. The process officially begins with the village chair appointing a nominating committee to interview potential nominees and make recommendations to the full committee. Candidential offers made to individuals by a chair or other interested parties before going through this process are resented by the leaders even though they may concur with the choice. Once the full committee has approved the selection, nominations go to the caucus of enrolled Democratic voters, which by election law must be held within a stated period of time.

In the not so distant past, this process has sometimes gone all the way to caucus before a full slate has been constructed. More recently, but still when Democrats were more likely than not beaten at the polls, people on a preferential list were either visited by a delegation from the nominating committee or—as the regrets accumulated and time ran short—called on the telephone. Old hands at the nomination job regarded the annual presentation of a full slate as a minor miracle made possible, at times, only by committee members giving in to pressure and filling the void. One such candidate was Pepe, who ran for mayor of his village while in India. "You need a lot of guts," he says, "to do it in vain. I remember when you couldn't get candidates. Now they're all over."

Candidates are not really "all over" but with the growth of the Democratic enrollment and Democratic wins in the villages, candidates have not been quite so hard to find. Let Hastings stand as an example, recognizing that in a larger village (Tarrytown) there are more potential nominees and in a smaller one (Elmsford or Ardsley) there are fewer.

In 1978, for the first time there was no search for a candidate at all. Two individuals offered themselves to the nominating committee for the one trustee slot still open. The other was filled by an incumbent running again. The nominating committee divided itself, half interviewing Cedric and half William, an unenrolled voter calling himself an independent (they appear on the rolls in the county as "no's"). William had judged that the Republicans would not nominate him and had already started campaigning for the Democratic nomination before most of the leaders had heard of him. The nominating committee, split about the choice to be made, called both men back to be interviewed by all of its members together. Impressed with William's vigorous presentation, they asked him to be the candidate. The full committee and later the caucus endorsed the choice—and victory ensued. From that time nominating committees have invited potential candidates to appear before them, only in extremis calling on them personally. Nevertheless, the search goes on.

With one exception, the Hastings committee has always accepted their nominating committee's recommendations unanimously (with perhaps one or two acquiescing by silence). Not so the Democratic caucus. The caucus is usually a ritual of solidarity, but not always. As far back as 1964 a caucus surprised the committee by rejecting one of its candidates and electing another nominated from the floor—a secretly and carefully planned event. Within the time frame of this study, there have been two other caucus conflicts in which the committee did not have its way.

In the first instance the village committee, under Charlie's leadership, attempted to weld a slate for trustees consisting of Bud, a native Hastingsite and Democratic incumbent, and Duke. Bud was a home town favorite, but his winning opposition in his first term to a proposed municipal fair housing ordinance had dimmed his luster in liberal eyes. Moreover, Bud and Duke, both "blue collar" men, had a short political history of antipathy and neither wished to run with the other, as a team. Nevertheless, the committee voted to ask them to do exactly that. Duke agreed but Bud remained adamant.

At the caucus Bud and Duke were put in nomination. Bud said nothing, and no explanation of the state of affairs was given the caucus. During the mingling as people lined up to have their enrollments checked and deposit their paper ballots, it became evident that supporters of Bud were present in substantial numbers. A leader in the most heavily Democratic and liberal district made a few telephone calls to counter Bud's weight. Sufficient people rushed to cast their votes before the polls closed. The result was that Duke out-polled Bud by a healthy margin. Bud then took the floor and declined his nomination.

The Republican committee promptly asked Bud to run for trustee on their line, and he accepted. A committee to fill vacancies is always appointed by the chair at a caucus in case a nominee for some reason cannot or will not run. After the Democratic caucus, this committee met and Vi was asked to run with Duke. Bud and his Republican running mate swept the election, with Bud achieving a personal triumph. After the election Bud advised the village Democratic committee on how to win: "Take off your liberal hats." He soon took off his Democratic hat and enrolled as a Republican, served three terms as mayor of Hastings before losing in a fourth try against a Democrat—the first woman to seek that position.

The second instance of conflict at the caucus occurred six years later, while Tess was chair, and it concerned William's third bid for his trustee seat. The focal issue was cross-endorsement, therefore it is described below in that context. In brief, the Democratic committee (in a split vote) did not nominate William. The caucus overwhelmingly did. In both of these cases popular incumbents rebuffed the committee, were nominated in caucus and finally won their elections. In both instances, partisanship apparent at the higher political levels of town and county is not evident at the village level. Both instances also indicate relatively weak links or different role perceptions between district leaders and incumbents. Charlie, looking back, comments ruefully, "You either couldn't get your candidates elected or if you did they wouldn't talk to you."

Cross-overs and Cross-endorsements

Republicans may be friends, neighbors or acquaintances of the district leaders but not, in the order of things, Democratic candidates for office. Any other Greenburgh Democrat can blithely climb aboard a "Democrats for (name the Republican candidate)" campaign and Republicans can do the reverse. Published lists of supporters enrolled in the opposite party or not enrolled in any are a staple of campaign practice. Such public support is tabu for district leaders. Some do, however, find less ostentatious ways of expressing their opinions, which range from "sitting on their hands" during a campaign to making not-so-discreet telephone calls of opposition.

Within the time frame of this study, three state or national office holders from Westchester changed their registrations from Republican to Democratic and then ran for office as that party's candidate. Two of them won. A third lost in the general election to one of the other two, who at the time was still a Republican.

Two of the new cross-overs were from Greenburgh and the town committee accepted them as their candidates, although not without a struggle. Both nominations went to primary. Ella and Fred are representative of leaders who say they do not like "turncoats," and Vi agrees: "I don't switch that easily." In the event, these leaders had few objections to the cross-overs, and Ella became an ardent supporter of one.

The case of Paul is the most complex and highlights the leaders' mixed reactions when asked to support a man they had long seen as a political villain. Paul, congressman and ex-mayor of one of the villages, had over the years successfully repulsed bids for congress from Democratic opponents. Environmental advocates had named him one of the House's "dirty dozen"; the Concerned Democrats deplored his defense of the Vietnam War; and he was late in congress in admitting the significance of Watergate. Then he became a Democrat and decided to seek the same congressional seat under that egis.

Paul's past congressional election opponents and Democratic colleagues in the House of Representatives encouraged him in his venture. The Westchester and Greenburgh Democratic leadership, including Becca, held a press conference endorsing him. It was widely assumed that the Republican candidate, from the city of Yonkers, would take the whole turf. Apparently for this reason no candidate other than Paul was willing to run.

It was with mixed emotions that the Greenburgh town executive committee met with the prospective candidate. Some accepted his candidacy as a given, some remained wary. John was silently hostile and Zoe refused to shake Paul's hand. Afterwards Paul made formal and informal appearances in various Greenburgh communities in order to garner support. A few leaders looked fruitlessly for a willing Democratic alternative. At town convention Paul's name alone was put in nomination, and he won by a voice vote.

Unexpectedly, it was publicly dislosed that the popular Republican candidate had lied about his military background. Brad, a young, aggressive liberal district leader, now found that he was interested in competing for the candidacy and various colleagues lined up to support him. A second convention was requested to annul the past action and nominate Brad. The town leadership refused on legal and moral grounds. Paul won the ensuing primary and then the general election. A few years later, when Paul was gerrymandered out of a reasonable chance to win his seat again, his record as a Democratic congressman—particularly on civil rights and women's issues—had converted most past critics into supporters.

On looking back, Ralph says that he had no problem supporting this "past Republican office holder trying his luck as a Democratic candidate" and he opposed "the doctrinaire group that held his previous stands on the Vietnam War and the environment against him." Looking back, Charlie is not so forgiving: "But I can still see him riding down Main Street with Nixon [during the 1972 presidential campaign]!"

The forty-seven are in more agreement about cross-endorsements than about cross-overs. The town committee takes a stand against Democratic-Republican cross-endorsements except for judges, and some leaders do not exempt them. The case rests on the fact that cross-endorsements by the major parties deprive the electorate of a choice.

In Westchester some Democrats have traditionally sought and received the Liberal line and some have sought and received the Conservative line, with repercussions in the opposing wings of the party. Gradually these other-party endorsements began to be seen as a dependence on small and erratic county constituencies that may cost as much as they gain. The rise of the Right to Life party in the state increased intra party friction on the issue of cross-endorsements, now particularly in the case of judges.

There has never been any possibility of the town committee running Republicans or unenrolled voters as their town candidates. At the village level, however, partisanship sometimes pales.

Leon, Ardsley's chair, once broke ranks with the town committee on its tabu on cross-endorsements. In an executive committee meeting after the election, Leon, made angry by jibes about his action, walked out of the meeting refusing to answer questions. Yet as he later made clear to leaders individually, there was logic in what Ardsley did, given the small village context.

Leon describes the Ardsley mayor, a Republican running for re-election, as someone "who did a good job of collecting the garbage." On the other hand, Leon believed that the sole willing potential Democratic candidate was totally unqualified. He told his committee, he says, "This guy will be our candidate over my dead body." They accepted his decision and endorsed the Republican. Leon explains: "The Democrat might have won and they would have had to hide their faces." In the villages, committee people may be pushed to weighing the caliber of whom they can offer as a candidate against their perceived duty to provide the voters with a choice instead of what amounts to a deal to shut them out of the selection process.

The Hastings Democratic committee also faced a cross-endorsement crisis, but of a different nature. It developed out of two practices that had been gradually accepted over the years: running its candidates on additional lines and running unenrolled voters.

The custom of petitioning for an additional party line on the ballot is to accrue votes from people purportedly averse to pulling a lever on the Democratic party line. The temporary parties—"Independent" was the favorite label—were entirely party-backed entities. That is, although non-Democrats were involved, the effort was organized and supported by the Democratic committee. Any voter who has not voted at a party caucus can carry or sign nominating petitions. This leaves a large population from which to recruit workers and signers. Even so, Democrats, including leaders, have been known to withhold their votes at their own caucus in order to work for the additional line.

The other pertinent custom, running unenrolled candidates, was initiated by nominating committees loath to prolong their duties by passing up a good choice because of partisanship. At different times, Duke and William were the beneficiaries.

A decade prior to the caucus fight about William, Hastings Democrats ran their first and last Republican, under unusual circumstances. Two Democratic candidates were elected trustees and were to join two Democratic incumbents on the village board. However, one of the new trustees had campaigned, not like Pepe from a foreign land, but like Pepe expecting to lose. He could not serve because he had already accepted a job and arranged to move from Hastings. With nonpartisan gallantry, the Democratic majority on the board selected the best person they could think of to serve until the next year's election—Naomi, a Republican. The choice somewhat mitigated the bad effect on the public of the false campaign. Both major parties nominated Naomi in the following year, and she was elected to serve out the last year of the term.

That year saw a controversy between Bud and his colleagues on the board who favored a proposed fair housing ordinance. The Democrats nominated Naomi again, but the Republicans refused to endorse her and she lost the election.

In spite of this precedent, and the cross-endorsement one year by the Republicans of the Democratic village justice, the Democrats settled down to running their own—except for William, who retained his unenrolled status.

When William ran for his second term the party chose Cedric to be his running mate. Sheila, a Republican and immediate past-president of the League of Women Voters, and Naomi and several others had become regular "board watchers," thus accumulating some expertise in local issues and government. Sheila made a candidential bid to the Republicans, who refused it. She then decided, with substantial backing, to petition for a place on the ballot as the candidate of the Hastings Choice party—the Democrats having already snagged the so-called Independent line for William and Cedric. William won the election and Sheila and Celdric split the normally Democratic vote; Morris, a Republican, won.

The following year a victorious team of mayor and two trustees was fielded by the Democrats, including Sheila (now an enrolled Democrat) as one of the trustee candidates. The issues in this election were far from "garbage"; they involved the fiscal management and integrity of the village. Tess, the Democratic chair, asked some of the Democrats who had been active in the prior Hastings Choice party for Sheila to organize the extra line for the Democrats, which they did, this time in tandem style with the Democratic committee.

On the new board, Morris accommodated himself to the Democratic majority, and they to him. Prior to the following year's election— William's third run—the threads of party solidarity started to unravel. Tess saw three revolts that were to plague the selection process and the election.

First, some leaders and members of the nominating committee questioned renominating William. Although there had been conflict between William and a few leaders in past campaigns, doubts about him now were more pervasive. Then, the committee having decided to swallow its doubts, he and the other Democratic incumbents showed signs of wanting to continue the board as constituted, with Morris (whose term was also up) still on board. "They don't want to rock the boat," said Tess. Third, Naomi and the other core people who had worked for the Independent line for the winning team the previous year seemed to feel the same way. The suggestion appeared in the letters to the editor column of the local paper—in effect, both parties should nominate William and Morris.

The nominating committee, chaired by Craig, met with William and asked him to run. He and his friend, Gene, asked the members to consider cross-endorsing Morris. The committee got the clear impression that the mayor would like this, too. After the two men had left, members discussed the matter and decided that it was their duty to search for another Democratic candidate and not settle the election then and there in Tess' living room by cross-endorsing. At a subsequent meeting they interviewed a second candidate and accepted him.

The Republican nominators apparently came to a different decision. Moreover, they offered their nomination to William even without the Democratic quid pro quo. And William accepted it.

The nominating committee met again with William and asked him to forgo the Republican cross-endorsement. They emphasized that they did not think his personal arrangement was fair to the candidacy of his Democratic teammate. He was not persuaded. The committee then interviewed another potential nominee, Betty, and decided to run her instead of William. The full Democratic committee met, and by a split vote accepted their report and got ready for the caucus.

The mayor and trustees did not accept the report and they got ready for the caucus, too. The meeting hall was packed. Craig gave the committee's report, and nominations and seconds were made for two Democrats. Then Gene and the mayor nominated and seconded William. The balloting was top heavy for William, but two nominees were being chosen and Betty was nominated also.

The erstwhile "Independents"—first for Sheila and then for the Democratic team the year before—had in the meantime constituted themselves in a much more independent mode. They decided to interview both Republican and Democratic nominees for positions on their own slate. They opted for William and Morris. (In the end, the County Board of Elections ruled that William could not run on that line since, with the two major parties, he already had the limit.) In reaction, a group of Betty's supporters, including some Democratic leaders, organized to achieve an additional line for her. After a campaign crammed with ironies, William and Morris won.

After the election William admitted to feeling some embarrassment about running as a team with two people opposing one another. As another postscript, there have been no cross-endorsements by the major parties since.[1] The seasonal "Independent party" continues to structure itself as a force to be recognized in campaigns: they audition the major parties' candidates, select their nominees from among them, and publicly urge that votes for them be on their line in support of nonpartisanship!

The Greenburgh district leaders have their "piece of power" in the selection of town and village candidates. In the latter case, the process may be more onerous than honorific due to the limited number of people aspiring to village office and a feeling among many voters that partisan politics is minimally important at that level.

CAMPAIGNING

Most district leaders can go for weeks or even months at a time without giving much thought to their party duties, but an election campaign has a galvanzing effect. Faith describes her village committee as coming alive at election time and says this is the period during which she most enjoys her political work and the camaraderie involved. In general, the memorable experiences the forty-seven talk about derive from campaigns. They believe that what they do in a campaign does make a difference in the outcome. Lewis articulates the motivation: "To be effective you have to elect people. Once you choose them, you have to work heart and soul to get them elected, short of lying and stealing. That's what I see politics as all about."

The party's nominees are on the whole dutifully supported, no matter how bitterly a primary has been fought (Nathan: "I tell you, once the ticket is put together, I'll support it"). Leaders respond variously, however, to particular candidates and this is reflected in the zeal with which they work for them. In addition, a candidate's relatives and the current committee chairs and campaign managers will work at peak levels in one election but when this personal motivation or status is missing they lose some or all of their momentum. It is difficult for leaders of many years' experience to maintain the same excitement every year—or, in the case of village leaders, twice a year—or more if there is a primary.

There are roughly two kinds of campaign activities. One is shaping strategy and the exploitation of issues. The other is carrying out the overall plan through media publicity, name recognition tactics (signs, buttons and other election paraphernalia), getting mailings out or making "literature" drops, fund-raising (in order to pay for the above), and exposure of the candidates by escorting them door-to-door or at train stations and shopping centers.

These activities are centered at rented (or proffered) headquarters during general elections and leaders are encouraged to make their enrollment lists canvass-effective there. This means highlighting Democrats and unenrolled voters for easy identification and supplying tele-

phone numbers. Many leaders prefer to do this job at home, and do—
or don't, as the leadership fears. Volunteers are recruited for headquarters work and to cover districts without active leaders.

A good number of the forty-seven have been deeply involved in
elections and have experienced a campaign as exhilaration. Winning
of course helps. The campaign most often referred to in the interviews
is the 1973 campaign with its culmination in the victory of Vince and
the whole town ticket, as well as Doris who was the county legislative
candidate. Zoe, who was Vince's co-campaign manager, recalls the
excitement of the campaign but particularly the night the votes came
in: "It was the first time in seventy-six years that the Democrats had
won and I was on the phone getting results. And I was a basket case.
I went bonkers. It was just a great feeling."

Mandy, Hanna and Becca have similar recollections. Orson sums it
up: "It was an emotional, intensive experience, and then it turns out
your way!"

Others who have exulted over campaigns include:

Nathan: I love the campaigns, all of them I have been part of. As
campaign manager [of a town election] I enjoyed the power, and spending
such large sums of money. And, of course, winning.

Sid: My peak experience as a leader was being campaign manager for [a
winning town clerk candidate]. I delighted in helping in primary strategy
and tactics.

Lewis: I like being in the middle of things and knowing what's going on.
Particularly I liked managing the two campaigns in Hastings.

Not all of the forty-seven are so exuberant in recollecting campaigns
and their roles as district leaders in them. Nora says that at times she
feels as if she were pulling the vote for candidates "who don't make a
difference. . . . But you have to be patient. That's the system." And
Nora is proud when her district shows up well in the final tally. "When
you win one," Hanna points out, "you feel naturally that as a district
leader you did something, that you've been part of it." As Arthur puts
it, "Election night is the moment of truth. You find out whether you
did it right or not."

Even when leaders do not particularly admire candidates that they
work for, they may find the campaign process itself, including problems
and personalities, interesting. Dennis takes a professional view of all
campaigns. He says he likes to size up the way different candidates
present themselves to the public. Jodie remembers her service in one
village campaign as manager as "mind-boggling" and remarks that "It's

difficult when you have to deal closely day to day with candidates, it's easier when it's an issue linked with a candidate at a distance." Tess, too, finds the campaigns that she has been active in "most interesting, with all the mistakes and tribulations—and candidates who have to be handled."

Ella's memories reach farther back in her village's history and touch on a different concept of "winning" as well as on a recurrent pattern in some village campaigns:

> During the campaign the committee just sat. Nobody did anything. My reward was getting a line, that was victory. Someone said to me, "How can you stand losing and losing like that?" I said as long as we field a ticket we are not losing. We are building a party, learning about issues. It makes them sit up and take notice if they have opposition.

A conflict between district leaders and candidates and their managers is almost classic in the villages. Ilse describes a recurring situation in Dobbs Ferry in which, on the one hand, committee members accuse the candidates of going over their heads in making decisions and spending money, and on the other hand, the latter accuse the former of "doing nothing" for the campaign. "The conflict can become pretty heated," she notes mildly. Chester, Dobbs Ferry's chair, agrees that there seems to be a perennial division between elected officials and committee members. The former, he says, see the leaders as showing little or no interest in village affairs or campaigns. Marge and Nathan tell similar stories about Irvington and Tarrytown elections. Ann recalls a variant experience in which the Ardsley committee tried to supplant an incumbent Democrat for being ineffective but failed because the caucus overruled the committee and nominated him. She suggests that he subsequently lost the election for lack of committee support.

In Hastings, too, the committee has now and then been accused of insufficient devotion to the current cause, the campaign. Lewis consistently suspects other leaders of failure to go all out for the ticket. Also, his philosophy as a village campaign manager was that during a campaign his judgment—which in one case included wanting to initiate a lawsuit—superseded that of the committee and chair. This idea led to considerable friction with the chair. Neither enjoyed the "emotional exchanges" (Lewis' description) that ensued. Comparable issues never arise in town elections, where the area committees are not faced with lower level elections.

At any campaign's end there are always the losers—the unsuccessful candidates and the coteries that worked hardest for them. Many village candidates go into a campaign expecting to lose, but as time goes on euphoria builds. People, no matter how they plan to vote, are in general kind—even warm—to canvassing candidates and wish them luck in their races. Surely this accounts in part for why so many candidates recall their campaigns as rewarding.

Losers take their lumps with chins up, even in those cases where faces pale and tears well. No matter how difficult it is, most manage to project grace.

By both the party's and their own reckoning, the essence of the leaders' job is choosing candidates and working for their election. In spite of some public flirtation with the idea of "independent" or non-partisan local elections, the Democratic political system in Greenburgh, including its villages, depends on party leaders. They operate not as well oiled cogs geared to a party machine's desired ends but as individuals of varied motivations, energy, and political dedication. They use the party to achieve some version of their own visions of the future, playing the party's game to the extent that they agree with its goals–and find it more fun than frustrating.

DISCUSSION

Certain structural properties of the two major parties are explained by the collective adaptive behavior of their functionaries, and without resort to speculation about individual materialist-idealist mixes. This is the stratarchical nature of political parties in the United States (see p. 17) and the integrative role of the people at the base of the system.

According to Eldersveld, who researched and developed the stratarchy idea, statuses in the party system are hierarchically arranged but authority is not. Control of the business at hand—electoral politics—is diffused to each of the strata, where the relevant committees make their own decisions. Relationships between each organizational level are loose. Since each rung of party activity is particularly concerned with its own province—nation, state or various kinds of localities—the ties it hopes to bind are horizontal: with party people in government, political interest groups, and other political associations.

Such a party structure has little in common with the bureaucratic-pyramidal model of most large organizations, public or private, in which authority and responsibility peak at the top and deference defines the base. In the case of the party "pyramid," the national committee is relatively powerless in its relations to the widely-scattered party base.[2]

The link that holds the party organization together vertically, tenuous as it may be, is the worker at the election district level. Greenburgh district leaders, for example, are active primarily in village or town politics, but through their horizontal political brokerage they are also involved—the bottom line—with campaigns at the other levels, including the apical presidential. Within the party, micro level workers have macro level roles because "all politics is local." A vacuum at the local level disconnects upper party levels from their reason for being— aggregating votes. Where party organizations are weak or non-existent, or when candidates are independent or distrustful of them, campaigns must rely on resources outside of the party structure—rich candidates, ad hoc recruits, and the media. Where they are relatively strong, however, these part-time activists literally are the party.

Lower strata party organizations are so inclusive in their appeal that they are characterized as "porous," "permeable." The willingness to soak in a diversity of potential activists is countered, however, by scarcity in the market place. Lack of political interest at the grassroots leaves party-base members at an advantage in their relations with proximate higher levels, and indeed their own local leadership (unless they are after patronage). Again, Greenburgh is an example: orders are not given and sanctions are rarely applied to district leaders. As for the county and the state, most leaders have only a dim idea of what the status superiors there actually do. As in much of the country, mutual tolerance is the mode of adaptation, and persuasion is the means to ends. Similar patterns occur between higher rungs. And so is born a stratarchy.

The system is inherently inefficient but it is democratic and, through intra stratum activists with inter strata rapport, a good deal of the work gets done. How this outcome is affected when the views and personalities of the Greenburgh district leaders clash head on is the subject of the next chapter.

The Forty-Seven: Part Four

LEON

Leon, an engineer, and his wife came with their two daughters to Ardsley over twenty years ago. His parents were native west side New Yorkers, and he grew up in the city, too. Both parents worked, his mother in the public school system and his father as a salesman and bookkeeper.

Leon attended a private day school with an active student body. He joined student protests against sending scrap iron to Japan, and once picketed a clothing store selling silk stockings. Leon says that growing up during the Depression and coming of age aware of inequities at home and abroad radicalized him. That he was Jewish was also a factor, even though "I was hard put to feel Jewish, I had no religious upbringing. It was more a political thing."

As early as his teens Leon wanted to be a union organizer. At college he joined in various political and union activities—organizing protests, picketing and leafleting. Later while studying engineering the pattern continued as he took his political work with the American Student Union as seriously as his academic work. During and after World War II Leon moved around working as an engineer and a union organizer, with the latter role sometimes leading to an abrupt cessation of the former.

At one time Leon joined the American Labor party, and even ran as their candidate for a congressional seat "just to have a chance to debate one of the 'real' runners." Later, he involved himself in Henry Wallace's 1948 presidential campaign.

Leon thinks the two-party system in the United States is a "flim-flam and for the rich." But he is a practical man and in order to reach people on the issues—the Vietnam War was paramount for the duration—entered party politics. He chose the Democratic party "because it makes more of a pretense of being the party of the people than do the Republicans."

ABBY

Abby is an ebullient, angry, independent young black woman with many community involvements and deep religious commitments. Her mother, aunts and grandmother were strong women who packed her off to college "when all I was expecting was to get married" (she has not). Her grandmother was particularly influential in shaping her activism since she was the principal caretaker and took the child with her on her various community rounds. Abby says, "I can't remember not carrying petitions."

She is a district leader in the community in which she has always lived. She says her district is mostly Republican, but usually "votes well" (that is, her way). "God has graced me, I am very persuasive in my presentations. I'll talk you to death until you give me what I want, you know." The peak of her political experience was running for, being elected and attending the 1971 Democratic mini-convention in St. Louis as a delegate—"The blacks in my district didn't turn out to vote for me but middle class whites couldn't tell I was black from my name so I won anyway."

Nevertheless, Abby's main interest is radical black movements and not partisan politics—"Neither party gives blacks a damn thing so it doesn't make any difference." She deplores the lack of unity and political initiative in the black community and her consuming desire is to see this changed.

RALPH

Ralph is from northwest Kansas, coming to Washington, D.C. in 1935 to attend a university there, first its school of foreign service, then its law school. He spent the years of World War II in Brazil with the Office of InterAmerican Affairs as special aide to the ambassador on war-related matters. After the war he worked for a law firm in New York City which, after a year, asked him to represent them in the Philippines. Because dependents were not given air space at the time and apartments were almost impossible to find, Ralph bought a house in Greenburgh for his wife to wait until she could join him.

Ralph had always been attracted to politics, particularly in Brazil. When the family came home, he discovered a friend was running for office in Greenburgh and he plunged into the fray, soon becoming a district leader. He played a very active role in the town committee— campaign manager, area chair, vice town chair and so on. Seven years later he concluded that local politics was "just entirely too absorbing.

I was neglecting everything but politics." So he resigned and picked up on his many other community and professional interests, which included various boards and commissions in Westchester and the Bar Association and Chamber of Commerce on the national and international level. He was still interested in politics, however, and took time to help found both the old and the new Greenburgh Democratic clubs.

After more than a decade Ralph returned to a district leadership. "I don't really know why. I guess somebody said something needed to be done." He has not resumed his previous active role, however, and is only waiting for someone to get interested enough to take over the job.

Ralph says that although he comes from a staunchly Republican family he has always been a Democrat. Until the third term, he voted for Franklin Roosevelt but never really trusted him. While in Washington he had difficulty identifying himself with the New Deal, but even more with the Republicans, so he fudged by sometimes saying he was "independent" or "Democratic but. . . ." Nevertheless, he used to regard himself as a liberal, but now says he gets less and less so every year. "I had no patience for the Concerned Democrats. I thought they were wrong, and I still think they were wrong."

FAY

Fay is a professional, community-active black woman who describes herself, in spite of her Fairview residence, as a New York City person at heart. She traces her activism to her parents' influence. Her father was a Garveyite and her mother was devoted to her church, so one Sunday the children would be taken to Garvey Hall and the next to the church. Her father's Back-to-Africa movement stories made her "want to do things." During the Depression her mother "set a big table" so that their many friends who were down in luck would at least have a good supper. "This sort of environment inspired me to go out and be a part of the community."

As an adult in the city, Fay worked at a variety of jobs, eventually owning a laundromat and becoming a realtor. She worked as an accountant for the Ugandan mission to the United Nations, and through this and other African mission contacts she began presenting African and Afro-American art shows. Fay also became acquainted with city politics and political figures. Her husband (later divorced) was a Democratic district leader and she helped him in his duties. Fay built a house in Greenburgh and moved there, living alone but close to cherished family members. She got a graduate degree at a local college in health care administration and took a job for a time with the Greenburgh Neighborhood Health Center and the Community Action Program because she wanted to work with organizations "trying to help black kids." She became a district leader through the urging of a black leader who met her at one of her art shows. Fay thinks of herself as a liberal Democrat. "But when I came up here they said, 'Oh, you've got to be a Republican.' Shucks, after a while I said that's getting me nothing. So I changed back to being a Democrat." Which, Fay says, is still getting her nothing.

NINO

Nino is an Italian American and extremely conscious of his ethnicity. He says that to know "what makes Nino tick" one must know that he comes from peasant stock, from people who were discriminated against in the old country and came to the new one ready to work hard and raise their children to work hard. He attributes his individualism and strong need to be successful to these antecedents and to his own youthful experience of open conflict with Irish-Americans—"My group was looked on as the Puerto Ricans are today."

Nino's father, a businessman, demanded from his only child complete compliance with his rules and instilled in him that he must "accomplish, succeed." Of an age for high school, Nino was sent to a strict Catholic boarding school where most of the students were of German and Irish descent. While there, Nino was always uncomfortably aware of his minority status. Although destined by his parents for a career in medicine, on graduation Nino applied to a range of professional schools "for a lark." As a result he entered law school in New York City and is now a successful maritime lawyer and, he remarks, a not-so-successful politician.

Nino lives in the Edgemont section of Greenburgh but his heart belongs to Brooklyn where he was born and brought up, and where he has strong political and other institutional ties. Nino has always been a Democrat because "if you wanted to accomplish anything in Brooklyn you had to be one." His early attempts to break into the circle of regular Democrats were rebuffed. Bitter, he joined those fighting them, the Independent Democratic Club of Brooklyn, a membership he maintains.

In Greenburgh, Nino joined the newly formed Democratic Club, nominated himself onto its board, and soon became a leader in his own district. In his political activity, he has two goals. One is individual success. The other is to unify his ethnic community. His relatives, however, distrust politicians and do not share his hopes.

Nino's general view of himself is as a strong family man ("My children are my purpose for life") and a patriot ("I'm very nationalistic, I have a great sense of loyalty to my country"). Politically, Nino sees himself as a moderator, a conciliator, one who can talk to all sides on an issue and bring people together. He says, "I am willing to give in order to take, I am willing to deal." However, "Extreme liberals will not permit you to have a thought of your own."

DENNIS

Dennis is a young man, a native Hastingsite, who comes from a traditionally political family, and who has made politics his career. His father is a Republican district leader, but on the other side his mother "was the little girl to present roses to FDR when he came to North Tarrytown after his elections."

In 1960, when Dennis was a teenager, the whole family went "gung ho" for John Kennedy, and he dates his penchant for politics from this period of campaigning. His mentor was Ella, then the Democratic chair. "She took me everywhere. I must have seen Robert Kennedy fifty times." Before and while in college, Dennis worked for a successful Democratic candidate for congress and for the same man's later unsuccessful senatorial campaign.

After an unhappy work stint in the garment industry, Dennis decided to go with his bent and "walk the halls of Congress" for a job working for a representative. Shirley Chisholm gave him a job. "I was very lucky. But then I maximized what I was doing, being neither black nor a woman." He then attached himself to the campaigns of other congressional candidates and when interviewed was the local representative of Paul, the current congressman in his district, who understands that he has political ambitions of his own.

Dennis moved to Irvington and almost immediately became a district leader there because, in his professional role, "I went to those meetings anyhow. . . . I like this nonsense, and the village seemed right for a little action" in which he could use his considerable campaigning skills.

Dennis identifies himself as a liberal Democrat now, although he says that during the Vietnam War he was confused, and could probably have been considered a "regular."

GOLDA

Golda is a native New Yorker from the Bronx. Her parents, of Russian Jewish descent, were business people and politically conservative Republicans. Golda remembers family conversations being dominated by business and political affairs. Business and politics continued to be main interests in her adult life. She and her husband (now divorced) ran a successful enterprise for which she handled the business end.

Today Golda lives with her two children in Dobbs Ferry, and she talks of her joy in living in a small community. Since settling there she has acquired an M.A. in political science from a New York City university and teaches there part-time. She also works part-time for a marketing research firm.

Golda has found an outlet for her fascination with politics in Dobbs. At first she did not enroll in a party because she was "unwinding from my Republican background." It also suited her role as a researcher for her master's thesis for which she interviewed both Republican and Democratic office holders. However, after working in Democratic Dobbs Ferry campaigns Golda enrolled in the party and accepted a leadership outside of her district. Within a year she became a candidate for trustee and won. She failed in a try for re-election, was appointed to the village committee and became active also in town-level politics. A later try for a trustee's seat was also unsuccessful.

Golda describes herself as a practical rather than issue-oriented politician. As a Democrat, she says, "I'm not radical. I wouldn't put my body on the line, but I'm liberal and open-minded—not the rough stuff."

CEDRIC

Cedric was born and brought up in Yonkers. After serving in the air force during World War II he went back to college and then worked as a reporter for the *Yonkers Herald Statesman*. He covered the city's political scene, getting to know and ultimately working in the campaigns of a rising Democratic politician. Although he and his family of orientation had always been Republican, Cedric changed his enrollment to Democratic and, three years later, ran an admittedly hopeless race against a popular Republican incumbent for the state Senate.

In the same year Cedric married a nurse, and they moved to an apartment complex in Hastings. He entered business in New York City and, when the job lessened in demands on his time, renewed his political interests with the express purpose of running for village office. However, a between-elections vacancy occurred on the Greenburgh town council and Cedric, now a leader in his own district, threw his hat in the ring and was appointed to fill the vacancy. He failed to retain his seat, however, and the next year ran unsuccessfully for village trustee.

Cedric describes himself as a moderate Democrat—"not activist enough to be a liberal, but neither am I conservative—I'm open-minded."

HANNA

Hanna is German-born, having left the country in 1938 at the age of nineteen to be safe with cousins in Florida. Her father had died three years earlier in an accident on a "Boycott Day" (boycott of Jewish firms). Her mother and her older sister were deported three years later and, she discovered long after the fact, were shot on transport to Riga. "Now it's a whole different life. We turn the switch and it's gone—we try to turn the switch."

Hanna is married to a man she knew in Germany who also came to America to escape the Nazi regime. They moved with their two children to Hartsdale over thirty years ago. Hanna became intensely involved in school and political affairs.

In Florida Hanna had worked in the presidential campaign of Henry Wallace. Then in Hartsdale she campaigned for Adlai Stevenson. She found it hard to break into the Greenburgh town committee, which seemed to her "a tight little group." After eight years of trying to become a leader in her own district, during the Concerned Democrat insurgency she took a vacancy in a predominantly black area. Her co-leader was also white and "I felt very foolish about the two whites getting out the black vote." Now she is a leader in her own neighborhood.

Hanna has always been a Democrat and thinks she is "way to the left," but not as far left as some of her friends.

JOHN

John was born into a working class family who lived in Brooklyn and then the Bronx. His parents came as young adults to this country, seeking a better life. When John grew up he was aware of political issues but considered himself apolitical, except for voting for Democrats who, he felt, had the working man's interests at heart.

A businessman, John came to Greenburgh with his wife, Lotta, and two sons for the suburban surroundings. He was still politically uninvolved except indirectly through Lotta, who was the secretary of the Democratic county chairman. But the couple decided several years previous to the interview that in the interest of better town government they would fill two of the many leadership vacancies in their area. John is also area chair. He thinks he and Lotta have been successful leaders. Their district he describes as tripartite; the section they live in—apartments—is ninety-eight percent Jewish and Democratic. The other sections have mostly Republicans and independents. "So what I do is I concentrate, I don't tell the other two areas there is an election."

PEPE

Pepe was sixteen years old and living in Paris when the Nazis invaded France. He describes his family as being completely assimilated, "far away from Judaism," but the young boy was asked "the grandfather questions," then told he was a Jew and must wear a star. After a time his mother and father were sent away and Pepe, left alone, joined the French underground.

Under cover of being a woodcutter (vital labor to the Germans), Pepe worked in the underground passing convoys into Switzerland and Spain. Finally he was "fingered as a leader" and jailed in Spain. Upon his release, he promised himself not to return to France because, "The French were bastards. They were collaborators. After the war everyone was a big hero, when so few really were."

Pepe made his way to the Middle East and joined the British Army, spending the last years of the war there and in Italy. He then went to Palestine, on the way meeting the woman he soon married. After the birth of his first child, the family came to the United States for economic reasons. There, three more children were born. Now a successful businessman, Pepe says, "This country has been great for me."

Pepe describes both his job and his location in Elmsford as accidents, and his identification as a Democrat, too, since the village was a Republican stronghold whose political elders treated him rudely. "Elmsford is the most bigoted, backward town I ever saw in my life. It's like Europe, new people have no rights. I was not going to let a bunch of bigots guide my destiny." Pepe ran unsuccessfully for village office twice, became a district leader and then served several years as the village Democratic chair. Still, he says, "I have nothing in common with the people's way of thinking and of life."

Pepe considers himself "a fighter for democracy," fervently anti-Communist and in favor of a strong defense against Russia, a regular Democrat who survived the takeover of the party by the "Concerneds." Well travelled and speaking eight languages, Pepe feels that other people do not understand the meaning of democracy. Speaking of the Middle East, he says:

They have a tendency to take advantage of it instead of protecting it. . . . I saw the British officers. They were slapping the Arabs in the face, kicking them in the rear. I said, you can't treat people like this, they're human beings. They said, you'll learn, and sure enough I learned. They tried to rob me, they tried to cheat me. I finally got mad and slapped in the face and kicked in the rear and got respect. They understand only strength, power. This is their way of life.

Pepe says he is in politics out of a sense of duty, not ego, because "we are all people, we should get together, you can't build a society where hatred exists." He is proud of being a founder of the Westchester Community Opportunity Program, and the work he has done for improved housing and the community center in the Fairview section of Greenburgh.

CHAPTER 6

Factionalism

While Greenburgh district leaders share a basic unity of purpose that one would expect of any essentially self-selected group, they are also aware that, in Brooke's words, "we are a unique group of great diversity." The diversity includes such overlapping categories as race, culture, class, religion and minority. The most striking divisions among the leaders, however, are transient alignments—factions—based on issues or personality clashes.

"Race" has become an outmoded word for many anthropologists, primarily because of the difficulty in attaching clear-cut significance to it. "Minority" entails a similar problem if not applied to locally circumscribed areas instead of to second class status regardless of the relative size of the group. At times "minority" and "majority" seem euphemisms for subordinate and dominant groups. In the face of these difficulties, "ethnicity" has become a popular usage among social scientists to include various categories of heritage and cultural identity.

A minimal definition of factionalism, as described by anthropologists, is political conflict in which the contending groups are temporary, randomly recruited by a leader or leaders, informally organized, and lacking a sharp ideological focus (Nicholas 1965). This type of conflict is contrasted with "ongoing corporate groups with fixed structural properties" (Lewellen 1983:109), although some think that actual cases are apt to be less fixed, found somewhere on a continuum between ideal types (Bujra 1973: Aronoff 1977; Strauch 1983). In this instance the local Democratic organization is the corporate group and the factions are described below. In the discussion, ethnicity and class describe *categories* of people; factions describe *groups* of people made up of varying population categories.

ETHNICITY, CLASS AND POLITICS

Ethnicity implies a homogeneity of behavior and belief that often, in ethnographic fact, does not exist. In spite of the traditional salience of ethnicity in the United States political system, each ethnic demographic slice is apt to be remarkably diverse. In particular, ethnic populations themselves are cut horizontally by class (some anthropologists think that much ethnic research is ethnically-tinged class research); Barnouw (1985) points out that although ethnic foods, parades and picnics do not a culture make, ethnicity may be important as an identity symbol, and this is the case in Greenburgh. As town demographics change, this symbolism takes on different political connotations in the community that affect factionalism on the Democratic committee.

A clarification is in order in turning to the forty-seven's viewpoints about ethnicity, class and politics. No one was asked direct questions about ethnicity or class. No one was asked questions such as "what class do you think so-and-so belongs to," or "what is your experience with anti-Semitism in local politics." These subjects did emerge, however, in conversations about family background, careers, and especially factionalism. Several of the forty-seven, all males, were specific about their "working class" or "lower middle class" origins.

The questions addressed in the following pages are: What, if any, political correlates of ethnicity and class do the leaders see in Greenburgh? To what extent are ethnicity and class reflected in factionalism? What processes are involved in the making or breaking of short-term political alliances?

Village, Hill and Ethnic Whites

Polly states that she finds the line between factionalism and ethnicity in the town committee very fine; her comment refers to a generally perceived ideological gulf between conservative ethnic Catholics and liberal Jews. The facts that substantial numbers of district leaders fall into neither category, and that many Catholic and Jewish leaders confound the attribution do little to shade the perception. The image, however, does reflect community attitudes that are widely expressed by more comprehensive labels: historically, old residents and newcomers; geographically, village and hill—"village" in this case referring not to the whole but a segment of it.

These attitudes are more evident in the villages with their older ethnic populations than in more recently settled areas of the town outside. At town committee meetings differing political stances are debated but ethnic associations with them are not voiced. The observations below about anti-Semitism were made by non-Jewish leaders. None of the Jewish leaders referred to the subject.

Jodie comments that one of the biggest problems facing the Democrats is resentment of Jews by non-Jews—"It's a problem in the town and in Hastings. It's ingrained." In the village, she says, it is about the only subject of comment about the local Democratic committee. And about the town committee, "It is always said first that Greenburgh is run by Jews." Evan supports this observation, saying that when he hears comments such as "the damned liberals run everything," he translates "liberals" into "Jews."

All of the Democratic leaders—indeed, all of Hastings—speak of the split there as being one of village and hill. According to Fred,

> The hill-village split is getting worse, not better. Hill Democrats are not trusted at all in this village. They are considered elitist and inflict their social attitudes on others because they can afford it. There is an undercurrent of anti-Semitism, anti-black. I'm surprised the Democrats do as well as they do, given this feeling. The fact that we win at all must be because the Republicans are doing such a lousy job.

Such statements are common. Perhaps the situation is epitomized by the description of a hill district circulated at a volunteer firehouse: "Kremlin-on-the-hill."

Vi and Jimmy, among Hastings leaders, are the most class and ethnicity-conscious. Vi explains that, having grown up in Hastings, she has a strong sense of hill and village. "In the thirties and forties I wouldn't be invited to a hill house for a chat." She believes that she has been discriminated against all her life because of her ethnic background and the family's early limited means.

Jimmy also traces his awareness of class to a childhood of comparative poverty and ethnic identity. In his interviews he dwelt on family background, pinpointing when he discovered that his family was poor and so became "class conscious." He faults his village committee for not encouraging more village participation in its meetings. He recalls the experience of young Ed, an ethnic Pole, who resigned as a district leader after only a few months because he was "conscious of class distinctions." (Young Ed, himself, at the time of the resignation gave the chair another reason: "the boys at the firehouse were giving me a hard time about being on the committee.") Jimmy also says that he encourages village-based inspectors (who in Hastings are part of the committee) "to show up and speak up" at committee meetings in order to balance the hill input with their own. But to no avail. "They say it's no use."

Faith remembers her early days on the Irvington Democratic committee when it was seriously split between Italian and Irish Catholics on the one hand and the newer, liberal Democrats on the other. "You never knew when you were talking to a Democrat whether they were

pro-church or a conservationist." Dennis, more recently come to Irvington, describes his committee as split between "regulars" and "reformers." The former are the older mainstream Democrats who supported the Vietnam War and the latter the War's opponents. He adds
that the committee as a whole is always concerned about the effect of
anti-Semitism on Democratic prospects, to the extent of worrying about
the election of a Jewish chair. (In fact, they have so elected, twice.)

Marge agrees that there is anti-Semitism in Irvington. Two personal
exchanges underlined this for her. A Republican friend advised her to
resign from the committee before she became tainted by association
with Jews. Another friend once remarked how nice one leader was,
carelessly adding, "It's too bad he's Jewish." Unlike young Ed, Marge
stayed on.

A similar situation prevails in Tarrytown, except that the committee
itself seems to be more split than elsewhere. One district leader says
of another "He thinks God is an Irish Catholic." Nathan remarks that
"some of the young liberal women on the committee are out of touch
with the mainstream of the village." Laura's ambition is to bring the
racial and ethnic elements in Tarrytown together, "but I know that
such unity is hard to achieve."

Undercurrents of ethnic attitudes surface now and then in the villages
in conflicts over particular issues. These conflicts are emotionally charged
not only within the communities, but within the Democratic committees themselves. In Hastings, for example, proposals for urban renewal
and a fair housing ordinance have been igniting issues. In both cases,
however, the majorities defeating the proposals were far more representative of the village than just the solid "village" opposition. Similar
issues have split leaders and communities in Irvington and Tarrytown,
and probably Dobbs Ferry, although the evidence there is not so
explicit.

As Greenburgh's demographics continue to change, so do the historical lines of cleavage, in both committees and communities.

Black Issues

Black district leaders care about civil rights, affirmative action and
improving the lot of black residents of Greenburgh, among other matters. So do the white leaders, although some are more passionate about
it than others. Factionalism in the town committee does not break on
white-black lines but it does break on perceptions of black issues. One
such issue is black representation on the committee and in town jobs.
Another is the extent to which black officials should represent black
constituents vis-à-vis their entire constituency.

Fay complains that there are very few blacks in the local party leadership. "We have no clout here. I'll be very frank, I'm very discouraged with the whole setup." She criticizes not only the white leadership but some of the black leaders who, while personally active, she says, are not sufficiently organized to achieve black goals. She thinks about vying with one such leader for his place on the town executive committee. Fay and other black leaders also distrust the administrator of the town government's affirmative action program and have raised questions in and out of committee about the filling of particular jobs. The supervisor, Vince, defends his appointments, without diminishing black wariness.

If Polly (who is black) in considering factionalism thinks in white ethnic terms, Abby thinks about practically every political topic in stark black and white. "Blacks should stick by blacks, period," is her credo. Abby is eloquent about why she is interested in partisan politics:

White America can say, "We're benevolent." Every ten years they can say, "Here's a crumb." I'm a child of God, an inheritor through God for this earth and what is on this earth. He didn't put me here to ask any man for anything. I have a right to as much as any other individual.

This leads Abby directly to her decision that "until there are more black people elected in Greenburgh, I'm a one-issue person."

Abby is so targeted in her interest that, ironically, she sometimes misses the import of a situation and acts in a way that she later regrets. For example, when given designating petitions for a judgeship, she carried only one for a white candidate she admired, neglecting one for a black candidate in trouble. After several losing campaigns, this man had chosen to shore up his chances by taking the Right to Life as well as the Democratic line. Many pro-choice leaders consequently refused to circulate his petition. Abby missed the whole conflict and was unaware that a black was running. As she remarked about her own election, "You can't tell we're black by our names."

Greenburgh's Fairview Community Center, a multi-million dollar facility located in the black community, became a source of conflict, first, among black officials and district leaders. The problem was what to do about a series of budget overruns incurred by the administrator of the center, a popular black community leader. Some of the blacks concerned seemed to feel, much as Abby proclaims, that blacks should stick by blacks; that the administrator should not be pressured about remedial action. Eleanor, the only black on the town council and also its liaison with the center, took the position that the administrator could and should take responsibility for the overruns and reduce the costs. After what she felt was a long period of trying to influence the remedial process, she publicly suggested that the center advisory board resign and be reconstituted to better help in the administration of the center. This intensified the criticism by the blacks on the board and widened it to include liberal white district leaders also on the board. The latter, including Rita, were incensed by what they considered Eleanor's cavalier action.

The town executive committee took up the matter at their next meeting. Eleanor explained her view that neither governmental nor party leaders had responded to her concerns until she went public. Other leaders, both black and white and on and off the center advisory board, including Mandy, decried her action. One black leader was so enraged that she spat at Eleanor. Although other leaders quietly accepted Eleanor's reasoning, the local newspaper's report that the executive committee had "chastised" the councilwoman was close to the mark.

This meeting was only a prelude to what Eleanor faced at the next town council meeting attended by a number of hostile black community leaders as well as by some of her supporters. A minister told her that black politicians represent the black community until they get elected. "Then you become an oreo." A center board member said, "You are not one of us. You say you're black, but you're not my kind." The attacks continued while Eleanor coolly defended herself. The supervisor and the other council members sat mute throughout the bitter confrontation. (This sequence of events preceded those described on p. 116 above.)

In this instance the executive committee leadership was angry with Eleanor and did not protest her colleagues' silence. Two years later a political enemy assailed her at a council meeting as a "plantation nigger" and other opprobriums, with her colleagues still silent. This time the executive committee objected to the supervisor, Vince, that these personal attacks should be gaveled out of order, should not be tolerated. Vince agreed and one councilman apologized for his silence.

There were three separate but interwoven issues at the base of this conflict. First, the black-black factionalism over what to do about the admitted financial problem. Second, the division among white leaders about Eleanor's culpability in her approach to the problem (which was resolved by her overwhelming support for renomination to the council). The third strand is not evidenced by any statements made but seems self-evident to local politicians. However politically involved whites might feel about the substantive issue, they would find it difficult to alienate an aroused black constituency that steadfastly voted Democratic.

There are black issues, then, and black factionalism. There is doubtless a pervasive suspicion of whites by blacks. But there is not black-white factionalism. None of the forty-seven perceive black leaders as a group as being "liberal" or "conservative," as is the view of ethnic whites. On any particular issue resulting from black or general concerns, black district leaders scatter.

TAKING SIDES

Whether factionalism is valued or deplored, it is a part of the political process that has received an abundance of journalistic and social scientific attention. Anthropological studies tend to be value-neutral and descriptive, but also concerned with either fleshing out or constricting the concept itself. Most accounts have focused on conflicts between one group or groups in non-Western societies, large or small. The factions in the field here—small-scale, with one exception (the Concerned Democratic movement)—are situated firmly in a modern political party system. Yet the general characteristics of factionalism framed by action-theory anthropologists in other fields seem applicable if expanded upon.

This framework starts with the "mobilization of political capital" when competition and conflict are evident. That is, various people are positioning themselves for a struggle by gauging resources and seeking support from others. Many tactics are used including exerting personal influence, participating in intrigues, making threats and promises, and trying to cut off support for rivals. This aspect of factionalism is described as undercurrents here and is a sharpening of competitive strategies suggested previously. Subsequent confrontational and adjustive phases form what has become in the literature a classical progression.

This general patterning of the factional process provides some of the background against which the subject is explored in the following pages. The views of the forty-seven are canvassed and then a particular episode of factionalism is presented, leading to answers to such questions as: What kinds of things cause the leaders to divide themselves into contending camps? Are issues divisive? What are the roles of personalities and power motivation? How is the conflict joined, carried out, and resolved?

Views About Factionalism

Without exception, the forty-seven recognize factionalism as pervasive within the Greenburgh town committee. In talking about it they refer mainly to the pre-phase of mobilizing support. The undercurrents of rivalry and ambition are soon noticed by the greenest of leaders, as when Nora remarked early in her tenure that "there seems to be a lot of infighting and backbiting going on." This atmosphere makes some uneasy. Jodie refers to "all these politicians in a room in intimate conversations saying rotten things about people." Sid says it makes him uncomfortable to be in a room with people making believe they like each other—"but I've done it too." (The political kiss may add to the sense of hypocrisy as well as to a sense of camaraderie. An anthropologist commented after attending a Greenburgh political fund-raiser that she had never seen so many people kissing one another.)

The second phase of factionalism—open conflict—is not always seen as such by the leaders because it is provided for by the rules of the game. A leader is supposed to take sides on an issue and to support one candidate or another. Bailey (1970:224) describes the situation:

> Rules, customs and conventions define political arenas. They regulate conflict by laying down who is eligible to compete, what are the prizes for the winner, and what the competitors may do and what they must not do in their efforts to gain the prize.

When the rules of the game are perceived to be broken, however, the contest becomes charged with accusations and bitterness. This kind of breach of the peace is more rare than the ongoing simmering factional undercurrents.

Most of the leaders are relatively unaware of schisms at the county level, and at the area and village levels the stage is too small, the cast too limited, and the prize too insignificant for any heavy political wheeling and dealing. For these reasons most of the following description is about the town level of conflict.

Many of the forty-seven deplore factional divisiveness; it is called "an enormous waste of time," it is lamented that "we fight among ourselves when we should be fighting the Republicans," and "we must have a death wish." The open-break phase of factionalism considerably increases costs to the participants in resources, both energy and money.

Office holders and candidates not directly involved in a controversy and leaders close to them try to avoid loaded within-party alliances whenever they can. Examples are Brooke, who is the wife of an incumbent, and Ann, who works for one. Others, like Craig, say they don't know enough about most local rifts to take sides.

On the other hand, some leaders see rivalry and competition as givens in their political lives and accept that it will from time to time balloon into gauntlet-throwing proportions. A few see factionalism as a sign of an intellectually vigorous political party. Ken and Rita, for example, believe that this is true of issue-based factionalism, and even if the fight gets personal "it may become ugly, but that's life." John says that "factionalism creates the nature of the party, and from the mix, the competition, we get good candidates."

The question of whether factionalism is issue-based or personality-based dominates thinking about the phenomenon, and so the question was put in those terms to the interviewees. Most leaders weighed "personality" far heavier than disagreement about issues. For example:

Conrad: I have been aware of personality conflicts but blissfully unaware of differences on issues.

Nora: I see no issue-based alignments, only factionalism stemming from personal ambition.

Nathan: Factionalism is vicious, personality-oriented, almost knee jerk. The personalities almost automatically decide: because someone is on the other side, we'll try to bump him. It starts with personalities that create the issues. It never ceases at the town level—the jealousies and trying to step over people.

Orson: Today it is ninety-seven percent personality and it makes me want to chuck it more than any time before.

Lewis, however, himself issue-oriented, says "It's hard to separate the issues and personality components. Maybe it's seventy percent issue and thirty percent personality."

Disregarding his particular ratios, Lewis puts his finger on a key point. Issue and personality differences are motivational strands in both stages of factionalism, the undercurrents of individual political strategies and the ultimate showdown and resolution. Nevertheless, understanding the process requires separation of the strands even while recognizing that they are a deceptive—if useful—dichotomy.

Issue factionalism is couched in terms of liberals and conservatives, although it is probably more apt to use the word "regular" than conservative. It began with the nationwide polarization of the party over the Vietnam War in the late 1960s and the organization of the Concerned Democrats. The regulars included conservatives but also liberals loyal to Lyndon Johnson because of the Great Society programs. Concerned Democrats were very active in Westchester, and particularly in Greenburgh.

Among the district leaders in place at the time, Ralph, Jimmy and Pepe were regulars. Ralph refers to Concerned Democrats as "single-issue liberals who were grossly wrong to oppose the War once we were in it." He thinks Greenburgh's "Concerneds" continue to be divisive.

Pepe and Jimmy seem not to hold grudges. Jimmy felt at the time "my country right or wrong and bomb the hell out of them—our job was to win the war." He resented and resisted the Concerned Democrats' (he called them "brainwashed") infiltration of the town committee. But he gradually made his peace with them. "If it's *everybody* against the war, that's fine. At least these people are working." He is tolerant of the liberals' illusions: "The Concerned Democrats are younger people who make graft and corruption harder, but it's still there. They [sic] just get slipperier about it. Politicians are used to it."

The Concerned Democrats on the town committee included Claud, Leon and Charlie from the villages, and Hanna, Ken, Rita, Mandy, Zoe and Orson from the unincorporated area. For Orson, the presidential primary of 1968 stands as the high point of his political experience, contrasted with his dim view of current factionalism.

For a time the regulars and Concerneds were squared off in the Greenburgh committee, challenging one another for party office and candidate selection. The regulars held their ground at first but as Concerned efforts paid off and their cause became more popular, they emerged the winners. Although Becca explains that she was elected Greenburgh chair because she was not immediately identifiable as belonging on either side of the Vietnam issue, it was an ad hoc group of Concerneds (including Claud and Ken) who approached her about running. Becca does not see issues as very divisive today.

But several of the forty-seven do. They blame the liberals on the town committee for fracturing party unity. For example:

> Laura: Most of the factionalizing has been done by the liberals and their allies who force issues and organize people to back them. The liberal-conservative cleavage is getting worse.

> Duke: The exception to the open manner in which the committee is run is a strong, tight group within the committee who have a rigid, limited philosophical viewpoint.

> Nathan: I'm not from the aggressive liberal wing of the party and I feel that clique causes a lot of trouble from time to time.

> Chester: Unless programs are for the poor, black or green, you get objection from the liberals on the committee.

Other issues brought up that are sometimes resented are abortion and group homes. Views that blame the liberals for factionalism are usually selective about the liberals referred to and slip gradually into the more complex matter of personality attributes, as when Nino says:

Divisiveness stems from the activities of a group who are involved in politics for politics' sake—power. They use issues as a way of controlling other people. They are intelligent, knowledgeable, hard-working, but from my guts I doubt their motives.

Those leaders who stress the importance of personality apparently use the term to cover competing ambitions and differences about political tactics more often than incompatible temperaments. Of course, differences about issues and selection of candidates can be exacerbated by rubbing one another the wrong way and personal dislike can be loosely clothed in issues. However, many of the forty-seven see factionalism purely and simply as a matter of rivalry for leadership:

Marge: Factionalism is personality-based, with one side trying to get power from the other.

Pepe: It's all a matter of personality. One clique wants to take over the leadership and is willing to do anything to eliminate the opposition.

Faith: The town leadership is, by the nature of things, always hungry for power. Who else would want that kind of job? Opposing them is a group that always tries to get power but doesn't succeed. Some will always take sides against the leadership and whatever they want, are always dissenters.

Dennis: There are two basic camps on the town committee. [The chair] and the people who deal with her and those against her. Some leaders perceive that there is a controlling group and automatically set out to challenge it.

These comments come chiefly from those who support the chair in the power struggle and have nothing whatever to do with ideology or ethnicity. When Hanna states that "They are always after somebody," or Mandy says "They are out to get people who are personally vulnerable," the "they" are not often—if ever—conservatives but fellow liberals. This may explain why the personality basis of the clash is stressed in spite of the fact that "they" either do not like the quality of the leadership or "they" want to further their own political careers—or both. Obviously the career motivation is not given either publicly or privately and is inferred—mistakenly or not—as in some of the quotes above.

Hanna, considering anti-chair factionalism, says that she would never seek to be town chair in spite of her long experience in the second most important town party position because, "I've watched Mandy and Becca for years. I wouldn't be able to act like nothing had happened the day after they had done something to me."

Cali has a more flexible notion of factionalism than those who blame the liberals and those who lay it to power motivation. She was told before she came on the executive committee that there was one group that really ran things—the so-called Edgemont group—but she doesn't see it that way. "I'm still in the process of putting people in little holes, but they don't always stay in the holes." She finds that from issue to issue and candidate to candidate people shift personal allegiances and "I find myself doing the same thing."

As the liberal-conservative factionalism can be related to the rise of the Concerned Democrats, some of the attacks on the leadership also have roots in the past and do not all necessarily stem from ambition. Several leaders commented on the legacy of bitterness that resulted from simultaneous campaigns for the selection of a congressional candidate and a candidate for town council. Laura recalls the campaigns as "very dirty and very, very unkind" on all sides. In the council race between two well known district leaders, rumors about candidates and individuals on both sides were extremely harsh and charges of deviousness and misrepresentation circulated. There were reverberations long after the campaign, even though the loser refused to force a primary. (Zoe who supported the loser says years later about the winner, "I was wrong about him. We can all be proud of him.")

The race between the two main competitors for the congressional candidacy was even more divisive. Dennis, not yet a district leader but a campaign aide to the winner of the convention and the primary, remembers the "raw viciousness" of things said about his choice. On the other hand, Rita and Ken trace existing bad feelings to the tactics of the leadership on behalf of the winner. Although they advised the candidate they favored not to wage a primary against the choice of the town convention, he did so and they supported him. He lost. His supporters accused the leadership (Becca and Hanna) of consistently giving their candidate breaks over his rival, such as making the committee enrollment lists with inked-in phone numbers available only to him. Relationships among people who previously had been comrades-in-arms perceptibly soured.

Zoe is alone among the forty-seven in remarking on a town-village cleavage cutting across any liberal-conservative split as contributing to factionalism. She traces it to Greenburgh being "an artificial package" so that from time to time the interests of a village and the town conflict. She describes two or three village leaders and those they have recruited to their cause as standing in opposition to the town leadership clique of Becca, Mandy, Hanna and sometimes Zoe, herself ("The mafia, we call ourselves"). She thinks it is more "a matter of strategy in the infighting" than of important issues.

Although the forty-seven rarely state it directly, it is evident that tactics and reactions to tactics used in mobilizing support and in open conflict are usually subsumed under the "it's all personality" claim. It is ironic that Lewis alone recognized that tactics can become issues, when he said to the interviewer:

> I don't know if you call tactics an issue. You and I have a terrific clash, okay? I never understood that. I still don't. Is it an issue thing or a personality? I don't see it as personality, I never did.

The irony is because Lewis and the interviewer, who agree on most issues, were perceived by many of their colleagues as being a prime example of personality dissonance.

The tactics of factionalism range from feeling out attitudes and planting ideas ("We don't seem to be consulted as much as we should be," "I am worried about what has been happening lately, have you observed how badly X handled that matter at the last meeting?") to secret meetings targeted against unknowing colleagues and orchestrated surprises sprung at regular meetings.

One tactic worth mentioning is the use of clubs—as clubs. They have a tendency to flower when there is a threat against the current leadership and wither after the threat fails or interest in it pales. This does not mean that most members or promoters of the clubs have ulterior motives in its formation. Clubs are good in that they can widen participation in the political process. But it takes considerable energy to organize and keep a club going, and altruistic politicians tend not to provide it as often as potential rivals for leadership. For example, Orson was a founder of one of the recent town clubs. He came to believe, however, that its chief instigator and elected president was using his position to try to gain support against Becca. Even though Orson opposed Becca frequently on particular issues, he "found the various rabid anti-Becca statements offensive" and lost interest in the club. Apparently others felt the same way, or Mandy's elevation to chair assuaged them, because the club continued for only a few more years, winding down for lack of interest.

The town committee does not crumble away under its load of competing issues, personalities and tactics. It may even be the better for it. The following opinions, at least, are optimistic:

> Fay: Very few issues come up in the committee that they don't come to a conclusion, settle it, and it's more or less fair.

> Brooke: I know the leaders have a lot of disagreements but afterward there is unity.

Zoe: When we need to be, we get together. We're more alike than different.

The leaders' generalizations and explanations of factionalism are next tested against a showdown experience. It is a case in which things are not as they appear. It is a case featuring Cedric as a candidate in which he is more or less an innocent bystander.

A Classic Case

Factional undercurrents often funnel into a showdown: the breaking of a norm that had been considered binding within the political field may precipitate a crisis, covert hostility becomes overt, sides are taken and peace is broken as they vie in a public arena. However, there is still likely to be enough consensus to prevent the group as a whole from permanent cleavage and institutional change. Redressive measures then lead to a healing of the breach and a restoration of peace.

A forty-eighth district leader must be introduced here. This case was chosen as an example because the ethnographer has a great deal of information on it, having been a participant from beginning to end. Give her the pseudo-pseudonym of Sadie. Sadie is trying to be "objective"—or at least restrained—in recording the following events. But reader, beware! She took sides.[1]

Background. Add certain events of the spring of 1979 to the various undercurrents of factionalism described above. A town councilman was appointed by the Governor of New York to a seat on the county court with six months of his council term left. The supervisor (Vince) and the council agreed to fill the vacancy from a list of three people who would be selected by the town Democratic executive committee acting as a screening committee. It was understood that the person selected would run for the office in the fall elections with the advantage of his incumbency. Vince also made it clear that he wanted the appointee to be from a village, otherwise the supervisor himself would be the only villager on the town board. One or two leaders from the unincorporated area questioned the preference for a villager at the executive committee meeting where these conditions were made known, but after all it was the board's appointment to make and it could set the rules.

Leaders were encouraged to come forward as candidates or with suggestions. Several from the town outside asked to be screened, including Tim, a lawyer and the part-time prosecutor for Dobbs Ferry. Village leaders, however, were engrossed in their own village elections and had minimal interest in the council opening. Most of them knew little about the town outside and did not have much desire to know more.

At the Hastings post-election party celebrating their election of a new trustee (which gave the Democrats a majority on the village board because their defeated mayoral candidate, Mac, retained his seat as trustee), Cedric approached Sadie and requested that she, as chair, let Mandy know that he was interested in running for the town vacancy. Lewis had told him about the opening and suggested that he try for it. Sadie said she would forward his name but, being on the screening committee, did not promise support.

When Sadie called Mandy, the town chair told her that there was another Hastings candidate. Lewis, who had expected Mac to win his mayoral race, had now encouraged him to go for the town council seat. The first that Cedric, who had been something of a protégé of Mac's, knew of this development was when the two candidacies were announced at the next Hastings committee meeting.

All in all, the town screening committee interviewed eight candidates in the course of three evenings. Hastings had four members and three votes on the committee. Lewis and Jimmy as recording secretary and treasurer of the town committee, respectively, had a vote each. Sadie split her vote as chair (since she had to miss some interviews) with Jodie, Hastings' vice-chair. Cedric and Mac attracted a lot of consideration from the screeners because of the villager qualification. There was only one other villager (from Elmsford) among the eight.

After the candidates were interviewed and discussed, screeners voted, each member listing three names in order of preference. The top three were Tim with sixteen votes, Cedric with twelve, and Mac with nine. (This reflected precisely the order of Sadie's and Jodie's joint vote.) The names were forwarded to the town board with a unanimous recommendation that Tim be appointed. Vince and the council then interviewed each of the men before making their selection. All three were asked if they would accept the choice made and not run against him in the fall election, and all agreed.

Since the officials knew little personally about Cedric and Mac, Sadie was informally asked her opinion. She said that she would pick Tim, but that possibility apparently had been dismissed. Not only did he come from the unincorporated area but he lacked rapport with Vince. Sadie then said that she would rather work with Cedric than Mac. (Because of their relationship at the time, Mac would have returned the favor.) For whatever other reasons—including the screening vote—Cedric was appointed to the council and seemed to have clear sailing for the fall election.

Breaking Norms. The first norm broken was that Tim and Mac reneged on their pledge not to oppose the appointee.

The convention for the nomination of town officials was scheduled for the second week in June. One evening before the convention a group of leaders was called to a meeting in Edgemont. They were told that Tim could be drafted to run against Cedric for a council nomination and that the meeting was to widen support for such a move. Frank, a member of the screening committee, had taken the lead in this effort. He had prepared a letter to go out to all district leaders in which he called Cedric "unknown, inexperienced, new to the town and unknowledgeable about Greenburgh's politics and issues" and asserted that "Our FIRST responsibility is to endorse candidates who are in touch with the people of Greenburgh and who will add strength to the ticket. . . ." A petition of agreement was circulated that evening, accumulating fifteen signatures to go out with Frank's letter.

Mac's signature was at the top of the list and Lewis had also signed. Other signers were Zoe, Cali, Golda, Orson, Ken, Rita, Pepe, Ilse and five other party and public officials. All members of the executive committee except for Mandy, Hanna and Jimmy had signed, and six of the fifteen people were from villages.

Leon, invited to the meeting, argued there against the revolt and refused to sign the petition. He told Sadie about the meeting the next morning. That evening she contacted Hastings committee members and some other active Democrats, recited these events and asked if they would sign a leaflet of support for Cedric to be handed out to people in convention. All agreed immediately. Among the thirty-seven signers were all of the Hastings district leaders except Lewis and Mac.

The second norm broken was the nature of the speech made at the convention placing Tim's name in nomination.

The convention lasted four hours and was unanimous in selecting as candidates Vince for supervisor, the incumbents for two town judgeships, and Doris and Brad for the county board of legislators. The two open council seats were sought by four candidates: Eleanor, Tim, Cedric and Willy, the latter a black active in school and political affairs. There was also a three-way race for the town clerk nomination.

Sadie placed Cedric's name in nomination. Frank nominated Tim in an extraordinary speech. He had little to say about Tim. Instead he issued a blistering attack on Cedric, repeating some of the points he had made in his letter and leaving by words and intonation the impression that he had a mysterious and unsavory past. "He ran for trustee twice in Hastings," he said, "and lost both times.[2] I think Hastings is trying to tell us something."

Mandy, who was chairing the convention, described the screening committee's activities and added, "I believe that in politics all you have is your word. The town board kept its word to choose one of the three recommended by the committee. . . ." (But "Don't be afraid to vote the way you want to," Frank had said. "This committee is not a rubber stamp for the town board.")

Vince rose to address the convention before the vote, appealing on Cedric's behalf to those who had not yet made up their minds:

> To tell you the truth, I had no experience when I first ran. . . . All it takes is a decent individual who wants to learn. Through no fault of his own Cedric was the selection of the town board. It would be a disgrace and a sham on decency to turn him out now.

Vince went on to recall the agreements made just a short time before and stated grimly that when he made the choice of Cedric he had not been sure it was the right one. Now, in view of the action of those who had given him their word, he was sure it had been.

The secret balloting chose Tim as the town committee's candidate with sixty-three votes. Eleanor won with ninety-six, Cedric lost with forty and Willy with thirteen. Cedric was gracious in defeat, and after the meeting accepted Frank's handshake and assurances that there had been nothing personal in his speech. Sadie was besieged by questions asking what was shady about Cedric's past—"Nothing." She was glad that it was over and that the Hastings turnout had been good. The Hastings leaders (many of whom rarely attend town meetings) were glad that they had not left Cedric to face Frank's onslaught and the convention vote alone.

Some Hastings leaders were angry, however. The next day Charlie wrote a letter to Mac, with copies to Frank and Sadie, saying in part:

> I was outraged at the nominating meeting. I entered active politics 30 years ago because of my indignation at the innuendos of Sen. McCarthy. Last night, my last meeting as a district leader, I had deja vu. Frank in his nominating speech stated that Cedric had been rejected twice as a candidate by "Hastings" or by the "Hastings voters" or by the "Hastings committee." I do not remember the exact words. The innuendo and personal degradation, however, were very clear. I asked Frank why he had said this, and his reply was that you told him. . . . If you mean that Cedric was not a candidate for village office, that is true; but neither were hundreds of other people we have considered, presumably in confidence, over the many years I have served on the committee.

Sadie had Charlie's letter copied and delivered it to members of the executive committee at their next meeting. As an order of business she objected to Frank's attack on Cedric as exceeding reasonable bounds.

Other leaders also expressed disapproval. Rita commended Frank for his courage.

Breach of the Peace. To reporters, Cedric blamed his defeat in the convention on Frank's "falsification" and said he was considering a primary run against Tim. He planned to talk with other Democrats to get their reactions. He told Sadie that he was getting many calls urging him to go to primary and wanted to "feel people out." He thought Mandy and Hanna were for it, and probably Vince. So many people were reported to be in favor of a contest that one had to wonder how Cedric had lost in the first place.

The main argument for running against Tim was that there was to be a primary anyway. Willy had already announced his candidacy, and a town clerk loser was also set to primary against Susan, the winner. In such a situation onus for party conflict would not rest heavily on Cedric, and "anything can happen." Only two Hastings leaders advised Cedric to primary. Sadie was torn. She had been angry but not angry enough to give up the rest of the summer for a campaign. Tim's core of backers was known for energy and drive in elections. Leon and Dennis seemed to be ambivalent, too, for much the same reasons.

A meeting was called to weigh the matter and ambivalence melted away. The decision was made to enter the primary. Two weeks to the day after the convention, Cedric announced his challenge to the press.

Such were the events. But what was going on here? Aside from Cedric, who delighted in being a candidate, why did the leaders act as they did?

First, the leaders rallying to Tim had perfectly good reasons to think Tim a better choice than Cedric. The anomalous village-town relationship did not concern them. Nor did the breaking of his "word"; both Tim and Mac clearly had no real choice but to give their pledges not to run if they wanted to be seriously considered for appointment. Second, there was another and not-so-hidden agenda for some of these leaders. They were beholden to Vince for the Democrats' unbroken stream of victories at the polls since 1973 but not happy with his dominance in office. One leader said she "wanted a thorn in Vince's side" on the council and not another yes-man. They wanted Vince, but they wanted a chastened Vince, one who had been taught a lesson, one who would listen to them in the future. Lewis put it more colorfully to Cedric in explaining his own part in the revolt: "We wanted to give Vince a bloody nose." Chester, also on Tim's side, describes its leaders as supporting Tim "because they were mad at Vince."

On Cedric's side motivations were more varied. For Becca, Hanna, Leon, John and Nino it was primarily a case of teaching a lesson to those trying to teach Vince a lesson. Nino's feeling was that Tim's leaders "were surrounding the chief," and he wanted to help him. Leon goes into more detail:

> They went overboard in trying to give Vince a bloody nose. He maybe deserved to be told off a little, but not by giving him a bloody nose in public. He's abrasive—so what? He's doing a good job, whatta I want to do with him? I'm not prepared to decide my politics on whether a guy is abrasive. Some suave ones are utter stinkers.

Leon also thinks it is "poor politics to agree on a procedure all the way down the line and then say because one loses, all bets are off."

Finally there is Hastings' role in the case, which was almost accidental. At that time the only committee people who seemed at all interested in town outside politics were Lewis and Sadie. Cedric was possibly the least known of the leaders among his colleagues. Concern in the village about filling the council vacancy was at a bare minimum, to put it mildly. But turf is turf. Becca (who laughingly says the fight was about personality "but the question is, whose personality?") gives her view of what happened:

> The fact that Hastings was the cutting edge of one side of the fight was because they went for overkill [at the Edgemont meeting and again at the town convention]. There are times in politics where you have to make a stand and say, "that's dirty pool."

These voiced motivations, of course, are not inconsistent with the overall views of factionalism expressed by the forty-seven about power motivations and personal antagonisms.

Showdown. Once the decision to primary was made, the nature of the conflict changed. Who had outraged whom could no longer be the point. How the candidates had been picked became irrelevant, as Claud and Antonia pointed out to Sadie after they had decided to work for Tim's election. On the surface both sides had to appeal to primary voters on the basis of "may the best man win." Factionalism had to take on the face of substance and a factional fight had to use time-honored campaign techniques, a principal one of which is plain hard work.

Tim's side was in place due to their pre-convention activity. Golda became the head of a dedicated, enthusiastic team of workers. Most district leaders decided to support the cause of the convention designee, including Polly, Laura, Sid, Arthur and Chester, in addition to the petition signers.

Cedric's side was more diffuse and later in mobilizing support outside of Hastings. As town Democratic chair and town supervisor, Mandy and Vince did not publicly take sides. There is little doubt, however, that without their not-so-tacit support there would have been no primary for Cedric. Leon and Nino were chosen to head the effort. Hanna, Dennis (the congressman he worked for contributed his aide's time and services)[3] and Sadie (whose name and address were used for headquarters purposes) were also consistently involved throughout the campaign.

Before anything else, Cedric's supporters had to muster enough workers to carry his nominating petitions so that by a fixed date he would have enough signatures (around 745) to get on the ballot. Otherwise, no primary. Over thirty people, one-third of them from Hastings, knocked on doors to accomplish this goal.

Within the party organization the petitions—specifically a "truncated petition"—became a major issue because it hurt Tim by making Cedric's petitioning more successful. Every other year the petition listing the town candidates has a place for the district leaders in each election district to write in their names. This was one of those years. The challengers—this year Cedric, Willy and the opponent of Susan, the town clerk designee—and their workers carry single-name petitions. At an executive committee meeting Sadie had made an obvious point: she would not be able to carry her own petition because it conflicted with the one she planned to carry for Cedric. This also meant that she could not get signatures for Vince, Eleanor and Susan, whom she wanted to support, because the slate included Tim.

When the petitions were finally distributed by Hanna, the problem had been dramatically solved. There were two petitions available to the leaders, both with Vince's name at the top and space to write in district leaders. One carried the convention slate, the other listed only Cedric. Cedric's supporters could carry the truncated petition and were delighted. Tim's supporters were upset. There had been no discussion of the matter; apparently it had been settled between Hanna, who as vice-chair had always distributed the petitions, and Vince. Eleanor and Susan now had a problem. They wanted to stay out of the Tim-Cedric factionalism but did not want to give up their supporters who were for Cedric. Unhappy about the cost, they also published solo petitions, which most of Cedric's workers carried along with the truncated one.

The town's vacancy committee had been transferred in toto to the truncated petition and this added to the protest against it. Arthur, who was on it, points out that he had agreed to be on the committee for the full slate but had not been asked about the other one—"Vince runs roughshod over people."

At the time the leaders could do nothing except carry their petitions of choice. Some of Tim's people felt that they had been betrayed by the leadership and seemed out for blood—specifically, Hanna's.

Both sides more than made their quotas of signatures. That hurdle was over, and both Cedric and Tim (and Eleanor and Willy) were assured places on the ballot for council. They could get on with the campaign.

Meanwhile a not unrelated struggle was going on in Hastings. For the first time, one of the village's election districts was having a primary for a Democratic district leadership. Charlie was not running again. Duke, his co-leader, and Sadie asked Vi to fill the vacancy in the district (her own), which she had long been promised. Pat, Lewis' wife, decided to run, too. A group of leaders set up a separate "Committee to Elect Vi and Duke" to help in their petitioning and campaign. All three candidates made the ballot.

In the campaign at the town level, Tim ran as the convention's choice and Cedric ran to the last mailing on the desirability of having a villager on the council. This, in spite of the facts that Dobbs Ferry leaders were pretty solidly for Tim, and Elmsford's and Tarrytown's leaders partly for him. Other than the villager matter, only two other issues differentiated this factional primary from any "normal" campaign. They had to do with raising money and abortion.

Each side watched the other carefully to see that the ground rules were respected. One of the ground rules is that in a local primary the party cannot take sides and its financial resources cannot be used. Both sides, therefore, had to raise funds for campaign expenses. They used the customary methods—mailings to make money for more mailings and a fund-raising party. Cedric's party was on the grounds of the Democratic county executive's home. There was some grumbling that this was inappropriate but it was directed more at the county executive than at Cedric. One up for Cedric.

To cut expenses each side considered using a party bulk-mailing permit. This is clearly a violation of the ground rules, not to say the law. Cedric's supporters did not request use of the Hastings permit (and would not have got it if they had). But Chester, the Dobbs chair, did allow Tim the use of the Dobbs Ferry permit. This action paid off in savings and no challenge since Cedric's side, though riled, decided there would be no political gain in making an issue of such an offense. Rather, they might be considered stupid for not doing it themselves. One up for Tim.

The abortion issue was more serious and hurt Cedric, perhaps decisively. Tim was not only a pro-choice activist but contributed advice and legal services to pro-choice groups. Cedric and Mac were both Catholic and individually against abortion but not Right to Life partisans. During their screening they both tried to articulate the Catholic politician's standard distinction between personal belief and political stance, but neither was particularly good at it. Cedric got better with practice. He identified himself as pro-choice and refused to take the Right to Life line. Nevertheless, the rumor passed on by some of the screeners that he was a Right to Lifer followed him on the campaign trail.

The pro-choice organizations formally and actively supported Tim throughout the race. This was against their self-imposed rule that if both candidates were pro-choice they would not publicly endorse either. Cedric's side, again, thought there was no political advantage in making the point. Many ups for Tim.

Resolution. Hanna voted in the morning and then left on vacation. After the polls closed Sadie received the Hastings returns which had Cedric running far ahead of the other council candidates. Lewis reported that Pat had lost the district leadership to Vi by eighteen votes. Sadie decided, as usual, not to go to town hall for the tally. She had thought for some time that Tim would win and hoped only that it would not be a too humiliating win.

Later Dennis called from town hall. Tim, with fourteen votes more than Cedric (out of 2,941 cast) had come in second and so won a seat. A cheerful Dennis, Becca and Leon came to Sadie's house to toast the end of the campaign. They described the winners at town hall as far from jubilant. The contest had been much more of a cliffhanger than anyone had imagined.

Looking back, Nino agonized that "if I had only knocked on just a few more doors . . ." but most of the leaders in his faction were amazed at how well they had done. John, for example, says in bemusement, "I didn't think we had a prayer. It's interesting that people like us could have gotten Cedric elected with just a few more votes." Leon, Dennis and Mandy all felt that the attempt to teach Vince a lesson had cost too much for any more talk about bloody noses. Becca did not regret the infighting, thinking that "the idea that it just wasn't okay to do what they did" was communicated.

There were undoubtedly other rationalizations on the other side. Golda cherished the whole campaign experience and gloried in winning. Some of the other leaders, however, were not mollified by their victory. The truncated petition still rankled.

A few days after the primary, Lewis, Rita and others met with Mandy, Dennis and Leon to discuss the upcoming town reorganization meeting. Tim's group told Mandy that they planned to run Pepe against Hanna for executive vice-chair. Prepared, Mandy replied that if they did, Lewis and Rita would face an opposing slate themselves. (This was no idle threat; candidates had already been lined up to give their all for the cause.) Mandy later told Pepe that she would run with him and the others only if they did not oppose Hanna. Risking their own seats for the pleasure of punishing Hanna must not have seemed appetizing. The matter was dropped and plans for reconciliation were made.

Arthur suggested to Mandy that peace be symbolized by having factional participants on one side nominate or second those on the other. To an extent—not to the point of farce—this was done. Hanna returned from vacation almost on the eve of reorganization, was nominated by Sadie, seconded by Zoe and duly re-elected without contest.

The matter of the truncated petition was not dropped. In executive committee Lewis and Rita, in particular, protested it and tried to get to the bottom of how the decision was made. They argued, first, that there should have been committee discussion before the decision was made and, second, that the only thing going for the convention's choice was the imprimatur of the party. They believed that the leadership should be bound by the convention vote (but see p. 152) and that the committee should find ways of institutionalizing this. Exhausted by the subject, the executive committee agreed to appoint a subcommittee to look into the matter and make a recommendation. In the event, no others wanted to keep poking at the coals enough to join the subcommittee and over time the matter was dropped from the agenda.

Strong forces were moving toward further reconciliation. For all of the talk about personality, bitterness and outrage, many leaders prided themselves on maintaining friendly relations throughout. Leon, for example, says he tries "to avoid personality issues so when the tempest is over, I'll be able to talk to the other side without too much difficulty." Dennis describes Golda as being friendly and fair-dealing during the campaign. Golda, on her part, was happy to have Dennis call on her after the primary and describes this as the start of "the coming-togetherness." Mandy reflects that "there will always be factionalism in politics. The difference between us and other committees, we fight and then pull together in the end. Other committees, they fade away."

Greenburgh Republicans had been openly predicting that the much publicized Democratic factionalism could hand them the opportunity to return to power in the town. It did not. With the Tim-Cedric decision made and accepted, the Democratic leaders submerged any personal differences and united behind their slate. "Vince's team" won the November election handily, as usual.

Dire predictions had been made by some that Mandy would face opposition from "the same people" again and she was warned to protect her flanks at all times. But politicians tend not to indulge themselves in losing friends and supporters just for the sake of vengeance; they may need one another at a different time and over a different issue. In the following years new conflicts arose and new candidates led to new alignments. The precise taking-of-sides of the 1979 primary never recurred.

DISCUSSION

A rich ethnography of factionalism has accumulated, each case usually accompanied by explorations of the concept beyond the minimal definition with which this chapter started. In addition, the flow of information is frequently punctuated by theoretical reviews and typology-building. As a result, adjectival factionalism proliferates—pervasive, schismatic, segmentary, parapolitical, polycommunal—depending on the political culture, arenas of conflict, and instigating factors in the particular field of research.

Most of these categories apply to some aspect of the Greenburgh cases; parapolitical factionalism (Easton 1979:52–3; Bailey 1968) seems particularly apt, since it refers to intra institutional strife. However, Easton confines parapolitical systems to internal matters only, which is too narrow a concept for use here. Furthermore the institution can be university, corporation, party organization and so on; and such inclusivity does not provide a suitable comparative framework.

Two major genres of factionalism that do provide one are conflicts among patron-client networks in traditional societies and those within political parties in modern nations: pre-party and intra party factionalism (Landé 1977:ii).[4] In the transition from one kind of society to another, clientage adapts to the new political and economic verities or disappears. Weingrod (1977) emphasizes the latter, pointing out that a political party is much more than a set of dyadic contracts and political patronage is a party-maintenance system, not sets of patron-client ties. However, transition is as transition does (e.g. Scott 1977; Lemarchand 1977) and—recalling Japan—the issue seems open. Whether, or the extent to which, the phenomenon of political patronage, case by case, is functionally or structurally explicable by clientage is arguable. Less acceptable is the idea that in many communities in the United States, including Greenburgh, a declining political patronage system, with or without amorphous remnants of clientage, is related to a thriving factionalism.

A variety of researchers, from different angles, stress that studying the internal workings of local factions is not sufficient to an understanding of them; external relationships must be considered. Strauch

(1983:43) warns that "a typology that specifies a range of possible intra group relations [action sets, factions, parties, movements] . . . does nothing to help us understand the significance a localized group has for higher-level political entities and vice versa." In other words, tracing processual threads means less concern for constrictive definitions and more attention to external linkages. And Nicholson (1972:308–09) observes that in modern democracies "electoral politics, by linking local and national factional systems inevitably complicate[s] the analysis of formal and informal structures. . . ." Thus, the character of national integration changes the form of factional competition. For another example, Aronoff (1977) emphasizes external relations and uses preparty purportedly un-factional ideas in an analysis of factionalism in an Israeli political party: ideology is the basis of factional conflict and success in the power struggle depends on the ability of an at least semi-permanent group to act corporately and mobilize resources outside the party.

Both Greenburgh cases illustrate these conclusions. Separated by a decade, the political climates at the two times were as distinct as could be expected from a country at war and a country at peace—and so was the factionalism. The Concerned Democratic local factionalism emerged from a nationwide movement and external events continued to propel the action. In the Cedric-Tim rivalry, certain district leaders on both sides created the conflict out of internal tensions and played it out in a very small arena. As local events, it should be noted, the internal processes were much the same: the district leaders used the political resources and strategies available to them in order to prevail at relevant resolution-producing primaries. External relations, however, varied.

The Cedric-Tim case followed the classic form of factionalism outlined by the action theorists: alliances were temporary and recruitment was more expeditious than ideological; there was marshaling of resources, a breach of the peace and a showdown; and redressive adaptations followed the final resolution. Throughout, however, the conflict was shaped by national structural elements (party and primary), state structural elements (the township-municipality framework) and the peculiar version of it in Greenburgh (the town wide and the town outside), the political culture of the metropolitan area (individualism unfettered) and the particular local political history. These conditions were not mere backdrops to the action on stage, but integral to it.

If the Cedric-Tim case was embedded in its levels of structural context, the Concerned Democrats' struggle was to change the national power structure and public policy on Vietnam. As with factional politics in Israel, corporate action and external relations on behalf of ideology were imperative. Nationally, the issue was fought out in many areas by a wide network of individuals and organizations. In Westchester, Concerned Democrats—including many district leaders—organized much as were the parties, with local groups coming together, electing leaders, and sending delegates to meetings of a county convention with regional ties to plan the election of peace candidates. The local petition campaign in support of the movement was far more organized and successful than the supposedly corporate party effort. After the war— important among the factors ending it being so many middle class sons dead or with lives disrupted—regional Concerned Democrats tried to funnel their momentum into a permanent faction with a reform agenda. Greenburgh leaders found that activities to that purpose, added to their party responsibilities, were not feasible and soon dissolved their organization but continued issue-related activities within their town committee.

The nature and outcomes of ethnic struggles depend on two sets of facts: the cultural history, experiences and resources of the particular immigrant or native population, and the political economy, cultural history, and social structure of the society in which they live. Some social scientists see a trend toward assimilation in European minorities as third generation family members come of age; paradoxically, this trend has been accompanied by acquisition of political skills and a kindling of interest in roots—a combination that adds to ethnic power. Ethnicity thus becomes a situational political strategy, what Vincent (1971:10), in another context, has called "a mask of confrontation," one to be used when judged to be in the group's interests and to be played down when incorporation in the wider society is thought to be beneficial.

This kind of factionalism, called polycommunal by Nicholson, is recognizable on a macro level but not in the Greenburgh data. Local ethnic or class interests and attitudes are reflected in pervasive factional undercurrents among the district leaders but not in taking sides in showdowns on issues or candidates. In these cases, conservative or liberal ideology seems more explanatory—unless the observer does not know an ethnic mask when she sees one.

It is interesting that the rise in importance of issues in the nation's parties is not reflected in the continued emphasis in the literature on politics as amoral pragmatism and on factional politics as a particularly ruthless and selfish version of it, with power and spoils the only goals. Factionalism is inherent in a party that emphasizes inclusivity and participation; the resulting broad coalitions and shallow consensus inevitably lead to factionalism as part of intra party conflict and decision-making processes. This is not bad: Rosen (1983:61) has remarked that "if one is concerned with limiting the power of leaders [and who is not in the political culture of the United States?], a little bit of anarchy is no dangerous thing." About factionalism, this may be paraphrased to read that if one is concerned with participation and democracy, a sizable dose of factionalism is no dangerous thing.

CHAPTER 7

Summation and Surmise

An ethnography is people-centered, as contrasted with studies focusing on theoretical approaches and models. It is particularly true of this work, which has leaned heavily on letting the forty-seven speak for themselves. Years have passed since they were interviewed and changes have occurred. There is no need to catch up on their personal or work lives as presented in the biographical sketches, but it is appropriate to look at what their leadership experiences have meant to them and what has happened in their political lives. In doing this, the ethnographic present is 1986.

The linked themes of political participation in a democracy, the viability of the parties and intra party factionalism recur throughout this documentation of a special and little-researched political role. They bear on two sets of conclusions about the Greenburgh findings: descriptions and analyses that can be used in comparative studies, and the applicability of the data to practical political considerations.

LOOKING BACK AND GOING AHEAD

As Swartz (1968:6) has pointed out, the scope of the field under study changes as "additional actors enter into the processes or as former participants withdraw and as they bring new types of activities and/or abandon old types." Almost all of the forty-seven, looking back on their years in local politics, are glad that they have at least given politics a fling or at most made it a focal part of their lives. Leon says that his experience on the town committee has been mostly frustration, then adds, "Yet I don't see how you could not do it. That would be abdicating in face of the need, whether it made any difference or not." A few indicate that they feel more worthy as individuals for having been leaders. For example, Brooke says, "It's like being a part of the making of America," Laura that "I'm proud to think of myself as a politician," and Duke has more respect for himself and politics ("I get very defensive of the political system"). Jane, less enthusiastic, describes her leadership as "a wholesome outside activity."

All of the forty-seven say that they are more knowledgeable about government, politics and people than before their leadership. A healthy dose of cynicism is widespread among the leaders or, at least as Hanna, Vi and Chester express it, being "not so naïve." Hanna finds politics a gray area where one should be alert to hidden agendas. Charlie's cynicism has increased but he says that this has stemmed more from national than local politics: "I always thought the government would step in and solve all evil. The Nixon years destroyed all politics for me. After Watergate I was spent." On the other hand, Faith probably catches the spirit of many of the lesser cynics when she says, "I still have faith in people." On the whole, the cynicism seems thinner than the sense of having done something worthwhile. John, who once said, "I was cynical before I came to the thing and I've become more cynical," is an exception. He has now moved beyond cynicism and out of politics. He explains:

> I do not mean anything I said as John. I'm totally not cynical, but these are the facts. I thought I was telling you the truth but I know now that I was covering up the fact that I was like everybody else—after personal power and attention. . . . We have to start all over, re-educate people.

Few leaders think politics has wrought any profound changes in their lives, aside from learning the political facts of life. Those that do cite a greater ability to work with other people, primarily through tolerance of diverging views. As Ralph underlines it, "There's an enormous need for tolerance in politics." Examples are Becca, who says, "To grow, to react. It's been a wonderful experience," and Zoe, "I've grown up. I love the diversity. It keeps the juices running." More restrained are Gene, Conrad, Fred and Sid who think they have "opened up a little" or become "more well-rounded."

Leon thinks—leadership or not—that he has mellowed over the years: "I've had to adjust to the certainty that the political change I want is going to be a long time coming." Lewis is not quite that mellow. He says, "I don't think I can change the world as I did ten years ago. I do think I can slow it up."

The leaders, of course, are neither temperamentally alike nor have they had the same experiences before or after their leaderships. To exemplify the point, Ann and Nino have learned opposite lessons from their political activity. Ann says that now she does not have the courage of her convictions. She has learned not to involve herself with people or issues when it does not seem worth the effort. "I used to think I would never back off." Nino, on the other hand, says, "I more than ever won't back off. I *will* be involved in spite of adversity and defeat."

Most of the forty-seven see minor changes in their attitudes and beliefs due to local political activity. But Cedric says, "I haven't changed. Very few things have changed me."

Twenty-seven of the people interviewed are no longer members of the town Democratic committee:

Fay, Dennis, Leon, Marge and Ralph have moved away, out of the Greenburgh political field.

Ella, Golda, Zoe and Nathan, at different times, reluctantly resigned from the committee, as required by the Greenburgh Code of Ethics, in order to take jobs with the town government.

Gene resigned because he was first appointed and then elected to judicial office in his village.

Vi became disillusioned with some local Democrats and dropped her enrollment in the party.

Cedric changed his enrollment from Democratic to Republican. He immediately ran on that ticket for the town council and then for mayor of Hastings, each time losing.

It took a fatal heart attack to remove Lewis from his beloved politics. Pat, his wife, commented of his memorial service that it was too bad he had to miss the recognition. Elected officials and party leaders came from many corners to pay tribute to the energy and intelligence he dedicated to what he thought was politically right and possible.

For the rest of those who retired from the field, including Nino and Orson, time and interest had simply run out. As Ralph put it, "It's been a lot of fun but it doesn't turn me on any more." Some left with no backward looks but others maintain their interest in politics. It seemed a new era when even Jimmy thought it was time to quit.

Not quite a new era. Twenty-one of the forty-seven are still district leaders:

Becca, Mandy, Hanna, Rita and Ken, Arthur, Polly, Ann, Cali, Faith, Fred, Craig, Jack, Maria, Pepe, Brooke and Tess are still active.

Ilse and Chester, although mayor and trustee, respectively, of Dobbs Ferry, also retain their leaderships, as does Sid while continuing to serve as a member of the town council.

Hanna has been elected town chair with no opposition. Nor was there opposition to Tim succeeding her as executive vice-chair. Pepe retired from the executive committee and Ann joined it. A newly elected county chair has appointed Mandy, who supported him in his contest for the position, as a county vice-chair, in place of Becca, who supported his opponent.

To bring up to date political information about some of the people in the text who are not among the forty-seven:

Tim did not run for a second term on the town council, running instead for the county legislature. He was the town convention's choice, but a new Greenburgh political figure challenged him in a primary, won in an upset, and went on to best his Republican opponent in another upset.

Doris is still a county legislator but in a different district, which had been unsuccessfully gerrymandered against her.

Brad is now a state assemblyman, and Tess works as his local liaison officer.

Vince remains the town supervisor and Rick and Eleanor are still on the council. Eleanor has also taken on the job of being a district leader.

In Hastings, the Democratic majority on the village board holds, and Betty succeeded Tess as the village committee chair.

Greenburgh Democrats in the mid–1980s do not evince the exuberance of the years of the Concerned Democratic movement nor of the 1973 takeover of the town government. But the political system still functions at its lowest official level because, although vacancies occur, vacancies are filled.

THE STORY AND ITS IMPLICATIONS

Curiosity, idealism and pragmatism led the forty-seven into their part-time political venture. Once in the field, they adapted to an accommodating political organization according to their past experiences, individual styles, goals and available time. In fact, the new roles had to be shaped to these earlier attitudinal and behavioral patterns more than the leaders had to change their current life patterns.

The forty-seven were socialized by their families or resocialized by world and national events to take some responsibility for the common good. Over half were professionally or socially motivated to activism in the areas of education, welfare and civil rights. Politically, a third of the leaders trace their leanings back to their parents being "FDR Democrats," or to their own World War II experiences. Others found their way from politically neutral or Republican families. Five leaders had more radical political involvements in the American Labor party and/or support for the Henry Wallace-Paul Robeson presidential ticket of 1948. Later, the Adlai Stevenson presidential campaigns of 1952 and 1956 galvanized both liberals and radicals among the forty-seven. More recently, around twenty of them became heavily committed to the

Vietnam War protest and the Concerned Democratic movement during the 1968 and 1972 presidential primaries.

How does this social and political orientation of the Greenburgh district leaders, as exemplified by the forty-seven, conform to the model of political culture devised by Elazar and tested by him and other political scientists (see pp. 14–15)? Putting aside the European-born among the leaders, the majority of them (thirty-one) were enculturated in or close to the New York metropolitan area. Five or more came as adults from individualistic, individualistic-moralistic, or moralistic-individualistic states. None were raised in a moralistic state and only one is from a traditionalistic sector—southern Indiana.

Valid tests of the Elazar theory are large-scale and statistical, and this study is neither. The expectation from the above socialization data, nonetheless, might be for individualistic orientations to outweigh the moralistic among the forty-seven, whereas the reverse seems just as likely. A simple explanation is that the leaders are not a random sample of the metropolitan area but are to a large extent self-selected, reform-minded and issue-oriented. The Elazar hypothesis, then, is neither validated nor negated here, but accommodated.

Another hypothesis about political socialization is that if adult political experience agrees with what was learned during childhood, the political system will be stable; if early lessons and later experience diverge markedly, change occurs. The general or distal socialization of the forty-seven was not significantly betrayed by their leadership experiences. If their family or other proximal orientations led them to hope for having more impact on decision-making, they were hardly surprised when such expectations did not materialize. In spite of cynicism, politics close up turned out for most leaders to be a more respectable and rewarding pursuit than they had been led to believe.

The fact that the stability of the political system in Greenburgh is not threatened, however, rests on more than a lack of incongruity between expectations and experience. An interrelated factor is the legitimacy of the enveloping authority system, which is solid enough to withstand all but the most egregious failure of expectations.

The local political system operates within a larger social and political context. In one direction, this larger field includes local-level connections with stratarchical political layers and a widening of mainly local concerns into state and national issues. In another direction, at the local level alone, the field also includes various aspects of each leader's community of residence.

Some district leaders carry their party roles with them in nonpartisan social areas and personal networks. But much of life in a complex society, as compared with communities traditionally studied by anthropologists, is compartmentalized into various categories. Many leaders compartmentalize their political life so that it rarely impinges on other activities, is rarely reflected in their community life. A few are part of the political process so spasmodically that the attention they give their political rights and obligations is questionable.

The description of the leadership role in the District Leaders Handbook is ideal, goal-oriented, and of the grassroots. The leader is to bring the party's message to the people and what the people think to the party, with heavy emphasis on identifying Democratic voters and seeing that they get to the polls on time. "Know your district" and "work your district" are the proper guidelines for the leaders.

This role does not fit easily into contemporary life in megalopolis. The constraints on doing an ideal job as leader derive from the quotidian world. There are livings to make, families to take care of, and various other sets of social relationships to maintain. Most of the forty-seven find the grassroots ideal laudable but highly impractical, and they have spotty records of trying to attain it. Hardly any of the leaders are more than temporarily troubled by their failures in living up to the ideal. Whatever their weaknesses, they are aware that they are giving more to the political system than do most of the people they know.

The leaders are also aware that the political system is more flexible than its organizational structure implies—flexible enough to operate, sometimes flourishing and sometimes almost foundering, as disparate individuals pick their way through it. Since both the party strata superiors and the district leaders agree that finding and electing candidates is the main point of their political activity, the relationship between them is reciprocally dependent. The leader-election district relationship, however, is lopsided. In most Greenburgh districts, the political brokerage function is carried out at least to the extent of routine get-out-the-vote telephone calls and often, also, by passing on electoral-related information. But the role of carrying messages from the voters to the party is weakly developed, usually left to election tallies.

Although individually diverse, the leaders share common community values and goals. Or at least they act as if they do, whatever their motivations. The goals the leaders take with them into the field are three-fold, and variously emphasized. Societal goals are the good things they want for community, nation and world. Partisan goals are what they want to do to improve or strengthen their chosen party. And there are personal goals that range from political advancement to maintaining a mere toe hold in local politics.

The forty-seven define power as "influence" and agree that their small piece of public power is their vote within the party organization. The most important voting is in selecting nominees to stand for public office. Leaders relish choosing candidates whom they can help elect, and in a setting in which their input is individually more potent than at the polls.

This power to choose the party's candidates, combined with hard work to elect them, has its ancillary: the power to influence, toward each leader's particular desired outcomes, the people whom they have helped elect. Influencing incumbents is a less concrete activity than choosing candidates. Some incumbents, in the villages at least, give their Democratic committees poor marks in helping them act in office in a practical way. On the other hand, various leaders have experienced a candidate's perceived commitments wisp away from the incumbent's agenda.

The means and skills with which district leaders try to influence one another and public officials are so individual as to defy generalization. Basic to any personal artistry, however, is doing a comparatively good job as a leader and a willingness on occasion to make waves. (Almost any amount of roil will be accepted if it is accompanied by a modicum of activity in the election districts and the party organization.)

Rivalry and competition among individuals, often translated as a "need for power," are widely accepted as universals, although variously manifested both culturally and individually. If this need is indeed universal, it is reasonable to see it as a basic political motivation. In the Greenburgh political system, rivalry is a powerful stimulus to action. Evidence of this for several of the forty-seven is elusive but—and always granting complexity in motivations—it is readily seen among the more active leaders. Without them, there would be only a shadow of a local party organization.

Self-interest, ambition and expediency in political activism are attributes associated with the need for power. Only a handful of the forty-seven explicitly desire patronage, a few more are glad to accept it when the possibility arises, and still more either seek or respond to offers of appointments to non-paying positions on boards and commissions. Relatively few leaders have been willing to run for public office, even when—at least in the villages—their party organization is close to despair for a slate. Only those leaders running for or in elective office consider expediency problematic and discriminate among options in those terms.

If politics is a game, it is a complex one, sometimes fun but often not, and kept going by a host of interrelated cultural and psychological motivations and social behaviors. Among these are the adaptations that district leaders make to their part-time environment and that the party must make to them.

A constant problem of national, state and county party strata is how to exert influence on and extract effort from next level party workers. They do not choose, particularly, to hold so light a rein on local party activists, but adapt to the central fact of their scarcity. The low amount of participation in party affairs at the local level leads to acceptance of almost any participation at all. Greenburgh is an example, but also an exception in a substantial number of its districts. The potential at that level, then, is for a great deal of independence—and conflict.

Greenburgh factionalism is both lamented and indulged in by the forty-seven. Of the two perceptions of factionalism expressed, one is along liberal-conservative lines with strong ethnic or class overtones. In this view, there is a fuzzily-drawn line between white ethnic leaders, with liberal Jews seen to be on one side and conservative Catholics on the other. The former are blamed for the fracture by some leaders because of their activism on such issues as open housing, abortion, group homes, and some foreign policies. Blacks are not seen to be part of a liberal-conservative split, but as taking sides over how to deal with issues of particular concern to them. The other kind of factionalism is among the liberals themselves and is ascribed to rivalry for leadership status, usually in terms of the outs wanting in. In the event of an open break, personality factors, subtle partisan issues and power motivations seem variously mixed in each actor.

The many faces of factionalism depend on the social and cultural context in which the conflict occurs; in this case, the context is parapolitical. The process is an integral part of intra party influence and decision making. Aside from its substantive outcome, the issue-based conflict caused by the Vietnam War policy revitalized the town political organization in a markedly more efficient way. The Cedric-Tim primary of 1979 filled the air with emotion, charges and countercharges, but party unity ensued. Both sides had "taught lessons" to the other; each could afford magnanimity.

The predispositions, values and political activities of the Greenburgh district leaders negate the harsh caricature presented at the opening of this work. They have not noticeably filled their pockets through their partisan offices (unless a politically benign deity was smiling down on Polly when she won a New York state lottery), and their egos have been as often bruised as soothed. Nor can they be described as epitomes of civic virtue, motivated purely by altruism. They are as much amalgams of self-interest and good will as are the many who denigrate or the few who admire them. These low-level politicians are distinctive, however, in their willingness to use a political party to achieve some version of their own visions of the future.

OPINION AND SPECULATION

A study of one's own society, no matter how small the slice, should have potential social impact—again, no matter how small. Sometimes this potential is clear; in other cases the complexity and magnitude of problems in modern societies urge wariness, or at least decorum, in linking observations to advice. But I listen to Burling (1974:12), who urges differently: ". . . if political anthropology is to have any bearing upon our practical political lives, then the political anthropologist had better be willing to climb out on a limb and offer a few judgments and opinions." I will edge a bit out on that limb and offer some fairly strong opinions about political participation, the future of the parties, and primaries and factions.

The Greenburgh experience is uppermost in my mind in the following remarks, but they also reflect ideas gleaned from a sampling of material on party politics in the United States. No local field can stand as the national "type specimen," yet all such locales must share some features by virtue of structure and function—to what extent, we do not know. Few researchers have delved into the great variety of local party experiences. The importance of presidential politics, with its accompanying hurly-burly, absorbs our attention and all but obscures from serious notice grassroots party activity. Surely when the subject is participation, it is opportune to focus on local scenes.

Voting patterns are a lead to thinking about participation in party affairs at the local level. I assume that low voter turnouts impoverish democracy by reducing the accountability of public officials. Vote maximization is in the immediate interest of candidates. In the long run, however, it is in the public interest that the electorate include as many people from as many sectors of our pluralistic society as possible in order that varying and competing concerns be fairly addressed. (In the short run of each election, of course, as a district leader my mode of operating was to each his own.)

Political scientists tell us that two things increase voter turnout: galvanizing issues and organizational effort. Galvanization aside, the decline in voting has gone hand-in-hand with the fading of party influence. That the parties were institutionalized at the local level precisely to get people to the polls, year in and year out, may have some bearing on the relationship. Greenburgh leaders agree that when a district is worked, the vote goes up.

The quid pro quo for election district workers can no longer be simply party patronage—there is too little of it to go around. It must be something else, something that changes "worker" to "activist." It is the chance, because of the democratic environment of local party organizations (Greenburgh cannot be the only one; stratarchy prevails), to chip in on the decision-making, work with others toward common goals, perhaps influence events in one's community—in short, a chance to be listened to. The chance is often virtually there for the taking: the party organizations are in place and they need people.

Across the country, many areas have no party presence at all and even where organizations do exist, they are in likelihood undermanned. The national mood and life's complexities run against facile recruitment of leaders. It is widely believed that partisan politics is dirty, if not downright immoral; that the problems facing us are so overwhelming that no individual can make a difference; and that because the old party bosses are out of business and non-party activists and groups abound, the parties are therefore doomed. These beliefs tend toward self-fulfillment: if one believes that partisan politics is tainted, useless and doomed, why try to use the system? (The answer is a cliché— because it is there.) For the less fatalistic, there are other constraints. Earning a living and bringing up children requires an inordinate amount of time and trouble, and causes stress; and most people do not consider politics a recreational sport. Lives are crowded with choices to make and giving up politics is relatively easy.

Voluntarism is at risk, but it still exists. As the saying goes, there is life in the old party yet.

Organizations, including political parties, wax and wane, and maybe wax again in different guises. A political scientist and an anthropologist, one writing about organizational evolution and the other touching upon the subject in a wider treatment of culture and personality, offer views applicable to the parties.

Kaufman (1985), the political scientist, looks at the life spans of organizations and finds that some are long and others short because of luck—good or bad, in that order.[1] In either case, they usually die for the same reason: they run out of resources. They run out of resources because their "organizational medium" (their total environment, including other organizations and the debris of organizations past) is thick and volatile: "the organizational world bubbles and seethes" (45). Organizations naturally have a difficult time adapting to all that tumult and fall apart, with some bits accruing to other pieces to structure new organizations or—not accruing—left to thicken still more the medium. The evolutionary trend, then, is toward constantly increasing complexity.

I do not see the various organizations of the political pyramid as anywhere near the debris stage of Kaufman's hypothesis. National and state committees aside (nexus or no, my field is essentially local), and in spite of a shortage in the participating-people resource, local activity is a powerful factor. Party relationships with other organizations in the political medium are problematic, however, and adjustments among them are needed. Today's party organizations are not the parties of the past; neither do they appear to have punctuated their equilibrium by any great leap to a new formula for being.

In case I am wrong, and resource problems are about to dismember the parties, there are glimmers of a future, anyway. LeVine (1982), the anthropologist, in discussing change in complex, pluralistic societies,[2] describes ways that shifts in personality dispositions, over time, can result in altered institutional norms. One of the ways is through organizational competition and selection. The scenario: ideological preferences vary in a population; personal decisions are made about which organizations to join, and most of them will be for those whose ideological solutions are already normative in the society; but in time people may become discontented with the selected organizations; other groups, seeing the opportunities, will offer other solutions; and in the resulting competition, some of the innovations will be selected for.

It is easy to put the political parties in this picture, but here comes the glimmer; in LeVine's words: "diverse psycho-social solutions of potential adaptive value are often stored not merely as cultural memories . . . but as ongoing organizations, often small and sectarian in nature, that are ready to expand when conditions are more propitious to their message" (160). Faded institutions may hang around somewhere just long enough for innovators, out of need, to twist them into something more catchy with the public. Not perfect, but a making do with the cultural materials at hand (inclusivity, flexibility, pluralism, and so on) and finding ways to take advantage of existing opportunities.

The great political innovation of the century has already been made, imposed by reformers from outside the parties: the direct primary. It has not entirely lived up to its promise of more public participation in politics, but it is popular and its use is still spreading. Many politicians loathe the institution because it has weakened the power of the parties. For example, New York Senator Daniel Patrick Moynihan (1986), perhaps forgetting that it was a primary that put him in the political big time, warns:[3]

> The only reason serious people will give serious time to work for a political party is that by doing so, they have some say as to whom their party nominates, and with luck, elects to office. Reduce that possibility—

as the primary system does . . . —and the uses of a political party are two: debating practice or plunder.

This is not a point that plays at a local level (nor probably at higher ones). I see the competition of primaries as essential to a healthy party system, even before the edge provided candidates by wealth is solved: primaries are a means to make the parties responsive to public concerns, keep them on their toes, so to speak. In any case, no amount of grumbling will make them go away (maybe some tinkering with the rules. . .). Voting is light in primaries, but people would nonetheless surely fight to keep the right to that franchise.

Since I believe that competition in politics is good and there ought to be more of it, I do not look askance at intra party factionalism, as many party people do. I am glad, however, that pitched conflict is controlled to a conclusion by the mechanics of the direct primary.

A political commentator (Reeves 1982), back from an "American Journey," finds that the nation has become more democratic than it was a hundred years ago. In just a few decades, so have the political parties. If this makes them "weaker," so be it: muscle-flexing seems less appropriate in their country-cousin role as semi-official constituent parts of government than does the facilitating behavior of political brokers between government and polity.

My worry about the party situation is that so little is known about local organizations, the places where the largest number of the public, short of voting booths, can be politically involved—and thereby add validity to the political system in general. Aggregate polling and voting data and brief human relations news squibs on election eves are helpful but not enough. To get a sense of the country at large, it would be good to know what is happening in a whole array of micro political fields: social, economic and political milieux, contingencies, events, and above all, relationships. We should look at, in anthropologist Gallaher's words in another context (Clinton 1979:viii), "grass roots laid bare." This means that the field should be broader than the one considered here, and cover other than partisan political activity.

Anthropology's pre-adaptation to small scale research and its more recent interest in micro-macro linkages might well add significantly to political science's longer research record in the politics of the United States. Further, perhaps political anthropologists who are professionally interested in their own society can develop a surer and louder voice than they have to date to the debate about the nation's value choices— the future—and about the practice of politics.

Alternative Futures?

In my discipline there is a research effort called "urgent anthropology" that aims to catch ethnographically—before they vanish forever—other peoples' ways of making a living, getting along together, and thinking about the unknown. The idea is that every group's adaptations to its physical and social environment add to our understanding of the human potential in general. Its implementation is primarily through qualitative methods.

I am reminded of this by the concentrated attention paid the party decline thesis by many political scientists—urgent political science, one might say. In this case, the urgency results from the vital connection researchers see between the party system in the United States and democracy itself. The parties have had a constituent function in linking the people with the government; do they today?

During my years as a district leader, I was only marginally familiar with political science literature; my reading about politics ran to accounts by or about politicians—Edward Costikyan's "Behind Closed Doors," Mike Royko's "Boss," and the "Diaries of Mario Cuomo," for example. It was only while writing this ethnography that I realized how heavily I must lean on political science in making sense of my own practical experience. Now, the work done, it seems appropriate to turn about, to encapsulate what some political scientists portend for the parties, and reflect on these views from my admittedly narrow vantage.

In doing this I pass over certain past and current intra discipline debates about the quixotic possibility of creating "responsible" parties (that is, ones designed to decide on policy programs and to see that candidates and incumbents toe the party line), "realignments" (major shifts in the make-up of a party's electorate, thus power), and whether the effects of various party reforms have been good or bad. As important as these issues are, not enough in my experience qualifies me to comment on them.

I turn to two questions that continue to be relevant into the 1990s: What do plummeted voter turnouts and widespread disaffection for the parties mean for the political system? Are the parties in a death struggle with that strange mixture of concern with issues, media images, and manipulative political consultants that is called the "new politics"? I do not address the condition of the party in government because attention there is on legislatures and the presidency, again pretty much outside of my field of research.

The political scientists I selected represent a continuum from worst case scenarios to chipper don't-nail-the-coffin-shut-yet views. All of them are behaviorists who test their generalizations with quantitative methods and, in proof of their conclusions, present the data in banks of tables. But some are more, especially the first.

If Walter Dean Burnham is not the apical ancestor of the party decline theory, he is the most renowned of its lineage. This is not so much due to his priority in describing across-the-board party degeneration and the "disappearance" of masses of working class voters, as it is to the historical depth and socioeconomic breadth of his explanation of how this political crisis developed, what its significance is for a democratic state, and why there is scant chance of things getting better.

The explanation is complex. Most of it can be found in two publications: a work on critical elections and realignment (1978) and a collection of his articles (1982) dating from 1965 to 1981, the last of which is original. In these writings he weaves a comprehensive pattern out of causal strands of a core political culture, a class structure with political implications, and changing national and global social and economic conditions that led to the rise and fall of the "political capitalist state."

Burnham describes a conflicted political culture: on the one hand, a liberal tradition valuing individualism and property rights shaped the new United States constitutionally and continues to dominate the culture; on the other, a countervailing but weaker cultural theme has been and is mass democratic participation through a collectivising party system that has prevailed only after disastrous events affecting multitudes (the Civil War, the Great Depression). For historical reasons, socialist or laborite ideas are absent in the mainstream culture— "excluded alternatives," Burnham calls them.

The class structure depicted by Burnham is composed of an essentially nonpartisan capitalistic elite; a large, diversified middle class; and the lower and working classes, which are so split along ethnic and occupational lines as to be broadly unorganizeable. Because of this cleavage and prevailing individualism, the lower classes are not proportionately reflected in the electorate, and policy choices depend on middle class interests and elite power (Burnham notes that a class struggle is going on but only the rich seem to know, hence are winning it).

As the slicing of the nation's economic pie counts the lower classes out, Burnham believes, more and more of them count themselves out of the political system. The fact that the majority party that is supposed to aggregate power for the powerless either cannot or will not, leads him to place the onus of decline on the party organizations and the party in government instead of on a moody electorate.

Burnham calls the United States a political capitalist state because the political economy is managed in support of a capitalist version of democracy. This state of the state dates from the New Deal but it flourished during postwar conditions of a fairly stable world order, United States hegemony in it, and an economic boom that meant capitalist growth and private-sector affluence. Governmental policy consisted of encouragement of consumer spending and achievement of social harmony through welfare for the needy. As long as the state had a growing surplus, the strain between capitalist and democratic goals was camouflaged.

The bubble burst in the 1970s: decline of capital accumulation led to a debt economy; although savings were now the name of the game consumerism continued to climb; general well-being deteriorated and the poor suffered. As Burnham sees it, public policy choices now in the market place are some kind of a welfare state with dwindling resources or a neo-laissez faire economy—both choices supportive of capitalism. The "current crisis" is that neither of these choices will lead to a democratized, participatory polity.

Theoretically, political parties are the only forces capable of aggregating the interests of common people but, he believes, ours have failed us: the Republican party is in the throes of a crusade to revitalize industrial capitalism and finalize the class struggle; the Democratic party—with its elites part of the capitalist establishment, its intellectuals in sterile disarray, and its organizations ineffectual—lies in ruins.

Given this precarious state of affairs, Burnham offers some "if this, then that" possibilities, one wish, and a more probable development. First: if the great middle class is radicalized, then policy choices may change; if the Democratic party relates to the party of nonvoters, then meaningful change can occur; if the Republicans cut entitlements, then voters may turn to the Democrats (which would only make a difference if that party had some new ideas). In fact, Burnham regards all of his if-thens highly unlikely except this one: if the neo-laissez faire program is successful, then public policy would grossly favor the rich, have little effect on the upper middle class, and be very bad for classes below that, increasingly so in downward order.

Burnham's wish is that a social-democratic party will break the excluded-alternative barrier with an "agenda for a democratic collective purpose." A corollary is that the mass electorate change its ways and organize behind such a program. All this he also deems highly unlikely.

His probable scenario is one designed to make us sit up and take notice—even action. Burnham recalls that in the past, cataclysmic events have led to the setting and achieving of national goals through collective action. He sees the current crisis as our political system spinning off into disaster, or a series of disasters, either economic or military. Would cataclysm do the job again?

In Martin Wattenberg's behavioral study of party decline (1984) the gloom and doom is dressed up as good news: a growing number of the electorate do not dislike the parties, they simply do not think much about them one way or another. They are neutral, not hostile. Even people who distrust the government and are politically cynical do not necessarily think badly of parties. To Wattenberg, who is supportive of parties, this is good news because it leaves the door open to party renewal and a refurbished image.

His analysis, however, is heavily pessimistic. He describes an aura of nonpartisanship enveloping the legislative bodies and the presidency, in the latter case leading to expansion of its powers and demagogic appeals to the people. Believing in partisanship as a framework for stability and conflict resolution, Wattenberg finds that quality in deep trouble: ties between parties and candidates loosen as the campaign relationship between candidates and media strengthens; party identification as "perceptual screening" is replaced by a voter volatility that, in the contest for swing voters, leads to negative campaign strategies.

Wattenberg refutes the idea that issues and organization can increase the saliency of parties. Issues and parties have become so divorced, he observes, that however catalytic the issues, they cannot revive the parties. As for organization, Wattenberg states that "some local political organizations can play an important role in some electoral outcomes." But this brief nod is followed by the caution that the potential of these organizations should not be exaggerated since they have not been very active for decades and, in fact, are likely to become even more dispensable as political action committees provide services for candidates once given by the parties.

Apparently the news about the opening door of revitalization is not all that good. Wattenberg does, however, have a recipe for it, of sorts: improve the public image of the parties. Short-term concentration on candidates and issues must be transformed into long-term stability by re-introducing party into the equation; political leaders and the media might help by treating the parties more fairly.

After this mixture of faint hope and harsh fact, the only prediction— as opposed to what ought to be—that Wattenberg makes is anticlimactic: "There seems to be no danger that the parties will suddenly vanish from the scene and leave catastrophic political and social chaos in their wake."

Frank Sorauf and Samuel Eldersveld, both authors of well-received political science texts as well as other analytical works, form the middle stretch of my anxiety continuum, where a break occurs between pessimism and optimism. Sorauf (1967, 1984) comes first not because he is so much worried about the famous decline as because he accepts it with comparative equanimity; he faces squarely the difference between describing what *is* and what one *wishes* were true; and he wastes no sympathy on the parties in their decline-induced pain.

Sorauf complains that too many of his peers write too much about what ought to be—a fault he suspects is due to over identification with their research subject. He also thinks that even in their golden age the parties were not all that great, and that political scientists are oversold on the idea that parties are the indispensable agents of democracy.

The thrust of Sorauf's analysis is toward killing the dragon of "the party supremacy myth." He describes the parties as slipping into atrophy because of long range societal changes and the nature of the electorate. Parties change because the electorate changes, and it changes according to what choices are available in the environment. And there are a lot of political alternatives—"a vast multitude of organizations"— out there offering competitive ways of participation. The parties, their monopoly broken, are only one of them.

There seems to be something for everyone in all this fragmented specialization. Politically sophisticated voters can pick and choose as they please, the less sophisticated can depend on a televised charismatic smile instead of a party symbol, and candidates can even "rent a party" if they wish—campaign managment firms are also out there. Dependent variables that they are, the parties succumb; at least, Sorauf believes, their decentralized local organizations do.

Although Sorauf allows that predictions about politics in the United States "are very perishable," he does take a peek at the future. After his dismal picture of the parties, he asks a series of rhetorical questions: "What happens . . . when large numbers of voters repeatedly feel more strongly about a candidate and an issue than they do about a party? What happens when large numbers of voters decide that they no longer need the ready-made, all-purpose, prepackaged judgment of a political party? Above all, what happens when that voter disenchantment takes place at the same time that candidates find ways of communicating with voters outside the usual channels of the party organization?" Well, more decline and eventual fall, right?

Wrong. He is not talking death, he says. What is more, "there are signs that the decline of the parties is leveling off." The parties, it seems, are settling into a reduced but stable political role. And—edging toward that forbidden "ought"—he writes that "many observers" are troubled by the thought of what might happen to democracy if the parties weaken even further; what institution, then, will have the desire or the resources to mobilize for elections "sheer numbers" of the individually powerless to countervail strong minority elites?

Sorauf seems to be suggesting a party decline not unto death, but unto a condition of perhaps being eaten alive by the organizational denizens of Kaufman's seething political environmental medium. And when you come right down to it, he does not seem to really like the idea that the parties "do not have a guaranteed future."

If Sorauf represents an equivocal tag to the first part of the continuum, Eldersveld (1982) clearly calls for a more optimistic reading of the health of the parties. He does not bury and then exhume them for a walk-on role, but is a dispassionate defender of—although he does not use the term—party primacy. His analysis is fully buttressed by behavioral data, and also relies on "normative requisites" as to how well the parties work.

For the most part, Eldersveld is only inferentially predictive as he examines the strands of thought that make up the decline thesis and evaluates the evidence in support or refutation of them. He considers questions, first, about the party organizations:

"Had party organizations' activities declined at the local level?" No. Activism is probably greater and just as efficient as pre-decline activism. More people, and from a wider socioeconomic spread, report being contacted by party campaign workers.

"Are the local party activists less likely to be competent than previously?" This is asking whether they are more amateur than professional, more ideological than pragmatic, and Eldersveld sees no evidence of such a trend; the parties have always been wide open to participants of various bents.

"Is party organization at the local level less important today?" The data do not support the impression that local organizations have been superseded by the mass media or scorned by incumbents.

"Has party organization at the state and national level become weaker?" If they have, the evidence is lacking.

Obviously Eldersveld's conclusions about party organizations do not jibe with Wattenberg's and Sorauf's. The picture changes, however, with the last question: "Has there been a decline in the public affect for and confidence in the parties?" The data are overwhelming that voting has declined precipitously and so has public identification with and confidence in the parties. (In view of this, his earlier statement that a majority of the electorate still do identify with a party, and only a minority feel negative about them or do not believe in their problem-solving ability, is somewhat less comforting.)

Eldersveld presents his two sets of conclusions as paradoxical: why do not party performance and party image match? Besides mostly negative media blitzes, he believes that the messages sent by some local party activists may undermine the perception of party or even have a boomerang effect. And that when the organizations have worthy news, they often do not know how to communicate it. Efforts to carry out and improve party functions, he suggests, must be *visible* efforts. In short, the local party organizations need public relations skills.

Only once does Elderveld come close to making a real prediction about the future: "It is highly likely" that the parties will continue to undergo incremental rather than radical changes, and that they "will adapt to new societal conditions."

Eldersveld's conclusions about party performance are shared by and partly based on the work of a number of other researchers. Political science is awash in behavioral data on the party in the electorate and in government (tallies of elections and legislative votes are public information, and thoroughly analyzed), but research on party organizations is usually decades old. Recognizing this, some political scientists have set to work to fill the data gap with the intent of relating their findings to the decline thesis. They were more or less surprised to discover that the party organizations are getting along just fine—or at least as well as in pre-decline days—from the national committees on down.

One such group of scholars is John Bibby, Cornelius Cotter, James Gibson, Robert Huckshorn (for once in alphabetical order), and various others that these men, singly or in combination, have worked with. It is relevant to the task they assumed that three of the four are not only academics but practitioners at the national and state levels in party and/or government posts. It was from this vantage that they wondered if party decline were not a more complex process than had been thought.

Their papers and publications abound but I refer only to two of them: Cotter et al. (1984), in which their thesis is most fully presented and which deals primarily with state parties and secondarily with local organizations, and Gibson et al. (1985), which expands on the latter. Both are cross-national comparative studies based on responses to questionnaires and some interviews, in the one case of past and present state organization chairs and in the other of current county chairs (or their equivalents). Chair recall and questionnaire responses are the substance of their data base.

The studies led to conclusions that bear on the future of the parties: approaching the 1980s, both state and county organizations were stronger than in the 1950s and probably more active, and were at least as active as parties in the mid-1960s. This, in spite of having lost some of their nominating and campaign functions. The state parties were more professional, integrative with other party units, outreaching to other groups, learning to use new communication technologies, and in a position to react to societal changes.

The county study was longitudinal in that a 1964 national survey was comparable to the new data. County leadership, to a lesser extent than state, was also becoming more professional; its components (precinct, ward, district, whatever), although more personalized and voluntaristic entities, were also active. The researchers state that, contrary to conventional political wisdom, the counties were, in general, successful in filling their leadership positions from top to bottom. The 1985 publication sums all this up with a rather nice pun: its title is "Whither the Local Parties?" and its conclusion is that they have "neither withered nor are they withering."

In explaining the similar or increased strength (the language varies) of local party organizations, the authors suggested that state party strength is one of the revitalizing agents. The data did not bear this out, however; they came to the conclusion that local party strength is independent of state party strength, that local factors are determinate.

These researchers have doubts about reports of electoral hostility or indifference, but the doubts aside, they conclude that an umbrella theory of party change must include organizational success. Their prediction is that the parties will survive by innovating ways of handling problems resulting from the direct primary, other electoral conditions, and nonparty competition.

Another group of scholars puts the seal on at least some of these predictions. William Crotty (1986) and some associates (including Eldersveld, as well as Richard Murray, Kent Tedin, Anne Hopkins and Dwaine Marvick) have investigated parties in five large urban areas (Chicago, Detroit, Los Angeles, Houston and Nashville) by interviewing and using questionnaires for ward and precinct members (or their equivalents) in the 1980 presidential election year. Of this group, Crotty came directly from a published record (1984) of depicting the party situation as bleak, envisioning a no-party era unless the electorate shaped up and revived the parties. He repeated this prediction (1985), but in this case he was already fully involved in his urban research and now saw the possibility that the local parties, rather than being dead, may simply be unappreciated. He also weighed an alternative view that the parties might be in a cultural-lag mode, and had not yet caught up with the electorate's bad mood.

The 1986 research asked if party decline was so great that traditional party roles were drastically changing. The study group found a great deal of diversity among their research targets—which was expected because of historical and environmental variations of the selected communities (another political wisdom is that local parties respond more sensitively to the political culture of their communities than can upper level party organizations). Commonalities, however, led Crotty to the following conclusions:

The competitiveness of nonparty organizations vis-á-vis the parties is not seen by party people as very influential or active in most campaigns. In all of the five cities the parties carried out their conventional campaign duties with an impressive "intensity of effort." These conclusions were reinforced by the longitudinal research conducted by Eldersveld and Marvick: change, but no atrophy.

Whatever professionalization and bureaucratization that has occurred at national and state party levels, both the Cotter group and the Crotty group found local level party organizations in general (Chicago aside) conforming to the stratarchical model.

All of the political scientists cited in the epilogue have, in different degrees, a macro view of party politics, whereas my basic data are micro. I do not use this space to rehash my speculations in the preceding chapter or macro implications elsewhere in the text. Instead I try to understand the dissonance among the views presented, and only once juxtapose a place-specific observation and a behavioral finding.

Two or more political scientists have remarked that if we did not have political parties, we would have to invent them. The continuum selectees, with the barely possible exception of Sorauf, believe in the theoretical importance of parties for a democratic state, even while they see real-life parties as either beyond redemption, or in need of some piece-work reinvention, or doing well enough to ameliorate declinomania.

In discussing these differences, I put aside the circumstance that Burnham describes the parties as causing electorate shrinkage while Sorauf attributes the decline of party organizations to changes in the electorate. In fuller expositions both make clear that causal arrows are neither unidirectional nor limited to two sources. A more relevant matter is understanding why at one end of the continuum we have party degeneration and at the other, organizations clicking along on time. (Of course, I placed them there, but for a reason.) It seems evident that these researchers are using different criteria in defining success and failure.

Burnham's criterion is the ability to direct public policy by amassing an electorate behind a program for collective well-being. The parties' failure is defined by policies in fact enacted and symbolized by all those missing working class voters. It is a macro truth that socioeconomic justice in the United States is far from being achieved and at present is in a back-tracking mode; it is a truism that the rich are getting richer and the poor are getting poorer. The extent to which party organizations (and the party in government) buck that trend varies, but on the whole is questionable. Why else does Burnham see a party "in ruins" where others see strength? Whatever his awareness of local party activities and their resonance, the "crisis" looms.

It is interesting that while Burnham uses New York as the nadir specimen of voter turnout, Gibson et al. rank the state's local organizations with the three highest in the nation in party strength. In addition, New York political scientist Howard Scarrow (1983) describes the two major parties as the primary political organizations in the state and its county organizations as strong. Concerning voter turnout and the parties, he writes, "without them turnout on election day would be even lower."

Whereas the Burnham view of party is value-laden, the Cotter et alias and Crotty et ceteras have a technical goal—strong parties—and a long list of value-free criteria relating to bureaucratization and professionalism to assess how well campaign activities, organization maintenanace, and the integration of national and state parties are carried out. For local organizations the performance of "traditional" or "conventional" roles is cited.

If setting local agendas or engaging in factionalism are thought traditional, it is not noted. And neither lead authors Gibson, Cotter, nor Crotty, in summary remarks, make anything of the nature of leader-electorate contacts. For example, Eldersveld's puzzle about the relationship of party performance to party image is not taken up.

Wattenberg's and Sorauf's assessment of party organizations to the contrary, these researchers have amply demonstrated their viability in general (far from in toto) and the lack of symmetry in two of the party dimensions—the electorate and the organizations. What remains to be seen are the implications of a class-skewed, shrunken electorate and similarly class-skewed (no behavioral data; assumed), strong party organizations.

I cannot resist an anecdotal, place-specific postscript to one conclusion. Never thinking that party organizations had faded away, I am not surprised by their rediscovery. I am surprised, however, at the high level of participation apparently seen in them. Recruitment of district leaders in Greenburgh *is* often difficult, and once recruited, eliciting work may become a problem. Other party watchers agree. But the behavioral et als refute this because county chairs answered questionnaires to the effect that they have kept positions filled.

At least in Westchester the local chairs and not the county chair do the recruiting and have the difficulty, and all chairs are elected by their district leaders. A decade-later story also provides a clue to the difference in observational and behavioral conclusions. In response to a reporter asking about recent local elections, the Democratic and Republican county chairs agreed that political party participation was undergoing general erosion, and the Democrat added, "The problem is keeping local organizations alive. Forget about prodding. The political parties are semi-destroyed. . . . They're aging and dying" (*New York Times* Westchester Section 3-29-87). This sounds as if the Westchester organizations are in shambles. Doubting that the situation is quite that bad, I wonder how the county chair would reply to a questionnaire about the state of his organization. Maybe the same, but I like to think—mellowed—he would put aside his frustrations and remember mostly good things accomplished.

To conclude: All of the continuum scholars, except for Burnham, are remarkably prudent in predicting the ultimate fate of the parties; many bets are hedged along the way. As for acceptable *alternatives* to the parties, prudence gives way to collective failure of imagination, and none are suggested. Technology had its Jules Verne, but futuristic social fictions have been notably less successful.

There may well be a way other than the potential of the party system to collectively empower the individually powerless. If so, these political scientists have not thought of it. Nor have I.

Notes

CHAPTER 1

1. With few exceptions, material about or including our own political systems has been left to the other social sciences or consists of generalizations and historical data about top-level political phenomena (e.g. Burling 1974; Fallers 1974; Weatherford 1981). Ethnographic data on local level politics, species USA, are scarce except for what appears in research on particular ethnic or disadvantaged neighborhoods (e.g. Esman 1985; Susser 1982).

2. Moore sees people's actions (in events or institutions) as resulting from the interplay of two processes: regularization by normative ideals (the cultural rules) and social adjustment to particular situations (improvised interactions). That which is culturally regulated is "determinacy" and that which is not culturally regulated—that is, in areas of ambiguity and uncertainty—is "indeterminacy."

3. W. L. Bennett's article (1983) on elections as political rituals invoking mythic models of society, and characterized by circular rather than rational thinking, banal appeals, and personality cults is clever enough to stand as satire alone although it is presented as a cultural perspective of political processes.

4. This was the heading used for a section of the Letters column, *The New York Times*, 6–30–86.

CHAPTER 2

1. The only Democrat elected to the town council before 1973 was a black who won by a handful of absentee ballots. He did not serve long before his employment took him out of the area.

2. Had I been successful in interviewing the three black men who had agreed to it, my sample would have been very slightly above the black representation on the full town committee. However, one of the men died of a heart attack, another disappeared from the field for months, and the other turned out to be white.

CHAPTER 3

1. Quotations are from the Westchester Section of *The New York Times*, 9–16–79.

CHAPTER 4

1. In a news story in *The New York Times*, 4–16–83.
2. Election inspectors are increasingly hard to recruit, and the town has recently resorted to advertising for applicants to fill these party jobs.
3. Bailey's interest in gamesmanship has been termed "game theory" here and by others (Vincent 1978; Lewellen 1983), but that term has long been applied to an abstract mathematical discipline to predict optimal behavior of participants in games of strategy in various kinds of situations (Morgenstern 1968), and Bailey explicitly denies any ability in that direction. His idea of game as analogy or metaphor is only a very distant relative to quantitative game theory. In fact, some anthropologists have been interested in applying the latter to anthropological problems, without notable success (Kronenfeld 1970; Levinson and Malone 1980:24).

CHAPTER 5

1. This track record was broken in the 1990 election for two trustees. Concern about a development issue led the Democratic and Republican committees to agree on running the same slate of one Democrat and one Republican in order to defeat a possible third party opposition.
2. Since the mid-1970s, the national committees have tried to balance the power relationships between them and state and local party organizations by expanding their activities in helping candidates at those levels, making and enforcing rules for the national conventions, and increasing both their coffers and their staffs; nevertheless, both parties have been "forced to recognize the limits of national party influence in state and local politics" (Bibby 1986:79).

CHAPTER 6

1. It is only fair to point out that Sadie as a participant observer has appeared at other places in this work with no strain on her conscience to identify herself. For the record, however, she may be found on the following pages:
   p. 87. She was the queasiest of all.
   p. 115. She was the leader "who was impressed with a presentation."
   p. 121. She was the leader who made calls for Duke.
   p. 123. She was one of the leaders who looked for another candidate.
   p. 123. She was a converted past critic of Paul's.

p. 126. She was a member of the nominating committee strongly against cross-endorsement and for running a candidate against William.

As for Sadie's political sketch, she was brought up in a settlement house (Abraham Lincoln Centre) in Chicago, one of the three children of the Unitarian minister who was dean of the Centre, and his wife who managed its household affairs. Her training in anthropology was at the University of Chicago and, briefly, in Mexico, where she met her husband. His career was in the United States government in cross-culturally related jobs and in the United Nations. They had three sons and the family moved to Hastings in 1959.

Although always enrolled Democrats, Sadie's parents voted for Norman Thomas for president until Franklin Roosevelt's second term, and never again strayed from the Democratic line. She has always been a Democrat, but does not consider it a sin to split one's vote now and then.

Sadie held responsible positions in the PTA and the Fair Housing Committee in Hastings. She served as an election inspector for several years, then as captain in her district, and then as leader. She served as vice-chair of the Hastings Democratic committee for four years, and another four years as chair. She remained on the Greenburgh and Hastings committees for the next six years. Having decided in 1983 that she didn't do train stations any more and in 1984 that neither did she do door-to-door, Sadie decided to go cold turkey, and resigned as district leader in 1985. She retains a chair-appointed position on the Hastings committee, and volunteers episodically for the Greenburgh committee.

2. Frank later denied making exactly this statement. Whatever the words, it was clear to Sadie that the reference was to two Hastings nominating committee events, the first recounted on p. 120 and the second when Cedric took himself out of consideration for personal reasons.

3. It is pure speculation, but one that was widely made, that the congressman had not appreciated having his truthfulness challenged by Tim on the occasion of his own nomination in town convention.

4. Lewellen (1983:109) refers to intra party conflict as "common parlance" factionalism, an emic phrasing with an oddly dismissive tone.

CHAPTER 7

1. Kaufman's evolutionary model is not Darwinian, in spite of the "Natural Selection" in his title. It is the primordial process of chemical evolution before genetic heredity came into the picture. He does not worry about whether that theory is true or not; it just fits his idea of what happens with organizations.

2. LeVine uses the Darwinian variation-selection model (genotype plus environment results in the phenotype) not in a biological sense but analogically; his focus is on personality development and socialization. The personality genotype sets boundaries to individual functioning: probably basically genetic, it is also a set of enduring psychological dispositions to respond emotionally in certain ways as a result of early childhood experience. The personality phenotype is observable patterns of behavior and attitudes, which are conscious

responses to the environment. It is the outcome of the modification of the genotype by long exposure to the norms of the society through both experience and deliberate socialization.

3. The senator was reacting to two 1986 current events: the scandal of political corruption in New York City and the Illinois Democratic primary, in which twenty-five percent of the party enrollment voted, and elected two unknown, non-Democratic extremists to be their candidates for office. Since the Illinois party organization was apparently asleep from top to bottom, it is hard to blame the primary process instead of the organization for the discomforting event.

References

Adams, Richard N. 1975. Energy and Structure: A Theory of Social Power. Austin: University of Texas Press.

Almond, Gabriel. 1956. "Comparative Political Systems." In Journal of Politics, August.

Almond, Gabriel and Sidney Verba. 1965. Civic Culture. Little, Brown.

Antoun, Richard. 1979. Low-Key Politics: Local-level Leadership and Change in the Middle East. Albany: State University of New York Press.

Aronoff, Myron J. 1977. Power and Ritual in the Israeli Labor Party. Ansen/ Amsterdam: Van Gorcum.

———. 1980. "Ideology and Interest: The Dialectics of Politics." In Ideology and Interest: the Dialectics of Politics, Political Anthropology V I, Myron J. Aronoff, ed. New Brunswick, NJ: Transaction: 1-29.

———. 1983. "Conceptualizing the Role of Culture in Political Change." In Culture and Political Change, Political Anthropoloogy V II, Myron J. Aronoff, ed. New Brunswick, NJ: Transaction: 1-19.

Baber, Willie L. 1985. "Political Economy and Social Change: The Bisette Affair and Local-level Politics in Morlse-Vert." In American Ethnologist V2 N 3: 489-504.

Bailey, F. G. 1968. "Parapolitical Systems." In Local-level Politics, Mark Swartz ed. Chicago: Aldine: 291-294.

———. 1969. Stratagems and Spoils: A Social Anthropology of Politics. NY: Schocken.

———. 1970. Politics and Social Change: Orissa in 1959. Berkeley: University of California Press.

Balandier, Georges. 1970. Political Anthropology. NY: Random House.

Barnouw, Victor. 1985. Culture and Personality, 4th ed. Homewood, Ill: Dorsey Press.

Barth, Frederick. 1959. Political Leadership among the Swat Pathans. London: Athalone.

Bennett, John W. 1967. "Microcosm-Macrocosm Relationships in North American Agrarian Society." In American Anthropologist V 69: 441-454.

———. 1985. "The Micro-Macro Nexus: Typology, Process, and System." In Micro and Macro Levels of Analysis in Anthropology: Issues in Theory and Research, DeWalt and Pelto eds. Boulder, CO: Westview Press: 23-51.

Bennett, W. Lance. 1983 [1980]. Culture, Communication, and Political Control. In Culture and Political Change, Political Anthropology V 2, Myron J. Aronoff ed. New Brunswick, NJ: Transaction: 39–52.

Bernstein, Richard. 1983. Beyond Objectivism and Relativism. Philadelphia: University of Pennsylvania Press.

Bibby, John F. 1986. "Party Trends in 1985: Constrained Advance of the National Party." In Publius V 16, N 3: 79–91.

Boissevain, Jeremy. 1974. Friends of Friends: Networks, Manipulators and Coalitions. Oxford: Blackwell.

Britan, Gerald M. and Roland Cohen, eds. 1980. Hierarchy and Society. Philadelphia: Institute for the Study of Human Issues.

Buchanan, James M. 1984. "Politics without Romance: A Sketch of Positive Public Choice Theory and Its Normative Implications." In The Theory of Public Choice 11, James M. Buchanan and Robert D. Tolleson, eds. Ann Arbor: University of Michigan Press.

Buchanan, James M. and Gordon Tullock. 1962. The Calculus of Consent. Ann Arbor: University of Michigan Press.

Bujra, Jane. 1973. "The Dynamics of Political Action: A New Look at Factionalism." In American Anthropologist V 75: 132–152.

Burling, Robbins. 1974. The Passage of Power. NY: Academic Press.

Burnham, Walter Dean. 1967. "Party Systems and the Political Process." In The American Party System: Stages of Development. William Chambers and Walter Burnham, eds. NY: Oxford University Press.

——. 1978. Critical Elections and the Dynamics of Politics. NY: Oxford University Press.

——. 1982. The Current Crisis in American Politics. NY: Oxford University Press.

Clammer, John. 1985. Anthropology and Political Economy: Theoretical and Asian Perspectives. NY: St. Martin's Press.

Clinton, Charles. 1979. Local Success and Federal Failure. Cambridge: ABT.

Cohen, Abner. 1974. Two-Dimensional Man. Berkeley: University of California Press.

Cohen, Eugene N. 1974. "Political Conflict and Social Change in an Italian Commune." In American Ethnologist V 1 N 2: 243–253.

Cohen, Ronald. 1973 [1970]. "The Political System." In A Handbook of Method in Cultural Anthropology, Raoul Naroll and Ronald Cohen, eds. NY: Columbia University Press: 489–499.

Comstock, Anita Inman. 1984. "Rural Westchester to the Turn of the Century: Farmers, Squires and Just Plain Folk." In Westchester County: The Past Hundred Years, Marilyn Weigold, ed. NY: Westchester Historical Society.

Cotter, Cornelius P., James L. Gibson, John F. Bibby and Robert J. Huckshorn. 1984. Party Organization in American Politics. NY: Praeger Publishers.

Crotty, William. 1984. American Politics in Decline, 2d ed. Boston: Little, Brown and Co.

——. 1985. The Party Game. NY: W. H. Freeman and Co.

Crotty, William, ed. 1986. Political Parties in Local Areas. Ithaca, NY: University of Tennessee Press.

Dahl, Robert. 1956. "Hierarchy, Democracy and Bargaining in Politics." In Political Behavior, Heinz Eulau, Samuel J. Eldersveld, and Morris Janowitz eds. Glencoe, IL: The Free Press.

Davis, Marvin. 1980. "Two Dimensional Politics: Political Action and Meaning in Rural West Bengal." In Ideology and Interest: The Dialectics of Politics, Political Anthropology V I, Myron J. Aronoff, ed. New Brunswick, NJ: Transaction: 57–93.

Devine, Donald J. 1972. The Political Culture of the United States: The Influence of Member Values on Regime Maintenance. Boston: Little, Brown.

DeWalt, Billie R. and Pertti J. Pelto, eds. 1985. Micro and Macro Levels of Analysis in Anthropology: Issues in Theory and Research. Boulder, CO: Westview Press.

Dolgin, Janet L., David S. Kemnitzer, and David M. Schneider, eds. 1977. Symbolic Anthropology: A Reader in the Study of Symbols and Meanings. NY: Columbia University Press.

Dominguez, Virginia R. 1984. "The Language of Left and Right in Israeli Politics." In Cross-Currents in Israeli Culture and Politics, Political Anthropology V IV, Myron J. Aronoff, ed. New Brunswick, NJ: Transaction: 89–109.

Douglas, Mary and Aaron Wildavsky. 1982. Risk and Culture. Berkeley: University of California Press.

Downs, Anthony. 1957. Economic Theories of Government. NY: Harper and Brothers.

Easton, David. 1979 [1965]. A Framework for Political Analysis. Chicago: University of Chicago Press, Phoenix Edition.

Elazar, Daniel J. 1970. Cities of the Prairie: The Metropolitan Frontier in American Politics. NY: Basic Books.

_____. 1972. American Federalism: A Viewpoint from the States. NY: Thomas Crowell.

_____. 1982. "Steps in the Study of American Political Culture." In Political Culture, Public Policy and the American States, John Kincaid ed. Philadelphia: Institute for the Study of Human Issues.

Eldersveld, Samuel J. 1986. "The Party Activist in Detroit and Los Angeles: A Longitudinal View, 1956–1980." In American Politics in Decline, 2d ed., William Crotty ed. Boston: Little, Brown and Co.

_____. 1964. Political Parties: A Behavioral Analysis. Chicago: Rand McNally.

_____. 1982. Political Parties in American Society. NY: Basic Books.

Esman, Marjorie R. 1985. Henderson, Louisiana: Cultural Adaptation in a Cajun Community. NY: Holt, Rinehart and Winston.

Fallers, Lloyd. 1974. The Social Anthropology of the Nation State. Chicago: Aldine.

Fried, Morton. 1967. The Evolution of Political Society. NY: Random House.

Galbraith, John K. 1983. The Anatomy of Power. NY: Houghton, Mifflin.

Geertz, Clifford. 1973. Interpretation of Culture. NY: Basic Books.

Gibb, Cecil, ed. 1969. Leadership: Selected Readings. Middlesex: Penguin.

Gibson, James L., Cornelius P. Cotter, John F. Bibby and Robert J. Huckshorn. 1985. "Whither the Local Parties? A Cross-Sectional and Longitudinal Analysis of the Strength of Party Organizations." In the American Journal of Political Science: 129–160.

Harris, Marvin. 1975. "Why a Perfect Knowledge of All the Rules That One Must Know in Order to Act Like a Native Cannot Lead to a Knowledge of How Natives Act." In Journal of Anthropological Research 30: 242–251.

Herbers, John. 1979. "The Party's Over for the Political Parties." In the New York Times Magazine, Dec. 9.

Hopkins, Anne H. 1986. "Campaign Activities and Local Party Organization in Nashville." In Political Parties in Local Areas, William Crotty ed. Ithaca, NY: University of Tennessee Press.

Ike, Nobutaka. 1972. Japanese Politics: Patron-Client Democracy. NY: Alfred A. Knopf.

Kaufman, Herbert. 1985. Time, Chance, and Organizations: Natural Selection in a Perilous Environment. NJ: Chatham House.

Kellerman, Barbara. 1984a. "Leadership as a Political Act." In Leadership: Multidisciplinary Perspectives, Barbara Kellerman ed. Englewood Cliffs, NJ: Prentice-Hall.

———. 1984b. The Political Presidency: Practice of Leadership. NY: Oxford University Press.

Kelley, Robert. 1981. The Cultural Pattern in American Politics: The First Century. Washington: University Press of America.

Kincaid, John. 1982a. "Dimensions and Effects of America's Political Culture." In Journal of American Culture 5 Fall.

Kincaid, John, ed. 1982b. Political Culture, Public Policy and the American States. Philadelphia: Institute for the Study of Human Issues.

Kronenfeld, David. 1970. Review of Ira R. Buchler and Hugo J. Nutini, Game Theory in the Behavioral Sciences. University of Pittsburgh Press 1969. In American Anthropologist V 72, N 6: 1469–1471.

Landé, Carl H. 1977. "On the Dyadic Basis of Clientilism." In Friends, Followers and Factions: A Reader in Political Clientilism, Schmidt et al. eds. Berkeley: University of California Press: xiii–xxxvii.

Lantis, Margaret L. 1987. "Two Important Roles in Organizations and Communities." In Human Organization V 46 N 3: 189–199.

Lasswell, Harold and Abraham Kaplan. 1950. Power and Society. New Haven: Yale University Press.

Leach, Edmund R. 1965. Political Systems of Highland Burma. Boston: Beacon Press.

Lemarchand, René. 1977 [1972]. "Political Clientilism and Ethnicity in Tropical Africa." In Friends, Followers and Factions, Schmidt et al. eds. Berkeley: University of California Press: 100–123.

Leons, Madeline and Frances Rothstein, eds. 1979. New Directions in Political Economy. Westport, CT: Greenwood Press.

LeVine, Robert A. 1982. Culture, Behavior and Personality: An Introduction to the Comparative Study of Psychosocial Adaptation, 2d ed. NY: Aldine.

Levinson, David and Martin J. Malone. 1980. Toward Explaining Human Culture: A Critical Review of the Findings of Worldwide Cross-Cultural Research. Human Relations Area Files Press.

Lewellen, Ted C. 1983. Political Anthropology: An Introduction. South Hadley, MA: Bergin and Harvey.

Lewis, Herbert. 1974. Leaders and Followers: Some Anthropological Perspectives. Module in Anthropology No. 50. Reading: Addison-Wesley.

Lipset, Seymour Martin. 1960. Political Man: The Social Basis of Politics. Garden City, NY: Doubleday and Co.

Marcus, George E. and Michael M. J. Fischer. 1986. Anthropology as Cultural Critique. Chicago: University of Chicago Press.

Marvick, Dwaine. 1986. "Stability and Change in the Views of Los Angeles Party Activists, 1968-1980." In American Politics in Decline, 2d ed., William Crotty ed. Boston: Little, Brown and Co.

Merton, Robert. 1957. Social Theory and Social Structure. Glencoe, IL: The Free Press.

Moore, Sally Falk and Barbara Myerhoff, eds. 1975. Symbol and Politics in Communal Ideology. Ithaca: Cornell University Press.

Morgenstern, Oskar. 1968. "Game Theory: Theoretical Aspects." In Encyclopedia of the Social Sciences, David Sills ed. V 6: 62-69.

Moynihan, Daniel Patrick. 1986. "Links between LaRouche and New York Corruption." The New York Times Op Ed page: 4-1-1986.

_____. 1987. Letter to New York. Washington, DC.

Murray, Richard W. and Kent L. Tedin. 1986. "The Emergence of Two-Party Competition in the Sunbelt: The Case of Houston." In Political Parties in Local Areas, William Crotty ed. Ithaca, NY: University of Tennessee Press.

Myerhoff, Barbara and Sally Falk Moore, eds. 1977. Secular Ritual. Ansen: Van Gorcum.

Naisbitt, John. 1984. Megatrends. NY: Warner Books.

Nicholas, Ralph. 1965. "Factions: A Comparative Analysis." In Political Systems and the Distribution of Power, Michael Banton ed. London: Havistock.

_____. 1968. "Rules, Resources and Political Activity." In Local-level Politics, Swartz ed. Chicago: Aldine: 295-321.

Nicholson, Norman K. 1972. "The Factional Model and the Study of Politics." In Comparative Political Studies 5 Fall: 291-314.

Paige, Glenn. 1974. The Scientific Study of Political Leadership. NY: The Free Press.

Pitkin, Hanna, and Sara Shumer. 1982. "On Participation." Democracy 2: 43-54.

Pye, Lucien and Sidney Verba, eds. 1969. Political Culture and Political Development. Princeton: Princeton University Press.

Reeves, Richard. 1982. American Journey: Traveling with Toqueville in Search of Democracy. NY: Simon and Schuster.

Rosen, David M. 1984. "Leadership Systems in World Cultures." In Leadership: Multidisciplinary Perspectives, Barbara Kellerman ed. Englewood Cliffs, NJ: Prentice-Hall: 39-61.

Rothenberg, Randall. 1984. The Neoliberals: Creating the New American Politics. NY: Simon and Schuster.

Savage, Robert L. 1982. "Patterns of Multilinear Evolution in the American States." In Political Culture, Public Policy and the American States, John Kincaid ed. Philadelphia: Institute for the Study of Human Issues.

Scarrow, Howard A. 1983. Parties, Elections and Representation in the State of New York. NY: New York University Press.

Schneider, David M. 1980. American Kinship: A Cultural Account, 2d ed. Chicago: University of Chicago Press.

Scott, James C. 1977 [1972]. "Patron-Client Politics and Political Change in Southeast Asia." In Friends, Followers and Factions, Schmidt et al. eds. Berkeley: University of California Press: 123-146.

Shweder, Richard and Robert LeVine, eds. 1986. Culture Theory: Essays on Mind, Self and Emotion. NY: Cambridge University Press.

Silverman, Sydel. 1975. Three Bells of Civilization: The Life of an Italian Hill Town. NY: Columbia University Press.

Sorauf, Frank. 1967. "Political Parties and Political Analysis." In The American Party System: Stages of Development, William Chambers, and Walter Burnham eds. NY: Oxford University Press.

_____. 1984. Party Politics in America, 5th ed. Boston: Little, Brown.

Strauch, Judith. 1981. Chinese Village Politics in the Malaysian State. Cambridge: Harvard University Press.

_____. 1983. "National Politics at the Village Level: Paradoxical Perspectives on Chinese-Malayan 'Factionalism'." In American Ethnologist V 10 N 1: 41-58.

Susser, Ida. 1982. Norman Street: Poverty and Politics in an Urban Neighborhood. NY: Oxford University Press.

Swartz, Mark, Victor Turner and Arthur Tuden, eds. 1966. Political Anthropology. Chicago: Aldine.

Swartz, Mark. 1968. "Introduction" and "The Political Middleman." In Local-level Politics, Swartz ed. Chicago: Aldine: 199-204.

Tarrow, Sidney. 1978. Between Center and Periphery. New Haven: Yale University Press.

Town of Greenburgh. 1985. This Is Greenburgh.

Tucker, Robert. 1981. Politics as Leadership. Columbia, MO: University of Missouri Press.

Turner, Victor. 1957. Schism and Continuity in an African Society. Manchester: Manchester University Press.

_____. 1974. Drama, Fields and Metaphors. Ithaca: Cornell University Press.

Verba, Sidney. 1961. Small Groups and Political Behavior: A Study of Leadership. Princeton, NJ: Princeton University Press.

Vincent, Joan. 1971. African Elite: The Big Men of a Small Town. NY: Columbia University Press.

_____. 1978. "Political Anthropology: Manipulative Strategies." In Annual Review of Anthropology V 7: 175-194.

Wattenberg, Martin P. 1984. The Decline of American Political Parties 1952-1980. Cambridge: Harvard University Press.

Weatherford, J. McIver. 1981. Tribes on the Hill. NY: Rawson, Wade.

Weingrod, Alex. 1977 [1968]. "Patrons, Patronage, and Political Parties." In *Friends, Followers and Factions*, Schmidt et al. eds. Berkeley: University of California Press: 323–337.

Westchester Community Service Council. 1983. A Community Profile of Westchester County.

Wiegold, Marilyn, ed. 1984. Westchester County: The Past Hundred Years 1883–1983. NY: Westchester Historical Society.

Wilson, James Q. 1961. "The Economy of Patronage." *Journal of Political Economy* V 69 N 4.

Index of Pseudonyms

Index

Action sets, 71, 165
Action theory, 9, 165. *See also* Game theory and gamesmanship; Process
Adaptation, political, 10, 12, 117, 175
Almond, Gabriel, 13–14, 16, 37
Arena, political, 3, 71
Aronoff, Myron J., 13, 141, 165

Bailey, F. G., 9, 39, 71, 99, 148, 164
Behaviorists, political science, 181, 190
Berking, Max, 54
Bibby, John F., 186
Boissevain, Jeremy, 9, 71
Brokers, cultural and political, 71, 173
Burnham, Walter Dean, 13, 181–183, 188–190

Campaigns, 127–130. *See also* Candidates; Factionalism, Cedric-Tim case
Candidates, 109–119
  evaluation of, 110–113
  friendship in choice of, 117–119
  leaders as, 94–95
  selection of. *See* Nomination, process of
  See also Campaigns; Cross-endorsements
Caucuses and conventions, 112, 114–116, 120–122, 123, 156–157
Class, 6, 35, 141–143, 181–183, 189

Clientage. *See* Patronage
Cohen, Ronald, 3, 9, 37, 80
Community life of leaders, 39–40
Concerned Democrats, 149–150, 152, 165–166, 172
Cotter, Cornelius P., 19, 186–187, 189
Cross-endorsements, 21, 123–127
Cross-overs, party, 122–123
Crotty, William, 19, 187–189
Culture, concept of, 12–13. *See also* Political culture

Democracy
  and participation, 15–16
  and the party system, 182–184, 188

Elazar, Daniel J., 14–15, 172
Eldersveld, Samuel J., 14, 17, 19, 70, 130, 185–186, 187–189
Elections
  economic theories of, 110
  New York laws about, 20–22
Emics and etics, 5–7
Ethics, Greenburgh code of, 93–94
Ethnicity, 15, 34–35, 37–38, 141–147, 175. *See also* Westchester County, socioeconomic profile of
Ethnography, 2–3, 5–8, 16
Event analysis, 10–11
Evolution, cultural and political, 8, 177–178
Expediency, 95–96, 174